POLISHING
GOD'S
MONUMENTS

POLISHING GOD'S MONUMENTS

PILLARS OF HOPE FOR PUNISHING TIMES

JIM ANDREWS

Shepherd Press
Wapwallopen, Pennsylvania

To my precious wife, Olsie,
my partner *par excellence*
mother extraordinaire,
and the very embodiment
of the noble woman of Proverbs 31

Contents

Contents

Acknowledgments

Behind any worthwhile book are persons other than the author who, directly or indirectly, deserve recognition and gratitude for the result. This one is no exception.

To our friend and fellow writer, Patricia Roberts, I owe the embryonic idea for alternating chapters and letters, thus separating the theological motifs from the biographical content. Early on, Patricia also volunteered her editing talents to polish the first manuscript, and some fingerprints of her early work remain.

From there the book morphed into its expanded form with the help of a very bright and dear family friend, Lynne Mackey. The development and refinement of the organizational scheme I owe to her skillful and unstinting labors. Lynne is a natural editor whose time, instincts, input and ideas were just invaluable. She worked tirelessly with me to time and to tweak the flow of message and narrative so that exposition and experience would converge on the reader in natural and timely sequences. I would have settled for less, but she held my feet to the fire and the message of the book, I think, benefits greatly from her insistence on things fitted more neatly together.

I also want to thank my daughter and son-in-law, the suffering subjects of this living drama. I desperately needed their help, especially with the chronology of events and the medical aspects of the narrative portions. Fortunately, both are blessed with prodigious memories, good writing skills, and Paul in particular, is a fussbudget about medical accuracy. It just so happened, in God's providence, that during the home stretch, when I was buttoning up the manuscript, the Lord gave Juli and Paul a brief season of sufficient relief from her chronic miseries to allow the two of them space and energy enough to fine tune the content and make needed changes. That unexpected window reassured me that God's hand was in this effort.

Finally, I would like to thank my friend and former colleague, Dr. Bruce Ware, Senior Associate Dean of the School of Theology at Southern Seminary, for his enthusiasm for this volume as well as his timely helpfulness en route to publication. Without his encouragement and advice, the manuscript probably still would be buried in my files.

Introduction

A sober reality in the life of faith is that "through many tribulations we must enter the kingdom of God" (Acts 14:22b). In these ordeals God's people are buffeted in two ways: sometimes we suffer *for the faith* and other times we suffer *with* faith. Either way, our faith remains a work in progress. In the midst of troubles, our emotions can oscillate between hope and despair, our wills vacillate between submission and rebellion, and our understanding alternates between moments of comprehension and times of total confusion.

Right here, "Houston, we have a problem." Whenever faith is in the grinder, it may *seem* that God is not living up to his billing or performing as advertised. In times of distress, especially periods of prolonged suffering, his character may not *seem* to us to measure up to his biblical résumé.

So how do we keep the faith, sunny side up, in the face of this maddening mystery side of God? And how can we "recommend" a walk with God when, frankly, he *seems* to have abandoned us to wallow in our pain, to have shut his ears to our pleas, and to have heartlessly left the scene of the accident? What is an *honest* saint to do when God appears either indifferent or impotent?

This book confronts these issues head-on and offers believers in despair biblical perspective and practical direction that should reinvigorate the spirit of all who will regularly heed and apply them. It is about walking with God in times of trouble, about being tested to our socks, about what to do when extreme pressure threatens our very faith. And for illustrative purposes, it is about the multi-layered afflictions of a young woman, my younger daughter, and her devoted husband, who have faced it all (and then some) as a baffling, mind-boggling illness hijacked their youth and shattered their dreams.

A friend reminded me of that small figurine depicting a man sitting under a tree branch, looking up at a bird, which is about to do that dirty little deed all birds do. If you have ever felt like that fellow about to get dumped on, then this book is for you. When life circumstances make you want to say, as this ill-positioned victim does, "Go ahead, everybody else does," then this story will resonate with you.

This book aims to provide you with spiritual perspective and insight in suffering that will lift you above the destructive forces of adversity and help your faith survive any pounding on the anvil of tough circumstances. Equally important, whether you are physically ill or spiritually debilitated, burned-out, burned up, depressed, or distressed, this volume about faith under fire will arm you with a thoroughly biblical and absolutely critical coping strategy that I call "polishing God's monuments."

Now here is a caution. Our message and its interwoven story are for serious-minded Christians (that ought to be a redundancy!) on such intimate terms with serious pain and suffering that they sometimes feel like pulling out their hair, if not throwing in the towel.

The message unfolds between edited pastoral letters, mostly written to my congregation during some of the worst of our agony, recounting for them limited details of our plight, as well as insights we have gained—the light of God's Word illuminating harsh circumstances.

The first letter begins five years into Paul and Juli's illness, which was near the beginning of my ministry at Lake Bible Church. In a few cases the original letters were expanded to give you, the reader, the same context the first recipients had, and in other instances they were condensed. However, the intent, names, and events have remained unchanged.

Prologue

From the Cradle to the Crucible

Imagine peering into a kaleidoscope, twisting its barrel round and round, and then being asked to describe clearly and succinctly what you saw. There you have some idea of my sense of inadequacy in attempting to convey a cohesive account of what my daughter and son-in-law have been through for the past twenty years. I feel about the same frustration as a tourist trying to compress his vista of the Grand Canyon into a single snapshot—it won't come close to doing it justice.

Remarkably, it has only been within the last year or so that we have begun to see, at least from a distance, some of the physiological causes for my daughter's suffering. Medical science at last seems to be getting a small handle on some of the "whys." Unfortunately, we still have not identified a cure, as some of the major components of Juli's condition are in the research stage. However, at least understanding part of the problem gives us hope that eventually a solution will become available.

Symmetrical as well as strategic considerations require me to gut their story unmercifully. In fact, if I were to give you the whole nine yards, the litany of their pain and suffering would blow your mind to the point of incredulity.

I hope that what remains will suffice to paint this tried-to-the-bone couple in poignant, living color, accentuate the mystery of their plight, and set up a compelling platform for our perspectives on suffering. Most particularly, I want their story to sell you on the habit of monument-polishing as a coping strategy. This vital discipline, so thoroughly and profusely biblical, has reinforced our faith through many bitter, stormy passages of life

Juli is the younger of our two daughters. The older, Kristi, is married to a pastor, and she and John presently live in Spokane, Washington, with our grandchildren, Alex and Ashley. Juli, now thirty-nine years old, and her husband, Paul, live near us in Tigard, Oregon. Sadly, her health issues thus far have denied them the joy of a family.

From the womb, struggle and narrow brushes with death have strangely dogged Juli's life. In retrospect her breech birth seemed almost an omen of things to come. In fact, my wife Olsie and I have wondered if that irregular delivery played any role in her eventual troubles.

Early on Juli betrayed hints of musical talent. For Christmas when she was only three, she received a miniature piano with only one octave . . . the kind of toy usually quickly forgotten. Not in this case, as Juli spent hours plunking away on that little tuneless keyboard.

Around that same time, someone gave us a recording of international children's songs. Juli was so enthralled with the music that Olsie soon found she could put on the record and clean the whole house almost before the child moved a muscle.

Before long the little tyke could sing along with every single track in every language.

When Juli was five, something confirmed her musical gift. Our family was returning from vacation to our home, then in Lakewood, Colorado. Just as the car crossed the state line into Colorado, Juli lit up and exclaimed, "Oh, goody, I can't wait to get back to my little piano!" That did it. When we got home, my wife, a piano teacher, decided to let Juli take a crack at the real piano, which up to then had been forbidden territory to curious kids looking for something to destroy. But now Olsie just wanted to see what would happen. That day I'll never forget. Within a half-hour Juli was picking out tunes! Mom then knew she had a musically gifted youngster on her hands.

Olsie immediately took charge of Juli's piano training and did not relinquish that role until just a couple years before she entered the conservatory. In 1981, Juli began studying with Don Lehmann, an exceedingly talented pianist, performer, and teacher.

Practice discipline was never a battle. The child loved the piano, and had a fine ear and an uncommon feel for the instrument. In those tender years, schoolwork, however, was another story. Somehow, Juli just didn't come together academically. It seemed that when she had a teacher who thoroughly explained concepts, Juli rose to the top of the class. While our older daughter Kristi could thrive under any instructor, Juli couldn't. She had trouble following instructions, and her sense of direction was always so bad, I was amazed the kid could find her way to bed at night! (By the way, nine years ago neurological testing confirmed that Juli had a learning disability that made following instructions akin to solving a mental jigsaw puzzle. It was suggested that oxygen deprivation during her breech birth might have damaged the part of the brain that controls this process.) From grades three through five Juli became so discouraged that she gave up trying altogether, describing herself retrospectively as a "lazy slough-off."

Then at age ten everything changed—in one fell swoop. Juli had just finished fifth grade when we made our annual trek back to West Virginia to visit family. While we were there we ran up to New Martinsville to visit Olsie's sister, Barbara, her husband, Don, and their twin girls. One warm, sunny day we all decided to take the kids for a picnic and recreational outing at the famed Olgebay Park in Wheeling.

Somebody suggested we let the four girls go horseback riding. Seemed like fun, though Juli was just barely tall enough to qualify as a rider. For some reason, the trail guide put her last in line before the group set off on their English-saddled horses down the steep, wooded terrain for a long ride. Little Juli looked so elfish on the back of that big mare!

The moms sauntered off to a nearby park cottage to wait, while Don and I killed time chatting in an adjacent parking lot, stopping now and then to jab and poke aimlessly at loose gravel with the nose of our tennies.

About an hour later, the late afternoon stillness gave way to a commotion emanating from down in the woods, approximately where we supposed the horse trail ascended toward us. At first I didn't think much about the hollering except that finally the wait was over and we could go home. I just assumed everybody was having a jolly good time and yelling back and forth in the typical kiddish way.

No sooner had that thought crossed my mind, than out of the woods and into the parking lot bolted a big white horse charging at speed, straight for the barn. It was dragging, as though a sack of feed, a limp youngster whose foot was still snagged in the stirrup on our side. Her head and upper torso were bumping along on the ground, plowing through the loose gravel like a speedboat knifing through water. Instantly I recognized that small, dangling body. It was Juli.

From the point where she had apparently fallen off the horse and the spooked animal tore past the other horses with their stunned riders, the beast had dragged the child some three hundred ninety feet over rocky ground.

Who can describe the horror of a scene like that for a parent? Ironically, only the previous afternoon, as Don and I were chatting in his living room, Juli just happened to prance past us. For some reason, as my eyes followed her happy steps, the thought had flitted across my mind, "My, how I love that kid! I could never bear to lose her." Now almost exactly twenty-four hours later the threat of that very nightmare was unfolding before my eyes.

One thing I knew instantly. Virtually no one, especially a child, could survive an accident like that. To tell the truth, I pretty much gave her up for lost the minute I saw what was happening. Yet never-say-die parental instinct took over and I knew I had to stop that horse . . . cut it off . . . grab that tangling bridle . . . restrain the dumb animal . . . somehow save her—if she was still alive.

As a former athlete, I knew something about cut-off angles and by natural instinct took the best one available. The horse, however, already spooked, and now even more frightened by my sudden movements, stepped it up and took off at full gallop toward the barn. That sudden lurch and change in the horse's gait altered the position of Juli's dangling body, and somehow pitched her tiny head like a fragile egg shell underneath one of its back hoofs. Right before my very eyes that hoof clomped down on her diminutive skull.

Nevertheless, the very finger of God was in the moment and I have often wondered if a holy angel intervened. Amazingly, the horse's hoof struck her skull just lightly enough not to crush it, yet with just enough physical force to break her foot loose from the stubborn stirrup, and *a la* Jacob, leave a calling card in the form of a half-moon "hoofprint" permanently imprinted in her skull. Once her small body and the charging horse parted hostile company, her limp figure went skittering across the gravel, landing in a seemingly lifeless heap near a clump of weeds between the parking lot and the adjacent woods.

Frantically I raced to her, instinctively gathering her battered, bloody body into my arms. Her eyes were set, her face and head all cut up and bleeding, and her teeth clenched so tightly one couldn't have pried them apart with a crowbar. With no experience in such emergencies, I feared from her appearance that she was either dead or dying.

Jumbled thoughts ricocheted in my confused mind. "Oh, Lord, she looks so bad! What do we do? Need an ambulance quick . . . teeth are clenched . . . is she swallowing her tongue? . . . do I need to pry her mouth open . . . how ? Has anyone called an ambulance yet? Olsie? Where is she? Does she know this has happened? Can't let her see Juli in this condition . . . Juli's probably not going to make it . . . or is it over already . . . have to prepare Olsie . . . can't leave Juli . . . but gotta get to Olsie . . . those clenched teeth . . . is Juli strangling on her own tongue? . . . don't know what to do . . . gotta leave Juli with Don . . . gotta find Olsie."

Leaving my mangled child with my brother-in-law, I tore off for the cottage where Olsie and Barbara were, and broke the awful news. "Honey, Juli's been hurt. I don't think she's going to make it," I explained, trying to prepare her for the worst. As you can imagine, Olsie became distraught and fought her way through Barb and me to the scene.

Meanwhile someone had called an ambulance. After forever it finally arrived. Not paramedics, just a rude ambulance. In the back I accompanied Juli to the Ohio Valley Hospital . . . the toughest trip of my life. Every moment I feared the imminent prospect of watching my own little baby expire before my very eyes.

Obviously and thankfully, she didn't. As in all such cases, the next seventy-two hours were nail biters. Juli was in a coma, had multiple brain contusions, a broken arm, perhaps a broken facial bone, that ugly head wound, plus other cuts, abrasions, and bruises from her waist up. The child was so battered, so swollen, and shortly turned so black that no one on earth could have identified her for almost two weeks. She was unconscious for about fourteen days, and in the hospital for a total of twenty-three.

About two weeks after the accident, Don and Barb's pastor visited us at the hospital just after Juli emerged from intensive care. "She is looking so much better," we informed him with considerable relief. Later, I was told, the pastor just shook his head and told my brother-in-law, "Amazing! Those poor people . . . they think that child is looking *better*!" That comment was some indication of the terrible battering she suffered.

Though petite for her age, Juli was never a wimp. It said something about her tolerance for serious pain that not one time in twenty-three days, conscious or unconscious, did she ever cry out, whimper or complain—not even when the orthopedic surgeon was fiddling around with her broken arm to see if he could set it. In fact with some surprise he commented on her toughness.

Now comes the trigger in the change equation. When Juli finally regained consciousness, she was placed in a hospital room with a pitiful little youngster named Karen. Karen had been the victim—not once, but twice—of savage domestic abuse at the hands of her so-called "parents." One attack was so violent that they literally tore the "hide" loose on one side of her tiny skull! That second attack had forever reduced the little thing, then about Juli's age, to a living vegetable . . . a sight so pitiful it would tear your heart out and turn your stomach. There she lay day after day just existing; her somehow still tender, almost smiling, big blue eyes the lone residue of her original beauty.

Let any who blanch at the prospect of "sinners in the hands of an angry God" stand at her bedside day after day as I did and tell me the cruelty of mankind does not cry out for the retribution of a holy God.

Unknown to us at the time, none of this tragedy was lost on Juli. When she was alert, she was taking it in at every pore. Only later did she relate to us the impact. In that hospital bed adjacent to Karen, God imprinted forcibly on Juli's pre-adolescent consciousness what could have happened to her. After being dragged over Hell's half-acre behind a runaway horse, she, by all rights, should have been killed, disabled, disfigured, or mentally incapacitated from the appalling abuse her body suffered. Yet for some reason God spared *her*.

God used this impression and little Karen's plight as a providential foil to imprint upon Juli's ten-year-old mind that He spared her for some greater purpose than just extending time on her life meter.

I should insert right here this important notation about the strange and terrible medical complications that have ensued for the past eighteen years. Her current doctors all agree that this severe brain trauma is undoubtedly a major player in her ongoing medical problems. For one thing, they believe her brain is impaired, so it does not send the proper signals to her immune system, thereby allowing pathogens to thrive in her weakened body. We were warned at the time of her accident by her treating physicians to expect serious complications from the brain injury, including seizures, well into her twenties and thirties. But

22

we were too overjoyed to have our daughter back to pay much attention to these ominous predictions.

And we were further amazed to see the positive changes in our daughter resulting from this tragedy. From that time on, Juli seemed to undergo a personality transplant. Right there in the hospital she vowed to us, even as her lucidity was still coming and going, that she would never again slough off in school. She never did. From that day she morphed into a disciplined, purposeful, and single-minded child. In fact, if memory serves, she later graduated thirteenth in her high school senior class of about 500 and earned membership in the National Honor Society. That is not too shabby for a kid whose second grade math teacher thought she might be a mental turtle rather than an intellectual rabbit.

Some kids are precocious intellectually, some athletically, some artistically, but once in a while one is precocious spiritually. From an early age their level of seriousness about the things of God, even their understanding of spiritual things, their spiritual discipline, and their devotion to Christ run considerably ahead of most of their Christian peers. I think it is fair to say that Juli fits that description.

Juli, however, would be embarrassed if I failed to acknowledge that she too is a daughter of Eve and a full partner with the rest of us in the whole scandal of human failure. She knows her own sinful heart, her flaws and foibles, warts and sharp edges well enough to understand that God still treats her, like the rest of us, far better than deserved.

Growing up, Juli and Kristi had their catfights over the usual sister things, and it certainly didn't help matters that emotionally Juli was strung higher than a power line. Though as an adult she changed radically, in her early years it was a chronic battle to get her to clean her room and maintain order (though she did "scrape by" with a few domestic chores). Over those types of things we had wars and rumors of wars. Sometimes Kristi, with occasional justification, believed strangulation was the only final solution.

To top it off, Juli possesses a fiery, almost Latin spirit and a temper to prove it. (The painful disease process that now rages in her body hasn't mellowed this "personality trait" with age, to say the least.) And, except in the matter of perseverance, she can become unglued faster than a dry stamp.

Those flaws conceded, Juli is, and always has been, a serious-minded Christian to whom lip service and half-heartedness are perfect strangers. She has always been serious about her walk with God.

Her intensity about spiritual things came to the fore at a very early age. In our Lakewood neighborhood, Juli was the self-appointed leader of a little pack of kids, mostly boys. When she wasn't force-training them in gymnastics or rallying them for some other kiddy enterprise, she would gather them like a little hen on the roost (front steps) of one house or the other and proceed to teach them Bible stories—a kind of VBS home school.

One summer evening when Juli was nine, she explained the plan of salvation to her next door neighbor and best friend, Kenny Johnson. Afterward, she invited him to attend VBS. He liked it so much that his parents, Earl and Sandy, asked if they could attend church with us. Soon the whole family received Christ and was deeply involved in church life at Riverside Baptist Church, before they eventually moved away. Years later, when Kenny learned how sick Juli was, he wrote her a letter to encourage her that he, his wife, and his children were all walking with the Lord because of her witness.

Through the years, Juli also maintained a serious and potent prayer life. Let me illustrate.

All my women lose things—everything but their heads. Drives me bananas. At Columbine High School her freshman year, Juli had misplaced her math book (bad enough) and was forced to borrow a friend's (worse yet). Then she lost that one, too! Not only did she face the wrath of her friend, but worse by far, possible summary execution by her parsimonious mom, who entertained neither the desire nor any intention of restocking the whole annual supply of Columbine math texts. We're talking crisis here and Juli well knew it. She did not dare break this dire news to Mom! Olsie guarded her pennies like a Roman soldier guarded prisoners—let one escape and you pay with your life.

Knowing I was a safer confidant than Olsie about such economic-impact revelations, Juli told me about "the problem" before I left for work at the Bible college that morning and implored me with great passion to pleas-s-s-e pray that somehow, after these several weeks, she would find that missing math text in cavernous Columbine High School.

Truthfully, I could pray for this outcome with about the same confidence as asking the Lord to help me find a $10 bill dropped in the school hallway a week ago—except, admittedly, stray textbooks are hardly in the same demand as ten spots. This, I thought, was pushing it. But that honestly did not deter her simple faith. So, I linked arms with her petition and dutifully prayed with all the thin faith I could muster.

Later that day, at Western Bible College (now Colorado Christian University) where I was teaching, I received an ecstatic phone call from Juli. She had found the book! During an English class, when she was distracted and pleading earnestly with the Lord about that math text, she suddenly spied a familiar-looking book in a window well of the classroom. Jumping up spontaneously, she raced to the window, picked up the text, and lo and behold it was her friend's missing math book.

After high school graduation, Juli's piano skills earned her a place in the Wheaton Conservatory of Music as a piano performance major. The very first day on campus she spotted Paul, who was a piano performance major also.

Here again was the invisible hand of God. With her woman's intuition Juli sensed right off the bat this was God's man for her. She was so sure that she even gave her mom and me a heads-up. Olsie, after visiting Wheaton for Parents' Weekend, was duly impressed with the tall, dark and handsome young man who had a winsome personality and a smile like sunshine. Meanwhile, with time-honored feminine wile, Juli baited the hook, waited for Paul to bite and shortly reeled him in before he knew what hit him. Here Paul thought all along that it was his own idea!

Paul is a brilliant young man with near total recall. He was co-valedictorian in high school. At Wheaton he graduated summa cum laude with a double major. A gentleman in every respect, Paul grew up in a pastor's home. Both his parents, Gordon and Elaine, had been Wheaton grads themselves. Elaine, like her son, graduated summa cum laude. Gordon had gone on to take a master's degree at Brandeis and his doctorate at Boston University.

Paul himself was cut from the same soldierly cloth as Juli. The only difference is, to this day I honestly could not tell you what *his* warts are. The guy is a gem.

If ever a marriage was prearranged in heaven, this was one. God reserved for Juli a special companion with a rare, but utterly necessary, combination of intelligence, recall, meticulosity, patience, unstinting love, and unwavering faith in the most baffling circumstances. Besides these virtues, he also has the persistence of a yellow jacket at a picnic. Any lesser combination of attributes, and their love boat would have been swamped long ago.

Ironically for a conservatory student, Paul's goal was missions, not piano performance *per se*, which tells one something about him right there. With that in mind, he took a double major, combining ethnomusicology (study of non-Western music) with piano performance. His vision was to help indigenous believers create culturally authentic Christian music for worship instead of borrowing the hymns and choruses that Western missionaries had imported.

He prepared for his mission endeavors by doing overseas missions trips in two entirely different countries and cultures. Paul's command of the French language allowed him to share Christ personally with nationals during two trips to Haiti. He also spent one summer in Papua, New Guinea, doing ethnomusicology research as part of his major.

Pastor Jess Moody once wrote, "There is no use to carry a lamp to Malaysia that won't burn at home." Well, *their* lamps burned at home. Virtually every Friday night for four years Paul and Juli joined a group of other Wheaton students doing street evangelism in downtown Chicago near the Water Tower. This story will give you some sense of Paul's heart for people.

At some point on his Friday night evangelism forays, Paul had struck up a friendship with a Chicago bag lady. For weeks he had been sharing Christ with her. One particular Friday some school obligation prevented him from coming in with the rest of the evangelism team. She missed him that week, and the next Friday she told him of her disappointment. Paul was so pleased that his absence mattered to her, that he was intent on making up for it. He apologized and offered to buy her an ice cream. However, *she* wanted to do the honors. So the bedraggled lady walked over to the nearby ice cream stand and ordered a cup (not cups!). Then she came back, plunged her unwashed hand into one of her soiled bags and pulled out, like twin rabbits from a tattered hat, two used plastic spoons, whereupon she invited her honored guest to dig in. Loath to injure her feelings, even at some risk to his health, Paul smiled, thanked her, and without hesitation lit into their common cup. That's vintage Paul. For someone in the performing arts, I have never seen such a selfless and ego-free zone.

After her sophomore year in college, Juli spent the summer among the Meru tribe in Kenya where she duly impressed the nationals with her ability to pick up their music, rhythms, and even language. "You do it just like us!" they would tell her with admiring surprise.

Juli returned from Kenya mysteriously ill, the first manifestation since her accident of bad things to come. In retrospect, we understand she picked up some parasites there that for a long time went undetected. These, among other ailments, have contributed to her problems, though it is impossible to allocate primary and secondary causes. Thus, what is behind the tapestry of ensuing trials remains a mystery except for the one common thread that largely explains the breakdown of Juli's health—her earlier brain trauma.

Back at school for her junior year, she struggled with walking pneumonia. However, it wasn't until the last semester of her senior year that things started to unravel.

Ironically, the catalyst that set her troubles in motion was her participation in a communion service during which the partakers shared a common cup of grape juice. Apparently two young women seated near Juli had recently contracted mononucleosis, though it was unknown at the time. Shortly thereafter, when Juli returned from the Wheaton College Concert Choir annual spring tour, she was diagnosed with a bad case of mono and had to be put up in the college clinic. The severity of her case stemmed, I presume, from the fact then hidden from us—that her whole immune system was on the verge of implosion.

Though mono itself is hardly the end of the world, this sickness could not have been more ill-timed. Her particular case was so debilitating that everything became a big struggle, again a cameo of things to come. Besides, her senior recital was originally scheduled for two weeks after her eventual diagnosis, a nightmare for any piano performance major.

Still, with Paul's constant help, she battled through it. Even though he was beginning to show signs of becoming sick himself, the poor fellow was her tireless and ever trusty pack animal. In the end somehow, Juli managed to rise from the dead. At her rescheduled senior recital she gave the performance of her life—a monument of God's timely grace.

Complicating matters even further was the fact that their wedding was set for Saturday, May 16th, the day before graduation! This was going to be an elaborate ceremony with a large reception at a local hotel. How does a sick girl coordinate all that on top of attending to her studies? It was enough to devastate anyone's health.

On her wedding day, the fragile bride (mouth full of painful canker sores) was a living lump of walking exhaustion. As Juli and Paul repeated their vows, "in sickness and in health," both sets of siblings, who were bridesmaids and groomsmen, as well as all the wedding guests, laughed at the irony. At that moment, none of us had the slightest inkling how applicable those words would be for them. Nor did the families realize the supportive and sacrificial roles they would have to play in the years to come.

Through sheer adrenaline, Juli mustered enough strength for the "Big Day" and even managed to walk for her commencement Sunday afternoon. But how would a girl in these circumstances find the time to pack and ship all her belongings in preparation for her honeymoon trip immediately after commencement? She couldn't do everything, even with Paul's help.

Dad and Mom never even made it to graduation exercises. While J. I. Packer was regaling faculty, students, family, and friends with what I am sure was an eminent commencement address, Olsie and I were abruptly detoured to Juli's house in our graduation-best. Shortly lathered in sweat like two plough horses, we frantically lit in to sorting and boxing her possessions for shipment early the next day before our flight back to Portland. At least she received her diploma! Little did we know then that this disruptive mini-crisis would be a metaphor and regular feature of our lives for the next eighteen years (and counting).

After their marriage and graduation, Paul and Juli flew to Florida for an extended honeymoon and a desperately needed rest. Paul's grandparents offered them the use of their ocean-view condominium for a month so they could do nothing but relax and enjoy themselves.

With Wheaton and the stress of the last few months behind them, Olsie and I thought our worries were over. Juli and Paul would return refreshed, ready to start their new lives together and prepare to carry out their vision abroad.

Their future for the next couple of years was mapped out. They had enrolled in Western Seminary here in Portland, where I taught, with the intent of starting work in the fall on master's degrees in intercultural studies. They both planned to attend seminary while teaching piano to support themselves. After graduation they would head off to some third world mission field. This was a well-formulated plan and a beautiful dream, but the Lord had other ideas.

Upon her return to Portland, Juli had not revived nearly as much as we had hoped or expected. Fighter that she is, she attempted to "keep up with the program," but after just a few weeks, she had to drop out of Western. She still taught piano part-time, as her energy allowed. Then, as Juli's energy level continued its free fall, Paul too came down with mono! To ration his strength, Paul dropped two of his classes, but managed to continue teaching piano part-time. His condition eventually worsened to the point where he had to drop his seminary studies altogether. (By March 1989, they both had to terminate their piano teaching—a heart-wrenching decision for all of us.)

Desperate to find relief, they reached in many different medical directions, but found no help. Like so many others with baffling afflictions, they were waved off with that exasperating cop-out so familiar to frustrated patients, "There's nothing wrong with you," or "You're just depressed." I guess blaming the victim is a universal human evasion tactic when the person responsible for answers has none, and refuses to admit it.

Finally, in December of 1988, a viral disease specialist at Oregon Health Sciences University (OHSU) diagnosed the health monster they were facing. Since they both became debilitated after contracting mono, he concluded that they were suffering from Chronic Epstein-Barr Virus (EBV causes mononucleosis). The recently discovered manifestation of this post-viral syndrome was labeled this way at the time. Shortly thereafter, the disease was renamed Chronic Fatigue Syndrome (CFS), a name which belies the seriousness of the disease.

Unfortunately, taming this beast has proven almost impossible. Although there have been some advancements in this area, there is still no cure for CFS, also known by its more recent name CFIDS (Chronic Fatigue Immune Dysfunction Syndrome). At the time of their diagnosis, much of the medical community was still skeptical of its existence. For those who did acknowledge it, understanding this condition was still in its infancy. So even when the CDC officially recognized the disease in 1989, there was little any doctor could do to alleviate it. We were all facing a dead-end street.

When you're that deep in calamity, things can only go up from there, right? We had no idea back then that we had much further to go before hitting the bottom. With no treatment on the horizon, both of them continued to worsen, especially Juli. The specialist at OHSU had predicted that she would fare worse than Paul, due to the complexity of the female hormonal system. Now the dead had somehow to care for the dead.

Before long, however, Juli was beginning to suffer from another condition CFS patients are prone to. Whatever the underlying cause of this affliction, Juli was soon developing what would become a horrifying, out-of-control, and totally mystifying disease called Environmental Illness, now known as MCS (Multiple Chemical Sensitivities). In lay terms, MCS is a condition that varies in severity from patient to patient, and causes some people to react to certain chemicals that would never affect the average person.

A rough analogy would be to compare the varying degrees to which different people respond to prescription drugs. Some people have side effects, others have downright allergic reactions, and some poor souls even die. When neither you nor anyone you know has ever experienced reactions to any substance on the planet, you tend to think condescendingly, "Oh, you've got to be kidding!" This is the typical skeptical response that I, or even Juli, would have projected prior to our nightmare. As you will soon see, during the first years of Juli's CFS, she gave no more thought than you or I to chemical sensitivities. She had never heard of them.

However, though there are few who are as acutely sensitive as Juli became, other currently enigmatic phenomena, like the mysterious Gulf War syndrome, have raised the profile of this problem. Occasionally stories appear in the media about doctors and medical workers becoming hypersensitive to latex rubber, commonly found in many medical supplies. As a result, they can no longer tolerate any exposure to everyday items such as paint, tires, etc. Some people become so "sensitized" to any form of rubber that they become housebound. Also, there are scattered reports of churches setting aside "safe rooms" for attendees who are hypersensitive to perfumes and scented lotions. Increasingly, carpets and glues in new housing and office complexes have caused devastating health effects for some. The bottom line is that we live today in a chemical-intensive world that for a growing number of people is toxic. In the future, my guess is that what is strange today will become more commonplace.

What we believe triggered our journey through this new health nightmare was a treatment Juli started for suggested "hidden allergies." A naturopathic physician explained that these "hidden allergies" might be behind her CFS. Since she was beginning to experience a minor skin sensitivity to makeup, Juli and Paul thought this was plausible. Because traditional medicine was offering neither hope nor help for her CFS, she agreed to this treatment. His alleged approach was to desensitize the immune system by administering a series of chemical allergy drops containing small amounts of key chemicals to which her body was presumably reacting.

It did not take any time for this "treatment" to further wreck her already fragile health and impose an odorless, colorless, cheerless lifestyle that would devastate her pride of appearance. The day Juli walked into that misbegotten excuse of an office, though extremely ill, her father can assure you she arrived as a very pretty, petite, well-groomed young lady with hair tastefully coiffed, and all the right cosmetic touches in all the right places. To this point she had refused to allow her growing debility to steal her desire to look her best (or conceal her native good looks).

Within two days of beginning the "allergy drop" treatment, she had to drop her beauty regimen like a hot iron. Her body was suddenly unable to tolerate hairspray and makeup— even regular soap and deodorant! This was nothing compared to where things would eventually go, but that development was a major crisis. All her natural feminine vanity was still intact, even if her immune system was not. After just a few more days things had deteriorated to the point where a mere whiff of any ordinary household cleaner now caused shrieking pain like she'd never felt before.

Incidentally, we learned much later from a medical assistant who had worked for this naturopath, that his method of testing and treatment was highly inaccurate due to the almost continual malfunction of the machine used to formulate the drops. She related that they often just mixed these concoctions by hand, simply guessing about the dosage. It finally got so bad that the poor woman couldn't live with herself, so she quit her job in protest. We also heard from another one of his patients that a group of five clients was filing a lawsuit against him alleging medical malpractice.

Despite her well-established high threshold for pain, these reactions became unbearable. The excruciating symptoms she experienced when exposed to chemicals felt like burning acid was being poured into her veins and muscles. The list of offenders seemed to grow with each passing day. She eventually became so reactive to who-knows-what that she was almost totally isolated from mainstream life.

Unfortunately Paul himself was caught in this vortex of isolation for two reasons: 1) Juli required virtually constant care, and 2) the more he ventured outside, the more he increased the risk that he would become a carrier of things she reacted to. If this happened, her body would go into orbit. An even greater risk was that he would import something on his person into the house itself, rendering her very dwelling unlivable to her. So Paul kept his head down, as much as circumstances permitted, taking a chance only on a pick-your-poison basis.

Of course this meant that Olsie and I could no longer enter the house for fear of being contamination camels ourselves. The ways we improvised for dealing with this problem imposed on all of us lifestyles stranger than a box of bugs. Eventually the well-traveled story of the Bubble Boy would become all too real to us.

Over the past eighteen years, we have been far more intimate with darkness than light, felt far more pain than pleasure, and seen more mysteries than miracles. Still, this God of ours, who seems to hide himself, as Isaiah said, has here and there dramatically broken his silence and rescued us in stunning ways. The very discipline of rehearsing these monuments has again and again strengthened our faith.

That is why we begin our message with the story of Juli and Paul. It is bewildering to know these two kids, their spiritual timbre, their passion to serve Christ, their gifts and capacities to make a difference, and then to see them put on the shelf. At the same time, others their age enjoy perfect health and life under the sun, while being spiritually tepid, wasteful of their endowments, and unfocused regarding their purpose in life. One has to wonder, "Where, oh where, is God?"

That tension is why we bring this message to you.

Mystery and Monuments

We rightly boast of a God of miracles. What we must remember is that he is also a God of mysteries. This mystery side of God's ways is precisely why the monument-polishing habit is so vital to a stable faith.

Many years ago, this lesson was forever branded on my consciousness. In 1980, I was invited to take a new position at Western Seminary in Portland, Oregon, while still teaching at a Bible college in Denver. After agonizing over the decision, the Lord made his direction clear to us. I accepted the appointment, and we put our home on the market. Nice place, choice neighborhood, fair price. Unfortunately, the housing market had slowed, and to my dismay there were few prospective buyers.

Several months later I found myself backing out of my drive-way alone. It was the pits to leave behind my wife and two teenage daughters to fend for themselves indefinitely. Under cover of darkness I wept intermittently all the way to Fort Collins. I had never dreamed when I accepted the job that our family wouldn't make the move together.

At worst I figured our Denver home would sell soon. Week after week passed. The loneliness was oppressive for all of us. Absolutely nothing was happening on that house. I had not imagined that when I left in August, I would be flying back to Denver for Christmas break to visit my family. Still, I returned in hope, not because of any real prospects, but because of my own romantic notions about the way God works.

After Christmas break, I boarded the plane and headed back to Portland alone with a big lump in my throat. Bubble burst. Home not sold and husband wondering, how long, O Lord? How long? This is the mystery side of God.

As weeks passed, my situation evolved into something of a *cause celebre* around campus. The attention was both welcome and tiresome. I needed prayer desperately, but asking for it meant having to answer the same old questions the same old way. I was constantly reminded that heaven was brass, and the Lord, so far as I could tell, was doing absolutely zero to fix the problem.

Maybe it wasn't God's will for me to be at Western after all, people had to be wondering. In fact, a few of our friends in Denver did question whether the Lord was sending me a signal. One well-meaning student was really troubled by my situation because it blew his paradigm.

"God doesn't separate families," he offered.

Could have fooled me! I guess he overlooked Matthew 19:29 where the Lord Jesus speaks of the reward of any disciple "who has left houses or brothers or sisters or father or mother or children or farms for my name's sake."

After a couple of months my wife flew to Portland. During this brief visit she was able to observe me ministering in my new academic environment, meet my faculty colleagues, and talk with some of my students. Her visit coincided with the issuance of faculty contracts, renewed annually. Was I going to return next year with the housing situation still unresolved?

My wife has always been a tower of strength, one of those all-too-rare, battle-tested, whatever-the-Lord-wills spouses that every soldier of Christ needs at his side. God's will has always been her will and her heart has always been fused with mine. If Olsie had second thoughts about an open-ended commitment to this teaching ministry, it would cause me to revisit the issue. Under the circumstances, I needed to reconfirm God's will and her affirmation was critical.

Her answer did not surprise me. "Jimmy, I have sat through your classes and talked with students. It is clear to me that God wants you here," she responded with tears welling up and a slight tremor in her voice. "It just kills me to be separated like this, and the girls miss you so much, but you have to sign that contract and we just have to wait on the Lord."

With that bold step I hoped our resolution to follow wherever Christ leads was sufficiently established. Way down deep, I felt that this decision was the final bridge we needed to cross before the Lord intervened and blew the whistle on the trauma.

Fat chance. Time marched on relentlessly and days added up to weeks. Then one day, out of the blue, it happened—a phone call from my wife. Since long distance calls between us were strictly rationed, I knew this was either very good or very bad news. She informed me that there was a serious buyer, with cash, who said he would be coming back in the morning with his wife for another look. Mentally he was already remodeling the place and that was an auspicious sign.

The next day passed slowly. Distraction soon started biodegrading into a surly impatience. Late in the afternoon I convinced myself that this qualified as an emergency and called my wife.

"Olsie, what's going on back there?" I asked impatiently. "How come you haven't called?"

"Oh, Jimmy, I don't know what is happening," she explained sadly. "The man came back this morning with his wife, then left with no explanation."

Well, the potential buyers never returned.

Now that was a biggie, but by no means our first tribulation. And nothing compared to what lay ahead, which would include our daughter's strange and horrifying future illnesses. If we hadn't learned through experiences like this the "secret" of what I call monumental faith, I for one might have been a spiritual casualty. The Lord taught us a spiritual discipline known and practiced by God's people from time immemorial, but widely overlooked and neglected today.

Without it, the storm waters of adversity would have swamped our spiritual boats, and we would have found our faith too small to cope with those rogue waves of incomprehensible affliction that seem unyielding to any amount of prayer, and even appear at times to intensify with every breath of supplication. Without the ballast of a monumental faith it is likely that faith will capsize in the giant swells.

When that anticipated sale fell through, I lost it for the better part of a day. Call it my day of spiritual infamy. Thank God for his mercy that passes understanding, for I was very angry with the Lord—something I had never done before.

Why? Some of us are wired so that we cope better with flash floods than with slow, dripping, water torture. Another factor was my faulty preconception of the way God was supposed to operate. This trial violated my paradigm. It was something of an "out of the box" encounter with the mystery side of God.

In our walk with God we tend to elevate precedents, biblical and personal, into "laws." We get these neat little models in our heads of the way God is supposed to do his business. The effect is to put him in a mold. We like to have it so, because it furnishes us a comfort zone. We like predictability. We want to be able to anticipate with some accuracy what the Lord will or will not do. We like a God whose ways fit almost geometrical patterns. Therein lies a problem.

The plain truth is that sometimes it would be quite a challenge for us to go into court, unroll the recent tapestry of our experience with God, and convince a jury of our peers, based on what is going on in our lives, that we are the certifiable objects of divine favor or the beneficiaries of his power or wisdom.

When that long-awaited "buyer" left us stranded, I was exasperated with God. The previous day I had been running around campus singing his praises. Now it felt as though my premature thanksgiving had embarrassed even God himself. I just couldn't believe he would do such a thing.

He shattered my little paradigm like a rock smashing a clay pot. Everything had come together and the Lord so cruelly, it seemed, pulled the rug right out from under my joy and embarrassed my praise. What is one to say about such a thing?

Never before, despite many hurtful and harsh experiences in my life, had I experienced this feeling of anger toward God. Previously I would have been unable to relate to this emotion, but now I was so angry I could spit nails. The next day it was all I could do to collect myself to teach.

Between classes, uncharacteristically, an anti-social inclination came over me. I would stride angrily back to my office, slam the door to shut out the stupid world, and just sit there with almost clenched teeth, glaring defiantly at my hateful surroundings.

"Lord, I have served you faithfully. I have put you first and it just seems like you have put me last. Here, for your sake, I've burned my bridges behind me and you refuse to build any before me. Instead of helping, you seem to be teasing. Do I deserve to be jerked around like this? For two cents I'd just jump in my Datsun and head back to Denver."

That day I was a fool percolating foolish thoughts, a man reminiscent of Jonah himself. In the displacement of my irrational anger, I was mad at everything and anybody who might dare to violate my little spatial boundaries.

Let's face it. There are times when the Christian life doesn't seem to live up to its billing. God doesn't seem to perform as advertised. His behavior is maddeningly mysterious and He doesn't seem to be operating according to blueprint.

Never imagine that you are immune to a spiritual knockout. "Let him who thinks he stands beware lest he fall" (1 Corinthians 10:12). In dark hours of prolonged crisis, I have heard the finest of Christian men and women cry aloud, "Where's God? I don't understand. Where *is* God?"

Didn't the Psalmist say, "Why dost Thou stand afar off, O Lord? Why dost Thou hide Thyself in times of trouble?" (Psalm 10:1).

Wasn't a great saint totally mystified by the ways of God when he asked, "How long, O Lord? Wilt Thou forget me forever? How long wilt Thou hide Thy face from me? How long shall I take counsel in my soul, having sorrow in my heart all the day? How long will my enemy be exalted over me?" (Psalm 13:1–2).

Wasn't Job exasperated out of his mind by his falsely accusing friends when God wouldn't step forward and answer for him in the immensity and mystery of his sufferings?

Are we stronger than they are?

Once in a while that old philosopher's dilemma gnaws at our faith like a dog on a bone. If God is totally good, one ponders; he cannot be all-powerful since he isn't stopping the trouble. Then again, if he is all-powerful, he cannot be totally good and wise or else he would put a stop to all the misery and trouble we go through.

It's neither mentally nor spiritually healthy to be in denial. We must be honest with ourselves, but most of all with God about our thoughts and feelings. He knows them anyway. No use to hide them, so let's just agree to put away those phony "who, me struggling?" faces and get real. Before we go any further, let's just admit to ourselves that sometimes in our distresses such thoughts flit across our minds.

We may not like to admit it, but it is good for us to realize that in this flesh, our faith, however real, is a fragile thing and easily rattled. Otherwise, if like Peter (Matthew 26:33) we are too sure of ourselves, our faith is apt to get mugged in the alleys of reality. Moments occur when our theology blushes or bristles at the realities of our experience. We don't know how to reconcile the two. Times arise when God is thunderously silent in the face of our impassioned prayers and he seems unaccountably unresponsive to our predicaments. The operative word here is *seems*. The ways and works of God never deviate from his revealed character and promises. Never. In our human frailty and limited understanding, it sometimes seems that God is not measuring up to his résumé. How are we supposed to deal with that?

Is the answer just to trudge on in blind faith? No. Blind faith is not biblical faith. Biblical faith is rooted in revelation, which is grounded on historical testimony and evidence. The internal witness of the Holy Spirit confirms its truth.

No—blind, unthinking faith is not the answer. Blind faith is just another expression for gullibility, and this has nothing in common with Christian faith. Biblical faith is conviction built on facts, not irrational superstitions pulled mindlessly out of the air. The alternative to blind faith is what I term "monumental" faith.

What is meant by "monumental" faith? I do not mean "great" faith or heroic faith. No, this is a faith that has trained itself in the midst of adversity to *look back* at God's *past* demonstrations of his character and confirmations of his promises. These monuments are a testimony of what he will do in the present, regardless of the difficult things that are happening.

Sometimes our faith may be under such heat from the friction of affliction that we may find ourselves at risk of spiritual meltdown. Long before that happens it is time to practice preventive maintenance.

How? Whenever you pray, polish your personal monuments. Our tender faith often requires shelter. That shelter is the active memory of those demonstrations and confirmations of God's goodness, wisdom, power, and faithfulness that we have stored up from our past.

Whenever the mystery of our present experience of God obliterates any sign on our immediate horizon that God is who he claims to be, we need to hunker down under the umbrella of those trophies in our past. A "monumental" faith is able to look forward with confidence because it looks backward to the past. It discounts the baffling mysteries of present circumstances because it finds reassurance in his historical works, his uncompromising character, and his unchanging promises. Therein is strength and hope for the future.

The logic of monumental faith is simple. If God loved and cared for me in the past; if God displayed his power and wisdom for me in the past; if God in his essential and moral being is the same yesterday; today, and forever; if I myself am on the same spiritual page as before when the Lord showed his glory on my behalf, then nothing in this baffling instance has changed except his secret purposes.

God has not changed, and you have not changed, but his purpose is different this time around. Be still, rest in the shade of his monuments, and wait patiently for him to finish his work. In the end he'll be there just as he was before.

"God has said, 'Never will I leave you; never will I forsake you.' So we say with confidence, 'The Lord is my helper; I will not be afraid. What can man do to me?'" (Hebrews 13:5b–6).

As Alexander Maclaren once put it, "Memory passes into hope, and the radiance of the sky behind throws light onto our forward path . . . [the] past reveals the eternal principles which will mold his future acts."

Monumental faith is a faith trained to look away from the confusion of the moment to find security and confidence in the past evidences of God's character and faithfulness. The scriptures are replete with illustrations of monument building and polishing in the midst of the travails of God's people.

In Joshua 3, we find the armies of Israel poised at last for the impending invasion of the Promised Land. Their encampment lay near the banks of the swollen Jordan River, opposite Jericho. They were awaiting marching orders.

In front of them was a formidable obstacle. The Jordan and surrounding plain were in flood stage. But all this was providentially timed for God's purposes. One reason was to provide a miracle that would serve to accredit Joshua as Moses's divinely endorsed successor.

However, there was another important reason for the wonder God was about to perform. In chapter four we read that the Lord wanted a monumental memory that would be a foundation on which to trust him in the future.

On the previous day the people of Israel were given preliminary instructions. The first directive had to do with the order of march. The priests carrying the Ark of the Covenant of the Lord would move out first. Then the armies of Israel would follow. However, those following the priests and their sacred burden would at all times maintain a reverential distance of about 3,000 feet between the ark and the army.

The second instruction had to do with spiritual preparation. The next day God was about to perform a wonder that would link what he had done when their fathers crossed the Red Sea. At a specified point God was going to create a dam with his invisible hand so Israel could pass over to Canaan on dry ground. Note the word "dry" and marvel at the perfection of God's monument.

Such a close encounter with the presence and power of God calls for a consecrated people. Orders appropriate to that preparation were issued. The priests were instructed in their forward march to advance no farther than the spot where their feet touched the water's edge. There, in awe, they were to stand with everyone else while the power of God took center stage. Once the river basin cleared of passing water, the priests' orders were to take up their stations along with the ark in the middle of the riverbed, while the hosts of Israel passed by to the other side.

Joshua declared the Lord's intent to the people. God wanted to etch on their national consciousness an awareness of his presence and power among them. He did not want them to forget. In the future, he knew times would come when they might imagine he had deserted them or they might forget his grace and power.

He erected a monument, physically and mentally, to keep hope and confidence alive in their hearts. Whenever doubt cast its shadows, this monument would be a reminder in perpetuity that the God of Israel was the same yesterday, today, and forever.

Once Israel crossed over to the west bank, and before the priests withdrew from their positions in the middle of the river bed, Joshua ordered one representative from each tribe to return to the spot where the priests were standing. Each was told to pick up a big stone and bring it back to camp, where they were to pile up these rocks as a memorial to the miracle they had witnessed that day.

The import of this act is mentioned twice in chapter four, a repetition underscoring its importance in the divine scheme of things. This mound was created for all God's people to take note and learn the wisdom of memorializing God's past works.

Remember how Jesus' disciples, when confronted with the problem of finding resources to feed the 4,000, had already forgotten the earlier lesson in his feeding of the 5,000?

We are too lax about preserving the memory of God's mighty acts on our behalf. Those monuments need to be polished! Otherwise, our faith languishes under the load of affliction at those times when God, for his own good reasons, seems to be in silent retreat.

Let me share a personal example of how failing to polish my personal monuments created an unnecessary crisis of faith. It was on that day of shame, the day when I was so angry that God was allowing our family to remain separated.

However one wants to explain it, when I was having my little hissy-fit with God, the Holy Spirit broke into my space uninvited and seemed to force me into an internal dialogue. It was as if he said:

"Jim, do you remember a few years ago that you had a problem with your home in Lakewood, Colorado?"

"Yes, I remember."

"Do you recall the predicament you were in at that time?"

"I had forgotten."

The Lakewood house was a significant monument of the grace, power, and faithfulness of God that I had totally obliterated in this most recent trauma. How could I have lost sight of it? The Spirit of God was using my recovered memory to restore me to spiritual health.

You see, three or four years previous to this recent crunch, Olsie and I had decided to build the home we were now trying to sell. It was a similar situation. Our realtor, when the market was white-hot, had advised us to go slowly and avoid putting our old house on the market too soon. Otherwise it might sell while our new home was under construction, and we would have to move out long before we were ready. Seemed like good advice.

As things turned out, by the time we put it up for sale, the market had buckled considerably. Now we faced the grim prospect of owning two houses, having bridge loans, and other problems. On my Bible college instructor's income, that would have posed a severe hardship, if not a calamity.

But just as our realtor's contract expired, it came to the point where we, on our own, had one weekend to sell our house or face the ugly alternatives. If the pros couldn't sell this house in three months, what were our chances of moving it in a single weekend? With major prayer (but I must confess, scant confidence, for we had been praying all along) we ran an ad in *The Denver Post* and hoped for a miracle.

Saturday evening we were entertaining some missionary friends when the phone rang. Somebody had seen our ad and was interested in looking at the house. Great! The fellow wanted to come by on Sunday. I told him that Sunday would be fine, but it would have to be in the afternoon, since we were in church Sunday morning.

"I'll come by tomorrow afternoon. Hey, by the way, you mentioned attending church. What church do you attend?" It turned out that he was a member of the adult class I taught at Riverside Baptist Church. Unbelievable "coincidence"!

Sunday afternoon he signed on the dotted line. Done deal. Problem solved. The Lord saved the bacon. How could I have forgotten an act of God like that—the same way the disciples forgot and puzzled over how to provide food for another, yet smaller, crowd.

Now, a few years later, as I sat there stewing in my office over being separated from my family, the Lord gently coaxed my memory and brought to mind the fact that he had nothing to prove to me. In the past he had amply demonstrated his faithfulness, his goodness, his power and wisdom. How many times did he need to validate himself to me? Wasn't there a point where in the mysteries of the present I could fall back on the monuments of the past and trust his character and his promises?

If we have walked with God for any length of time, if we are veterans of the Christian life, then there must have been along the way some dark passages and deep valleys where God has created some rocks of remembrance. It is those monuments we must keep front and center in our consciousness for the stormy days.

When the Lord brought the sale of our former house to mind, perspective came into focus. Even through my emotionally blurred vision, I could clearly see the answer.

"Jim, have I changed?"

"Of course not, Lord."

"Have *you* changed? Are you still with the program? Have you stayed the same course?"

"Lord, you know *I* have not changed. If anything, your grace has improved and strengthened my walk. I know of no reason why, if you covered my back then, you would abandon me now."

"Then what do you suppose the difference is?"

"The difference must be your purpose. You had one design then, and another now. You are always the same. Your character is fixed. There is no moral variableness or dark shadow in it (James 1:17). What does change is what you are doing in my life at a given time, how you are training me. There may be some barnacles you are beating off my spiritual hull and this pounding is what it takes."

"There's your answer, Jim. Don't forget it. Polish your monuments for a rainy season when you can't see the Son shining."

Now, I did not have that literal "conversation" with God, but the Spirit did prompt an internal dialogue in approximately that vein.

All of a sudden my spiritual grip returned. Ashamed and humbled by my extreme immaturity and irreverence, I repented in sackcloth and ashes, as it were, resolving never again to forget God's monuments.

In a devotional by W. Glyn Evans, entitled *Daily with the King*, the following is written, "I will not demand that God explain himself to me at any time, for this is characteristic of the unregenerate man. I must be willing to let God be unreasonable, in my view, if necessary, because he is not concerned with my understanding, but with my faith. The unregenerate man sees contradiction in the world and demands that God justify himself before him; the believing man makes no such demand, but believes God supremely."[1]

That was a change point for me—one of those monumental illuminations that marked an important spiritual understanding. Right then and there I developed a little higher threshold for the mystery side of God. Since then it has gone even higher as we've experienced the horrifying and prolonged ordeal with Juli and her mysterious illness.

Exactly one week after losing our potential buyer, my wife called again. This time it was for real. A retired colonel and his college professor wife showed up at our door. They loved the house and offered us a higher price than we had been asking when we were so desperate to move. Is that amazing!

What God did back then still astounds me. That is why I regularly memorialize God's monuments of faithfulness. I store up in the "seven plentiful years" the great acts of God in my life, to feed my soul during those inevitable "seven lean years."

As you read about Juli and Paul's sufferings and what our family has endured, be assured that this habit of polishing monuments has played a large role in sustaining us. On many occasions when we were just about to lose our grip, this monument-polishing discipline was the difference between spiritual stability and utter calamity. For us it has been polish or perish.

So when, in the mysteries of God's inscrutable purposes, life turns into a monster, don't camp in the present. Take refuge in the past. Run to God's monuments. Lock your arms of faith around their testimony. Like the ark of Noah, they are there for you to ride out the raging floods and the deafening silences of God. Whatever the pounding, pummeling present may seem to say, he will never leave you or forsake you, even if he seems at times to hide from you.

In Isaiah 50:10 we are told, "Who is among you that fears the Lord, that obeys the voice of his servant, that walks in darkness and has no light? Let him trust in the name of the Lord and rely on his God."

Does polishing monuments bring a quick end to life's stressful circumstances? Hardly. Sometimes when snow falls, it piles up.

I remember in 1992 when we were about five years into my daughter's illness. Life at that point was very stressful. What significantly sapped our strength was that Olsie was needed to care for Juli, as her circumstances caused Paul to be a virtual housebound prisoner. At this point her illness began taking ugly new turns and complications just kept multiplying.

One morning at the church office where my wife served as our bookkeeper, she literally came apart. Suddenly she could no longer add simple figures—literally. Right there this blind man opened his eyes and saw that his wife, overwhelmed by more than any one woman could handle, was sinking fast and needed rest. I told her I was taking her home immediately. The very fact that she didn't object was a huge clue that she was not herself.

Once in the car, Olsie's rubber bands just snapped. For fifteen minutes solid she was irrational: writhing . . . kicking . . . screaming . . . and bouncing her head off the dash. I felt helpless and totally bewildered. I had no idea what to do and fear seized me.

I got her home, put her to bed and for the next six weeks or so she was in a state of classic clinical depression, staring into a black hole so deep she thought she would never again see the light of day. In the months leading up to her breakdown, she had gradually lost twenty-five pounds and was so heartbroken and drained at Juli's pitiful condition that all her fountains were dried up. She could no longer even cry. Now at last she collapsed emotionally in a fetal position on our bed. Occasionally she was tormented by literal voices taunting her and urging her to "Curse God and die!"

This happened to the most unlikely candidate on earth. Olsie has to be one of the strongest, most even-tempered, stable women alive. But even steel can bend and break under enough pressure. In fact, the doctor found her so anemic that she was near the point of needing a blood transfusion. How she stood up as long as she did is a wonder.

Thankfully, Olsie's sister Barb and husband Don flew out to assist us in the nick of time, because just when she needed less anxiety and my full-time attention, I had to undergo surgery for a herniated disk. And I thought all the usual pastoral pressures, including a new church building program, were enough. Yet, every new trial is an opportunity to establish a new monument.

Neither my wife nor I have ever been very good about asking for or receiving help—a streak of that hillbilly independence we grew up with in the mountains of West Virginia. Now this had to change somewhat. When Olsie went down for the count, it literally took twenty-three volunteers, in rotating shifts, to cover all she had been doing. Suddenly church people came out of the woodwork to fill in the gaps, as they poured out their love and care for our family.

Though Juli was unable to be with church helpers physically, the emotional vacuum for Juli and Paul was filled in such a way that the two of them ironically experienced a sense of family they had otherwise missed in our previous go-it-alone mode. This significantly alleviated their sense of total isolation.

How wise are the unexpected ways of our God! Yes, he is a God of miracles, but he is also a God of mysteries. When the God of mysteries shows up, just take refuge in the shadow of his monuments.

YEAR

5

July 30, 1992

Dear Friends,

Many of you have heard about the fiery trials my daughter Juli and son-in-law Paul have endured since 1987, as they both struggle with the debilitating illness known as CFS (Chronic Fatigue Syndrome) and my daughter with MCS (Multiple Chemical Sensitivities). We deeply appreciate your concerned questions and I'd like to explain the situation for those of you who are new to our church.

For the past few years Juli and Paul's life has been sinking like the doomed Titanic. Previously, they could each sit up for approximately two hours in half-hour increments, though Juli sat less than this. But they tried to keep their chins up and "the band played on." Unable to attend church or practice piano, they devoted their small portions of energy to decorating their rented house where the bed was always nearby. Juli and Paul have always been perfectionists—sticklers for color, order, and coordination. Before Paul became ill, he had already done the more extensive work of painting, wallpapering, laying linoleum, and carpeting. The small decorating tasks they undertook brought them a sense of normalcy and cheer.

Now even that is gone. Her chemical sensitivities worsened to the point where we had to strip the house down to everything except their bed. Just as we see in Job chapter one that Satan wanted to destroy Job's very life, God's protective hand allowed Satan instead to test Job by destroying his possessions, his family, and finally his own health. In Juli and Paul's case, the stripping of their house and other human comforts has become a metaphor for the Spartan existence forced upon them in every area of their lives.

Because of her CFS, Juli has become completely bedridden. With her energy descending down to minus zero, she can barely lift her head off the pillow and walk to the bathroom. She needs help even to take a bath. It's so hard to watch such a high-spirited, life-loving girl wasted by a total vacuum of physical energy. It's also heartbreaking for Juli, who loves sunshine and pretty flowers, to be imprisoned in her bed and to have no energy for a single creative outlet.

I'm often asked by well-meaning folks eager to understand Juli's plight, "Chronic Fatigue Syndrome? Is Juli just tired all the time?"

That is a natural question, given the name of the illness. This, by the way, is as cruel as naming Parkinson's disease "Chronic Shaking Disorder," or paraplegia "Perpetual Sitting Syndrome." Unfortunately, the symptoms she has in no way resemble the typical use of the word "fatigue." Let me try to explain.

Juli describes the sensation as a kind of "temporary painful paralysis," where every movement bathes her muscles in what feels like a paralyzing poison-causing pain, heaviness, and intense pressure. Continued exertion increases the symptoms until she has no alternative but to lie still and rest until the toxins break up and leave her system. Only then can she attempt another movement, which starts the whole process over again.

No, Juli is not simply "tired." Imagine for a moment having the strength literally drained from your body so that the slightest exertion leaves you utterly exhausted and unable to move for hours or days. Imagine living in constant pain, where every movement you have the energy to make is agony. Add to that a devilish sleep disorder, which makes it impossible for you to sleep, sometimes for weeks at a time. Mix in the pain of being misunderstood, labeled a malingerer, lazy, or simply depressed, making this whole nightmare somehow your fault and something you could fix if you simply had the will. Don't forget the pain of seeing your dreams for the future vanish like smoke, as year after year, instead of growing stronger, your situation grows more desperate with each passing day. Ponder well these things and you will have only a glimpse of what Juli and Paul have been enduring.

As if all that weren't enough, things have intensified with Juli's chemical sensitivities. She is now sensitized to almost any type of chemical (especially phenol and formaldehyde, which seem to be in almost everything). She detects and reacts severely to odors that only animals can smell at such distances. It is now at a point where she even reacts to Paul if he has one of these chemicals on his person.

Her condition and required care is almost beyond belief. It is a wonder that she, Paul, and my wife are in their right minds. If something doesn't give soon, one of them may go over the edge.

As I've told many of you, the burning and searing pain in her veins and muscles that these reactions incur is out of this world. Psychosomatic? Try to fool her system and her body immediately reacts from any place in the house. Although skepticism remains in the medical community, other people have reported the same phenomena, though it is something we had never heard of or could have imagined before this.

Here are some examples of the situation we face daily.

A few months back, she experienced a severe reaction to a shirt I was wearing. I had removed my sport coat but the shirt, undetected by me, contained a residue of dry cleaning fluids. Within minutes, with a barrier between us, she had a reaction. Who could believe such a thing?

On another occasion, Olsie bought some earplugs from a girl who was wearing perfume. When Olsie was approaching Paul so he could give them to Juli, he could smell the aroma. Since those earplugs would have thrown Juli into a painful tailspin, from which she wouldn't be able to recover, they had to be returned and exchanged for new, fragrance-free replacements. Unfortunately, this has become an all-too-familiar routine. To do anything for them, Olsie must go a hundred yards to take one step, so to speak.

Not long ago, Paul accidentally dried his hair with a stray towel that had fabric softener on it. For days he was unable to enter Juli's room, except to run her food in, then beat a hasty retreat. Trying everything, he finally cut off all his hair and resorted to coating his scalp with tomato paste, since he knew it worked on skunk odor. It dulled the "fumes" to a degree, but what a humiliating price! Eventually another patient shared the secret to finally neutralizing the phenol/perfume smell: Heinz Apple Cider Vinegar! Nobody but Paul is "safe" enough environmentally to be with her. He only leaves the house on a very limited basis, being extremely careful to avoid contacting any materials or odors.

Nevertheless, God's staying hand is in their midst. Even though Juli's condition has worsened, Paul has recently begun to make some major strides so that he is able to care for her and tend to their basic needs. However, he needs prayer. He is still not strong, very underweight, and afflicted with chronic infections that cause his eyes to get red and swollen.

People have trouble relating to the circumstances of this illness. They ask if we should hospitalize Juli. Are you kidding? The kind of environmentally protected unit that Juli needs is not available to us locally. The chemicals within a typical hospital could kill her overnight. Can we get help someplace else? Juli is so incredibly fragile that we would jeopardize what little health she has by taking her out of state.

On the other hand, if help could come to her, the "detoxing" procedures alone would be a challenge. They would involve purchasing special clothing, bathing to eliminate perms, deodorants, perfumes, lotions, and so forth. Who would be willing to go through all these contortions just to get near enough to examine or help her? So we are in between the proverbial rock and hard place. Now that we're in this situation, all sorts of horror stories come out of the woodwork. We confront the reality that there is an underworld of human misery and broken health that medical science is virtually ignoring. "Blessed be the God and Father of our Lord Jesus Christ, the Father of mercies and God of all comfort, who comforts us in all our affliction, so that we may be able to comfort those who are in any affliction, with the comfort with which we ourselves are comforted by God" (2 Corinthians 1:3,4).

As for our plight, God in his goodness has enabled us to complete construction on an environmentally safe home close to the church. This way Juli and Paul can receive help with errands from Olsie and Paul's folks, who moved here from New York. This building project was very complicated, extremely labor-intensive, and included many expensive materials. But Juli and Paul are now moved into their "safe" house. While they still have no furniture, their bed is placed near the French doors so she can look out into the pretty backyard with its abundance of trees and friendly squirrels.

For months Juli rarely sees or talks to any human but Paul. Both are almost totally cut off from the outside. Juli doesn't even have the luxury of reading, as she is allergic to the print and chemicals in the paper. For Olsie and me, all direct communication has been cut off for months. What an agony! She can't talk on the phone or see pictures of the family, so we communicate entirely through Paul. We miss her terribly. It's killing Olsie inch by inch to feel so helpless, knowing that Juli's frail body has dwindled down to eighty-nine pounds. God only knows how Olsie maintains her strength.

I have no idea how Juli and Paul keep their mental sanity. With every diversion cut off from them, they have taken to memorizing whole chapters of scripture. He memorizes a few verses when he is far enough away from her to read, then returns and repeats them to her. Yet, to this hour I have never—and I mean never—heard a word of complaint. There are wimps and there are warriors; Juli and Paul definitely fit the latter category. Their fight and endurance constantly astound me. However, there have been many tears of pain and confusion. There seem to be no answers—no way out. Believe it or not, I've only told you about sixty percent of their ordeal.

Still, their faith holds strong. How are they coping through it all?

Juli finally had an occasion to explain their spiritual perspective. The following are some excerpts taken from a letter she wrote for her mother, who at the time had succumbed to the inevitable and had an emotional and physical collapse. To give you some idea of the demands of this disease, every word was "dictated" by Juli from inside the house to Paul, who wrote them down on paper in the garage:

I wanted to write and let you know how I'm doing spiritually and about the extra measure of grace that God has given me to cope emotionally. I'm praying that the Holy Spirit will use my letter to give you that same grace. I emphasize Holy Spirit because only he can break through the darkness, gloom, and depression that you feel. I know this from personal experience.

A few days ago, Paul and I were talking about our ordeal. I was crying and he was trying to help me spiritually, because I had said to God in my prayers "How do you expect me to cope with all this when I can't see my parents, fellowship with your people, or pick up my Bible like everyone else and get perspective?" Paul said, "But that's exactly the enemy's strategy, to cut off your spiritual supply lines." Then the Holy Spirit brought to my mind a passage that we had memorized in 1 Peter 5:

Be of sober spirit; be on the alert. Your adversary the devil prowls around like a roaring lion, seeking someone to devour, but resist him, firm in your faith, knowing that the same experiences of suffering are being accomplished by your brethren in the world. And after you have suffered for a little while, the God of all grace, who called you to his eternal glory in Christ, will himself perfect, confirm, strengthen, and establish you.

Somehow just knowing Satan's strategy strengthened my resolve to fight the good fight, but I still needed to know that God cared about what I was going through. Then the Spirit brought the prior verses in 1 Peter 5 to my mind:

"Humble yourselves therefore under the mighty hand of God, that he may exalt you at the proper time. Casting all your anxiety on him because he cares for you."

He cares for you! At this point the Holy Spirit turned back on my spiritual light and gave me the extra measure of grace that has lasted me until now. Along with this I received the following insights:

How was Satan trying to devour me? By trying to convince me that God did not care, and therefore I would never be able to cast all my anxiety on him. He also tried to convince me that God would never exalt me and bring me out of this situation. Then Peter says to resist him. How?

By humbling myself under the mighty hand of God. I had to admit that I could not take care of myself, that God was in control and that he could bring me out any time he wanted.

I also resist Satan by being firm in my faith. How do I do that? By knowing that other Christians are undergoing the same kind of suffering as I am. That's what Paul was telling me that night. He reminded me that Satan tries to use isolation from God's word, from other Christians, or both, to devour believers.

I resist him by knowing that after I have suffered for a little while, the same God whose grace brought me to his salvation will also bring me out of this situation. He *will* perfect, confirm, strengthen, and establish me.

Satan has tried to use my illness and isolation to devour me. He is using your physical and emotional exhaustion to try to devour you. He is attacking your mind because it is chemically imbalanced with severe depression. I know that Luther and Spurgeon went through similar bouts with depression. Other men and women of God throughout time have gone through extreme torment with depression and it is this very point that I want you to see. Satan is attacking you because you belong to God and are valuable to his eternal cause.

When Satan asked God's permission to test Job, God said that Job was upright and blameless in his sight. Job went through severe depression for dozens of chapters, but God eventually delivered him. We all need to remember this. James 5 says, "You have heard of the endurance of Job and have seen the outcome of the Lord's dealings, that the Lord is compassionate and is merciful."

A few months back Paul told me that a verse you were hanging onto was, "My grace is sufficient for you." It is! But we also need to remember that, "My power is made manifest in weakness." It takes little perception to conclude that God wants our whole family, between my illness, Dad's surgery, and your depression, to be in a perpetual state of weakness.

I am reminded of the passage where Jesus was told that Lazarus had died. When he went there, Mary was so consumed by grief that she could only cry and say, "Lord if you had been here, my brother would not have died." That's where I was a few months ago, and that may be where you are now. Jesus never chastised Mary for weeping, but wept alongside her.

Jesus, the very God of very God, experienced every kind of human suffering. He doesn't ask us to go through anything that he did not go through himself. This is one of the few perspectives that helps me.

While my earthly mother is limited in her ability to care for me, my Heavenly Father is not. Every time I look out at our pretty birdbath, the Spirit reminds me of how little the birds do to care for themselves. They don't sow, reap, or gather into barns, and yet God feeds them. How much more does he care for you and me.

God continues to provide for my needs. Just when I think, "I'm getting allergic to everything on my plate; I won't have anything to eat," he provides a new type of food I can handle.

I've also begun to notice a slight increase in energy over the last few weeks. Even my ability to dictate this letter to Paul is proof that I have the mental energy to focus my thoughts. I feel like I have more and more strength to function.

And he has faithfully provided members of our church to take care of our ongoing needs. They are incredibly caring, consistent, and committed. We literally have a small army to help—and it takes one to keep our lives going. When the burden is spread over dozens of people, it is not only easier, but more efficient. Now you can spend all of your time caring for me in the way only you can, as my emotional support and sounding board.

Because we have so many people helping and coming by the house, I no longer feel so lonely and isolated. Even though I can't go to church, I feel like I have a church family. Just knowing that someone is running an errand for us or is out on the corner praying helps us hang on emotionally.

Please don't worry about my loneliness, Mom. It's still really hard, but not only are church people there for me but also God has provided me companionship in a way few women experience: the unconditional, undivided love and devotion of the godliest man I could have ever asked for. God may not choose to give us a family, but Paul is always by my side, loving me as Christ loves his bride.

As you can imagine, such wisdom and concern for the well-being of her mother, amid the swirling vortex of her own afflictions, evoked in me no small measure of joy and wonder.

Thank you for your prayers,

Pastor Jim

The "Peninnah Factor"

Monuments, like buildings, require a foundation. Our foundation is the verity that God has spoken. It is this revelation that informs our faith and defines the attributes of God. It gives us boundaries so we know what we can rightly expect of God. He has told us how he will care for us. He has shown us how he cared for his people in the past. Our personal monuments equip us with extra-biblical testimony that our foundation—our revelation—is dependable. We can rely on him in our trials to be as faithful to us today as he was in history.

There are many stories of suffering found in the Bible. One of these concerns a husband, Elkanah, and his two wives, Hannah and Peninnah. My concern is not about the morality, healthiness, or wisdom of being married to two women.

That is a separate issue. I want to focus on a situation that I call the "Peninnah factor."

Hannah was unable to conceive a child, while Peninnah was blessed with many sons and daughters. She never let Hannah forget it. The text tells us "Her rival, however, would provoke her bitterly to irritate her" (1 Samuel 1:6).

This happened year after year. As often as Hannah went up to the house of the Lord, Peninnah would provoke her, so she wept and would not eat. This woman suffered a human pestilence in her life, who took pernicious delight in needling her out of her mind.

On these occasions Elkanah would ask, "Hannah, why are you weeping? Why don't you eat? Why are you downhearted? Don't I mean more to you than ten sons?" To reassure her of his deep affection, Elkanah would double up Hannah's table portions as a token of her standing in his eyes.

Even so, Hannah continued to feel inadequate as a woman. She had failed to present her husband with the gift of a child, particularly a son. In that ancient culture, this was a huge deal for a woman. It is one thing to feel you are a failure. It is another to have someone around who takes cruel pleasure in rubbing your face in it.

You may not have a rival to tear you down, but you may struggle like Hannah with feelings of inadequacy or being shortchanged by God. Many must deal daily with some pit bull who constantly runs them down and tears at their sense of self. Some may face more than one "Peninnah factor." Whatever shape it takes, such psychological abuse makes its target feel like a social leper.

On one occasion when Hannah was attending the yearly religious festivities, she excused herself and headed toward the temple of the Lord. Eli the priest was sitting by the doorpost when she arrived. Greatly distressed, she began to pray and weep bitterly.

She cried within her spirit and made a vow saying, "O Lord of hosts" that is, Lord of armies. What armies? Heavenly armies, earthly armies—all the forces at God's command, human or supernatural. She appealed to the God of all powers, the God who is able in his sovereignty to marshal whatever forces he chooses to answer any request. Hannah implored the Lord God who is able to bridle the taunts of a mean-spirited rival.

"If you will only look upon your servant's misery," Hannah continued, "and remember me, and not forget your servant but give her a son, then I will give him to the Lord for all the days of his life" (1 Samuel 1:11).

Well, wouldn't you know it? Eli, observing, only got it half right and jumped to conclusions. Seeing only her desperate lips moving but hearing no words, he assumed she was smashed. Put off by such presumed excess, he said sharply, "How long will you keep on getting drunk? Get rid of your wine."

Hannah corrected his premature judgment, "I am a woman who is deeply troubled. I have not been drinking wine or beer; I was pouring out my soul to the Lord. Do not take your servant for a wicked woman; I have been praying here out of my great anguish and grief" (1:15–16).

Insensitive and sometimes crushing mistakes are inevitable when the rush to judgment arrives ahead of the facts. Partial knowledge can be more destructive than ignorance.

To red-faced Eli's credit, he quickly reversed himself and in his official position as a priest of God, he pronounced a blessing and said, "Go in peace, and may the God of Israel grant you what you have asked of him."

Hannah replied, "May your servant find favor in your eyes." Then she went out, took nourishment, and her countenance revived. Hope does that.

This reminds me of a recent story about how in Washington, D.C. they distinguish between an optimist and a pessimist. The pessimist says, "Things are as bad as they can get." The optimist says, "No, they're not. They can always get worse."

Sometimes we're like Hannah. We feel as though we're in a situation where things can always get worse. Circumstances continue to spiral downward. We feel abused, misused, and misunderstood. Life comes cascading down upon us with all of its burdens. We barely exist in a world of ache. That is where this dear woman was, along with her husband, who was hurting just watching her writhe in pain.

God allowed a situation in her life like one he might allow in yours. It may take a form that you, and the people around you, don't understand. I've been there and perhaps you have also. These are mysteries and it doesn't pay the bills to stand around and ask, "Lord, why? Why? Why?" Not that the question is wicked; it's just worthless. It gets us nowhere.

Misused and misunderstood. All of us will know this drill, sooner or later. Hannah and her husband walked with God, but she had this exasperating Peninnah factor in her life—and it was eating her emotional lunch.

Lest we overlook the obvious, let us remind ourselves that the most godly men and women are all certifiably human. In provocative circumstances, the best among us can roll out a whole gamut of unruly emotions. It does not necessarily mark you as a religious hypocrite if you temporarily react less than angelically when confronted as Hannah was with the vexations of a Peninnah factor. The most decisive thing spiritually in these situations is not where we start out, but where we end up.

Most men and women of God will experience passion surges when misused, misunderstood, and misrepresented. It's okay to acknowledge (not to say "approve") every blip on our emotional radar, from swells of anger to bitterness, resentment, grief, and despondency. Let's cut ourselves a little slack here and be human. Grace just means we're urban renewal projects in process.

Lord, deliver us from those "saints" who pretend to live in a passion-free zone, who always convey the impression they walk through these emotional mine fields with perfect equanimity. I'm sorry, but those "saints" are "aints." Such folk are either liars or zombies. As we learn from the Bible itself, and most especially from the Psalms, God's people in the Peninnah zone experience and express a torrent of mixed emotions. I am not suggesting we just shrug when our passions run riot and say dismissively, "Hey, look, I'm just fallen flesh here. Circumstances owe me the right to be a jerk if I feel like it. So if I go toxic, I think I can bank on a gracious, understanding God to overlook my excesses." No, not at all. I'm just saying that it's natural (that's the problem, however) at Peninnah time to feel these spikes of emotional distress, these sun flares in the soul. Hannah was there. But at the end of the day she handled it the best way.

The reason Hannah is such a symbol of hope for us is because we know her to be a woman of God. One reason so many of us love reading the Psalms is that the psalmists were utterly real. These servants of God laid bare the whole emotional anatomy of their humanness. They pulled no punches. With perfect candor they went before the Lord and said, "This is where I am and this is how I'm feeling." In the end, however, they always put their arms around their monuments of faith and clung to their original convictions.

This helps us because you and I can go to the Lord like Hannah with our Peninnah factors. There are times when we are distraught, depressed, oppressed, and provoked. "Oh God, help me!" we cry.

One difference between godly people and those who aren't is that the godly will intercept these emotions, bundle them up with their burdens, and lay both right where they belong—before the Lord. "Let us come boldly to the throne of grace, that we may find mercy and grace to help us in time of need" (Hebrews 4:16).

They don't allow these things to hijack their lives to the point of drawing them away from God and diverting them from the highways of righteousness, at least not for very long.

The struggle to keep aroused emotions within proper boundaries is won by putting a conscious leash on them and leading them like junkyard dogs right to the throne of grace.

Hannah, even though a godly woman, did make one natural, but serious tactical error in the way she related to her distress. Like many of us, she had a master's degree in self-pity and used it unwittingly to aggravate her pain. You see, victims always master the art of counting their burdens instead of their blessings. This habit can be a spiritual disaster.

Many of us are in the emotional tank much deeper than necessary because we have become burden-counters instead of blessing-counters. Spiritual honesty is a virtue—provided we can see God's blessings behind our burdens.

What was Hannah forgetting? She forgot a treasure, a blessing that many of us can never thank God for enough. She had a godly, immensely caring spouse, a husband who loved her more than life itself. Elkanah was for that day, or any day for that matter, uncommonly compassionate and understanding of her grief. To be married to someone who loves to the limit is a blessing that can lighten a multitude of burdens.

Though she lived with a constant tormentor and had every reason to be in pain, the burden of her existence could have been lightened if she had been mindful to add more and subtract less. It is extremely tempting to be preoccupied with what has been taken from us, as opposed to concentrating on what has been given to us. Many of us are more prone to wallow in the pits of life than to revel in its pinnacles.

Hannah, you see, would have been wiser had she said, "Lord, I'm really hurting. But before I tell you about my burdens, I want to thank you for my blessings. I have a home. I have a model husband who loves me dearly and provides for me." This, my friends, is what the Apostle Paul means when he says, "Do not be anxious about anything, but in everything by prayer and petition, *with thanksgiving*, present your requests to God. And the peace of God, which transcends all understanding, *will guard your hearts and minds in Christ Jesus*" (Philippians 4:6–7).

There was one event in my life that started me on the path to learning thankfulness. I began to learn the value of that discipline as a young pastor fresh out of seminary in West Virginia. My habit was to be in the office at 7:00 a.m. and spend the first hour praying in the church sanctuary, the perfect venue for my peripatetic mode of talking with God. On one particular day I was pretty much in the tank. I had been unveiling all my burdens to the Lord, when in a flash of self-consciousness I noticed, during my circuits around the aisles, my sluggish pace, which mirrored my sunken spirits.

Convicted by the Spirit of my preoccupation with my problems and my ingratitude for a veritable treasure of God's goodness surrounding me, I hastened to repent for counting my pains instead of my gains. I immediately rectified my error. Stopping to inventory the wealth of his benefits that I daily enjoyed, spiritual and temporal, I moved from tears to tribute. I thanked the Lord for His kindnesses, that in my light depression I had ignored. Soon after I switched mental gears, I experienced another brief window of self-awareness.

There was a dramatic change in my whole physical mien. The transition from "tears to tribute" had so unconsciously affected me that the slug-on-the-rug had morphed into a man-on-a-mission. My walk was now brisk and purposeful.

This is a lesson my daughter has been learning—one that has kept her from sinking irretrievably into the mire of depression and despair. You see, like Hannah, she too deeply desires children, as does Paul. Before they were married, he used to tease her by holding up four of her fingers as a fun-loving indication of the number of kids he wanted to have. Juli would tease him back by curling two of the four fingers back down inside her hand. Like most Christian couples, they naturally assumed God would grant them the joy of a family of their own.

God in his providence has not seen fit to grant this desire. All things are possible with God, but the sad fact is he probably has a different plan for them than parenthood. That is pretty painful stuff. But, even more wrenching is watching God bestow this blessing on friend after friend and family member after family member, not to mention all their peers in our church who are starting families. This is piling pain on top of pain.

Now, please don't misunderstand me. Neither Juli nor Paul begrudges this happiness to anyone, but it is difficult in such circumstances to rejoice at every new birth announcement—of which there have literally been scores. As Proverbs 25:20 so aptly describes, "Like one who takes away a garment on a cold day, or like vinegar poured on soda, is one who sings songs to a heavy heart."

But in her grief, Juli has been granted a blessing to help even the scales, so to speak. God has not seen fit to grant her a child, but he has given her a "double" portion when it came to providing a mate. He has not left her comfortless, but granted to her a unique companion who lovingly and tenderly cares for her needs and heroically shares her hardships and burdens. Polishing this monument doesn't lessen the pain of being childless, but it does help her put life into perspective. This lightens the load to a degree and makes her difficult circumstances endurable.

When you run into the Peninnah factor in life, when something is irritating your spirit and it's all over you like white on rice, there are four ways to go.

The first is to turn in on ourselves and become so bitter that nobody can stand us. Let me tell you something about anger. With this emotion, the safer person may be the one who wears his "heat" on his sleeve, who pops off steam before it builds up and everything explodes. I didn't say this person was necessarily safe, just perhaps safer than the fellow who represses it behind a placid exterior only to lose it in a volcanic explosion.

This is the kind of person who will show up at the office with shotgun in one hand and an Uzi in the other. There's normal anger and then there's pent-up rage. When dealing with this strong passion, don't be tempted to turn inward and fill up with smoldering wrath. This option is not a good one. Control and repression are two different things.

Then there's a second option. We can turn on those who are our enemies or provocateurs. Now, that would be not only godless, but it makes us just like them. Bad choice.

The third option is to turn away from God and abandon any hope for relief and redemption. As a minister, I've seen this happen in many pastors' families. People often wonder, "What's wrong with the pastor's children?" Well, they've seen dad get the whey pummeled out of him by congregational factions and they become disillusioned and bitter, and eventually displace the blame by putting it all on God. Consequently they abandon the Lord. Sad.

Hannah made the fourth choice. She turned *to* God and entrusted the resolution of the difficulty to his love, power, and wisdom. Meanwhile, she looked to him to sustain her until that time. This is the option for us.

We cannot let wild, unruly feelings have their way with us. Like smoke when it invades a home, it is nearly impossible to chase it all back out the door. You can open all the windows to air out the room, but the odor lingers. In time, fresh air will clear it, but you *do* have to open the windows. It's the same for negative or destructive feelings. We have to open up, let the refreshing breeze of the Word and Spirit of God circulate through the soul and let time assist in its way.

Like Hannah, go to the Lord and share your feelings. When your Peninnah provokes you with statements like, "If you were spiritual . . . if you were any kind of woman (or man) you would . . . ," take it to God's throne in prayer.

Let me share with you another monument from our past that illustrates this point. When Juli and Paul were still living in southeast Portland, before they moved into their "environmentally safe house," things got very sticky. Dealing with her medical problems was already too much for both of them to handle, but then one neighbor started piling on and compounding their misery, especially for Paul.

Clod (not his real name) lived almost directly across the street from Juli and Paul, idling away most days warming his backside in his porch swing or slouching on his front step, smoking, being snide and sulky. A miserable man, Clod loathed himself and liked to spread his bile around, especially to anyone who appeared better than he was—not a very high bar for most people.

With classic psychological projection, he began regularly railing at Paul every time the poor guy showed his face in public, having the temerity to assail *him* as a guy who was "loafing around all the time and doing nothing." The clueless misanthrope was totally ignorant of all the extremities Paul was dealing with, unaware that Paul was up on his feet when most people would have been down on their beds, and was desperately trying to hold life together for Juli and himself.

Paul could handle this, but it was ripping Juli apart emotionally, knowing the loud verbal scorn her husband had to endure every time he showed his face. To be perfectly honest, I myself would probably have walked over there and jerked a knot in his tail, but Paul's hands were too full to concern himself with Clod. Besides, Paul is by nature a gentler soul than his father-in-law. (I have learned to turn the other cheek, but it turns under protest like a heavy door on rusty hinges.) Juli's reaction was faithfully genetic. However, she was in no condition to play Terminator, a helpless feeling that only exacerbated her emotional tension.

Debility as much as piety forced on her the better alternative—prayer. As it turned out, Clod might have been better off had Juli played the shrew and come at him with a rolling pin rather than making him the object of her rolling prayer. She began to petition the Lord earnestly to get Clod off Paul's overburdened back. Still, the rest of that spring and summer they just had to put up with it.

Aggravating the situation, though owing to sheer insensitivity rather than hostility, was the annoying practice of the widow next door who babysat children to help make ends meet. Juli and Paul desperately needed long hours of uninterrupted sleep just as a newborn needs warm milk. The problem was that this lady was always turning her small fry loose right under Juli and Paul's window at 7:00 a.m., interrupting their sleep cycle. As much as they tried to explain the situation to her, she just didn't seem to get it.

So between Clod and Maude (not her real name), Juli and Paul's tortured life was doubly maddening that spring and summer.

The winter months brought relief, but as the next spring approached, Juli intensified her prayers, asking the Lord somehow to silence Clod and keep Maude's ankle-biters at a sleepable distance from their window.

Well, spring arrived, the time when restless kings and people like Clod go to war. Funniest thing though. Clod never showed up on his front porch. Blessedly strange. Not only that, but, for some reason, no kids turned up at Maude's place either. We all kept waiting for the other shoe to drop. This was too good to be true.

One day around mid-summer, the mystery was solved. Olsie was doing some yard work at Juli's when she encountered Maude, who had gone sight unseen this whole time. Curious about the whereabouts of Clod, Olsie inquired gently, "Maude, I haven't seen Clod. He is usually out on his front porch. Where is he?"

"Oh, didn't you hear?" she asked in surprise. "Early this spring he went out camping and dropped dead."

Whoa! Can you believe that? Not that we take pleasure in someone's death *per se*, but our faith had to be lifted by such a timely marker of God's sovereign exertion in our behalf and his tender compassion for the helpless and oppressed. Experiences like that pump air back into the tires of flat faith.

But that was just part of the story. That covered, Olsie delicately mentioned to Maude that she had been kind of invisible. Maude then related that her nephew had been seriously injured weeks earlier in some kind of street scrap, as I recall. His care required her to suspend for that summer her day care operation.

Amazing! Just when we felt heaven was a brass ceiling, God broke through the overwhelming darkness with timely relief. These shining monuments, combined with others in our past, reinforced our faith and reminded us of God's promise, "I will never leave you nor forsake you" (Hebrews 13:5b). When shortly thereafter God seemed once again to disappear behind the clouds of crisis and disregard our pleas day after day, such memories from our past served us as sustaining monuments in the lonely present.

But there is more that we can learn from this narrative. Have you ever noticed that when things come into your life, they tend to come in lumps? Whenever there is a plane crash—that's when I don't want to fly. It just seems like things come in triplicate. Probably not, but sometimes it just seems that way. The point is, if blessings sometimes seem to come in clusters, so do burdens. Shall we call them "cluster bombs"?

Well, here is Hannah who has all that she can handle. She is doing a good thing the best way that she knows how. Yes, there is a tactical omission in not being thankful. But, hey, this woman is fundamentally right. She's taking her burdens and going to the Lord. She's saying that God is the one who can help her, that he has all knowledge, all power, and all wisdom. And she pleads for his mercy. Hannah was doing what was spiritually healthy, and here was this judgmental priest writing her off as a mumbling drunk hanging around the porch of the church.

You know, there are times when it's piling on. It's just too much. This is what Hannah felt. Sometimes it's well-meaning people, other times not so well-meaning. Sometimes those around us just stupidly aggravate our injuries like Penninah. In our daughter's siege of illness, my wife Olsie and I have lived close to the edge of total disaster for years. At least three different times I sat down to write a letter of resignation from my pastorate because I couldn't handle the piling on any more.

About Juli and Paul, and I say this with no irreverence, Job suffered more, but to this point he never suffered any better than these two young people. They continue to amaze me with their spiritual endurance and uncomplaining spirit. I must confess that at times my own response to this stress has been less than heroic.

There was unbelievable pain. So much that Olsie, as you remember, broke down emotionally around five years into it. Then out of the blue Juli started showing some signs of improvement. First she was able to get up every so often for about two minutes during the day. Next she had the strength to venture outside and sit on the porch for about ten minutes. This was big. Apparently the CFS component of her sickness was yielding. However, the savage MCS remained, as she was still a far cry from anything resembling normal health.

This temporary improvement did wonders for my wife's emotional health. When she learned that she could actually see Juli and talk to her from a distance, the water came roaring back into her emotional well. The transformation was about as dramatic as when Jesus told the paralytic to rise and walk!

Olsie rallied from these circumstances, but then the piling on started. Some who knew absolutely nothing conceded that there was an illness all right, but insinuated it was actually a *mental* illness and it was all in our daughter's head. That almost killed Olsie.

One well-intentioned, but woefully uninformed and egregiously misguided lady went to the trouble of forming a support group for us and invited Olsie and me to a first meeting to recharge our batteries. She somehow had it in her head that Juli's problem was an anxiety disorder. She had also found a book in a local library on panic attacks and presented it to us during the meeting. With the help of a well-connected physician in the group, she had, all on her own, arranged a bought-and-paid-for appointment for Juli with a biologic psychiatrist at Oregon Health Sciences University.

This lady had never seen Juli, never asked us about Juli, had almost no specific knowledge of her symptoms, yet made up her own mind about the nature of her condition and went to all that trouble to "help" us fix her. Even if she had some treatable psychiatric condition, her chemical sensitivities would not have allowed her to come within 1,000 yards of a chemically-intensive venue like a medical center. She would have nearly died on the spot. Such ignorance on the part of a "support group" was highly deflating.

But it was really piling on when this group, following this woman's lead, "informed" us of the psychiatric nature of our daughter's illness and cheerily announced the initiatives they had taken to get her fixed. I almost heard Olsie's heart shatter like manhandled crystal right there on the spot. For those young people to endure all they had gone through, and for Olsie to cope, and to have grossly uninformed people suggest such a stupid thing, was almost more than we could take.

When we got home, despite her brokenness, Olsie had the strength to read the book and almost went into shock at its impertinence. I then stayed up into the wee hours reading it myself and was incredulous that what these folk imagined our daughter suffered from was as remote from her symptoms as flu is from a stroke. Not one symptom in common. Not even close. Well, I knew then that if we continued with this kind of "support" I would lose my wife again to clinical depression and this time the rubber band may get so stretched it would break! So I had to find a way to opt out, but politically speaking it was not going to be easy. All but one of those folk became estranged and our original troubles were amplified until at last all broke ranks and left our church.

That is what I mean by piling on. That's part of the Peninnah factor. One layer is bad enough, but then some folk always find ways of making bad matters worse.

But that wasn't the end of it. Because Olsie had to be such a tireless caregiver, the rumor circulated that Juli had become overly dependent on her mom! Now that was vicious. Way over the top. But sometimes piling on goes with the territory of saints in suffering. Somehow inside there builds a fury that only the grace of God can stem. The hurt goes so deep that the pain hasn't left to this day.

I know a pastor who was serving a church of about 200 in the state of Washington. The salary was marginal. In fact, by state standards, it was just under the poverty line. The church, with its limited resources, did not pay for medical insurance. Thus the family was always just one hospital illness away from financial disaster.

Fortunately, Washington State offers a state-sponsored catastrophe insurance for which the pastor's family qualified. When someone in the church heard that the pastor and his family were on this state program, he took offense. So this member invited the pastor to breakfast and shared his concern about the alleged "abuse" of this state provision for folks in that low income bracket.

"Why is that?" the pastor asked. "I do need insurance, you know."

"Well," replied the man, "you ought to pay your own. You're taking money from the poor."

Of course, the pastor thought for all the world he was in that category, but he didn't argue. Instead he asked the gentleman what he proposed as an alternative.

"Well, I'd sell my home, and move to a lower income neighborhood, then use that money to buy insurance," offered the man with a straight face, as if the pastor's modest home (which his in-laws had helped the family buy) were Fat City itself.

Here a financially challenged young couple in the ministry thought they were serving and honoring God by not complaining or placing financial demands on the congregation. Instead of getting credit for trusting the Lord to provide their daily needs on a poverty-level salary, the pastor finds this shameless character discrediting him for ostensibly robbing the pockets of the poor! That's too much.

That's the way Hannah felt. What she was doing was right, but Eli piled on. In the midst of all this pain, instead of commending her for being a pious woman, he called her a drunk.

Life sometimes works like that. But in God's time, he answered Hannah and gave her the son she prayed for.

Hannah's experience reminds you and me that God's richest blessings are often molded from a crucible of pain. Godly perseverance through pain and humiliation seems, as we read in biblical history, to be answered with a gracious reward that minimizes the suffering.

People who bear their pain and misunderstandings, their abuse and misrepresentation, in a godly manner find that God eventually rescues great gain from the jaws of enormous pain, if not now, then in eternity.

So let Hannah be your monument of hope. Her God is our God. His character has not changed. His will has not changed. His purpose has not changed. Jesus Christ is the same yesterday, today, and forever. If God loved Hannah, yet saw fit to allow her to endure this pain and misunderstanding, then he will make us not just his blessing receivers, but his burden bearers, for his glory.

If he helped Hannah in his good time, then he will help you. God says, "He who honors me, I will honor. He who shows contempt for me, I will lightly esteem." Tattoo that on your heart.

Let him deliver us in his time, in his way, on his day.

Y E A R

6

September 1, 1993

Dear Friends,

In the midst of our ministry duties and the day-to-day madness—and sadness—resident in Juli and Paul's plight, I find it so hard to keep you current. At the end of my first update to you fourteen months ago, I included a letter Juli had written to her mom. She was able to write because of an improvement in her CFS symptoms. This was no accident. She had been treated with a medication for an additional health problem, and this therapy had very welcome benefits for her CFS. I won't describe here how she managed to tolerate the pharmaceutical for the short time she did, but the treatment had lasting effects.

Last September (1992), this gain in her energy enabled her to fly with Paul on a private plane to see Dr. William Rea, a prominent cardiologist who had recovered from MCS and subsequently set up an environmentally safe hospital unit for patients with this disease. After conducting a series of tests, he diagnosed her with severe MCS and informed Juli and Paul that the severely painful reactions to chemicals in her blood vessels were caused by a condition known as vasculitis. Upon finding remarkably high levels of toxic chemicals in her blood, he remarked to Paul, "Your wife has a real problem."

Dr. Rea also treated Juli with shots that alleviated many of her food sensitivities. Unfortunately, her insurance didn't cover any of the hospital bills, so when Juli was stable enough after two weeks, she and Paul relocated to a housing complex where other MCS patients stayed as outpatients. But even these exposures were too much for her system and she was forced to come home prematurely. Given that Dr. Rea had previously told Juli, "You're among the sickest patients I've seen," it was little wonder that it all went south as soon as it did. Murphy's law rules with an iron hand! Just when we were all convinced that because of her CFS improvement, her MCS would soon follow suit, the bottom dropped out. The whole thing was like a recurring nightmare almost everyone has experienced. In the middle of the night, the sleeper is descending deeper and deeper into a bottomless pit and the only way to end the horror is to jolt oneself awake.

For Juli, however, this was a real life nightmare, and it kept getting worse. When the isolation and boredom became unbearable, she tried to pry apart the jailhouse bars to experience a small taste of freedom as she prayed to God for any reprieve from her "sentence." Her greatest desire was to read the Bible, since she felt like she was losing her spiritual grip on their trial. Well, she touched the ultra-thin pages of an inexpensive copy, and her body went into orbit. What the layperson needs to understand is that it is not merely the pain of the day that is the problem. Once one's body is this toxic, there is a pattern that follows. One chemical exposure sensitizes the victim of this malady to many members of its chemical "family" and the dreaded domino effect begins. Thus, this became Juli's rude awakening to her living nightmare, that these related chemicals are the instruments of further torture, as they cause the "out of the world" pain called vasculitis. Now any chemicals related to paper and print have become a devilish problem. (I do wonder sometimes if Satan has an outpost on their rooftop.)

Guess what? Their unfinished second floor is covered wall-to-wall, ceiling-to-ceiling, yes, every square inch except for the windows, in dual-sided aluminum foil/kraft paper sheeting. Recently, a major leak developed in their two-year-old roof. As the water soaked down into the foil/paper, the glue began to emit gas and the paper started to disintegrate. Juli's "radar" had discovered the problem, as she began having reactions that lacked any explainable source. Paul snooped around the house to discover what was provoking her, and he stumbled upon the leak. When the roofers came to fix it, they discovered that the unconventional underlayment the contractor used had also begun to degrade. No problem, just redo the whole underlayment of the roof! That's right. Just a measly 7,000 bucks. One thing about this illness: it eats money faster than a paper-shredder. And if it weren't for the generosity of Paul's grandparents, none of us would have a roof over our heads.

However, we were grateful that God had provided Juli the strength she needed to leave the premises during the roof reconstruction that summer. They typically would seek refuge in the great outdoors . . . in a public park. But this avenue of retreat presented its own problems. You see, because of her sensitivity to formaldehyde and clothing dyes, Juli had lost the ability to wear normal clothing and both she and Paul, because of his close proximity to her, were consigned to wear only thin white cotton hospital scrubs. This was so ironically sad for a girl whose sister incessantly teased her about her affinity for Nordstrom clothes in high school and college.

Anyway, since they both looked extremely underweight in their gear and had to spend long hours parked in one spot, "responsible" observers often informed the local law about a suspicious couple living out of their truck. Police officers descended time and again on the shivering kids to check them out. Most often, because this illness is not as familiar to the public as Parkinson's or MS, these lawmen didn't believe their tale. It's just another example of the kind of humiliating circumstances God has allowed them to suffer.

Occasionally some forbidding situation at the park would force them to seek refuge here at the church, hanging around on the south sidewalk areas outside the building, looking like, as Juli laughingly said, a couple of lepers or two sit-in Hari Krishnas. Even though Juli could only talk to people at great distances and the small amount of fellowship with church members was good for them, I think it created a false illusion of progress. Exposed to Juli for the first time, many around the church were pleasantly surprised by her liveliness and energy and arrived at the premature conclusion that the worst was over.

I stress the continuing horror of this situation lest anyone imagine that we are over the hump. Right now, dear friends, we don't even see the top of the hill. They still need your intercession. The long and short of it is that the CFS is not nearly as bad as it used to be; the MCS is inconceivably worse than we ever imagined.

Let me just use one example to show you the havoc her sensitivity to chlorine has wrought—and this is not her worst chemical adversary. Though she was having trouble with this chemical in the tap water previously, it kicked in big-time during last summer's drought and heat wave. The City of Tigard temporarily increased the chlorine level in the public water supply, and even though Juli and Paul already had a whole-house filtration system in place, it proved inadequate. Because of the increased exposure, she reacted horribly every time the water was turned on. Suddenly she had no drinking water, and couldn't bathe or use the toilet.

What a setback this was. Juli had just "risen from the dead" with her CFS, and was on her feet to a limited degree. The encouragement "fixed" her mother emotionally and Olsie was now up and running at full-tilt. Though Paul tried to warn us that Juli had two related maladies, we were persistently optimistic that the break in her CFS condition presaged the recovery of her immune system. We thought that her environmental sensitivities would break up in the wake of her improvement with CFS.

Suddenly we were frantic again, and a mad scramble ensued to find suitable water. At that point we hadn't figured out what constituted "suitable" water except that it should contain a lower level of chlorine than the public supply. Some of our church people even drove as far as the coast in an effort to come up with water that Juli could tolerate. Finally, in Cedar Mill, a temporary supply surfaced. The "angel" responsible for it was a lady with environmental sensitivities similar to Juli's. Her husband, a retired professor of electrical engineering, had rigged a filtration system to her well that filtered the chlorine down to zero—where Juli needed it.

But her supply was limited and we had to find a longer-term answer. So we invested several thousand dollars in a new stainless steel filtration system with more capacity. This enabled the kids at last to return to filtered tap water for bathing and use of their toilet, a great improvement on the old-fashioned bucket method. But she still could not drink the filtered tap water.

Try as we may, we could not find an acceptable local source for drinking. Her supply had to be spring water stored in glass, not plastic, bottles. Every brand of spring water was not safe. Even these sources frequently were naturally "contaminated" with too much of one element (like sulfur) or another for her system to tolerate. After much trial and error (mostly error) we eventually tracked down a safe supply in Arkansas, so every three months we have been trucking in new provisions of drinking water.

The impact of these sensitivities on our daughter is mind-boggling—and she is not alone. It is clear that the experts are missing something when it comes to mysterious sensitivities. You know about all the so-called "safe" chemicals we have been using for decades. Sadly, we are just beginning to awaken to the insidious effects on our bodies of the omnipresent chemicals in our civilization.

So, the malady that afflicts our daughter and her fellow sufferers serves as an early warning sign of things to come. More and more people, I predict, are going to be struck with these dreadful symptoms. In fact, several people in our own church already are fighting some of these on a much milder basis. At their worst, reactions to these chemicals can send a patient into convulsions, a coma, or even death. The excruciating reactions Juli experiences affect her nervous and circulatory systems, and cause this perfectly endearing young woman to be deformed into ranting and writhing human agony in the grip of intense, unalleviated pain. It is difficult beyond words to watch one's daughter imprisoned in such physical torture.

I can illustrate the magnitude of this disease by relaying the experiences of a woman who once suffered this same affliction.

Eventually she got over the worst of it, only to fall victim to cancer. Later she died, after prolonged chemotherapy. When Olsie talked with her husband about his late wife, he remarked that in the midst of her chemo treatments, she told him that her suffering from cancer and chemotherapy was no match for the misery she endured as a former MCS patient.

I emphasize that for the benefit of armchair doctors who, like myself in my earlier innocence, may be tempted to prescribe simply a little more toughness. You don't know Juli. The fact is, as I've said repeatedly, she has always been one of those people with a high pain tolerance.

Let me illustrate the point. To top everything off, Juli's wisdom teeth recently became infected. As you can probably guess by now, her body has become so sensitive that she couldn't tolerate the various chemical exposures resident in a dental office. So a dentist in our church agreed to roll back the clock of time and make a house call. Right there on her back patio he set about extracting four wisdom teeth. A couple were more obstinate than he bargained for. Through that ordeal, and with twenty injections of a less-than-ideal anesthetic, Juli, like an English royal, maintained a stiff upper lip, though she did yield a quiet stream of tears. Her hardiness impressed the dentist too.

Trust me, this gritty little lady has many times gone toe-to-toe with monster pain that would make lots of big, ugly, tough guys I know flat-out faint. Over the years Juli established such a high benchmark for pain tolerance that we knew whenever she did complain of it, it was out of the margins. If an ordinary mortal could just "tough it out," you can be sure she would.

Now for the latest news. Juli has been reacting to the local water supply again this summer. A call to the water department confirmed that they have indeed raised the chlorine level. We are staring the old nightmare in the face again . . . except this time a new wrinkle is added to the scary mix.

Before Juli and Paul could, if necessary, omit bathing, but that is not an option now. Since both are outside quite a bit, regular bathing is essential to rid themselves of contaminants on their persons that might precipitate reactions in the confinement of the home. So what do we do now? We are back to the same indignity as before concerning toilet needs as well as bathing. They must now use their expensive quart-size drinking water for baths.

As a result of all this stress on her system, Juli has relapsed somewhat in her CFS. The constant shock of the elements, and the lack of sleep entailed in all this confusion, has set her back. Paul has had to carry her to the truck whenever they need to leave the house, and she has been able to stand up less and less. This setback has her terrified at the prospect of a complete relapse into that dreadful debility that had left her almost unable to lift her head.

We keep searching for answers, for some means of relief, and so far discovered little that significantly helps. Sometimes we feel right on the edge of despair. Keep praying. Eventually God will intervene, I am confident. He will not do this because he is obliged to, but because I believe he has a great purpose in all this suffering. This great purpose is still a mystery to us. What is not a mystery is God's goodness as revealed in Scripture. And that, folks, is what anchors our souls in the midst of such confusion.

Thank you for caring,

Pastor Jim

Is This God For Real?

A few years ago in the process of channel surfing, I came across a traveling antique show. People from different regions of the U.S. brought in heirlooms or old pieces they had picked up for expert appraisal. The show featured antique experts interviewing the owners about how long they had possessed the item, and what they knew about its history. They then offered an appraisal based on the condition, the origin, and the uniqueness of the piece. As you can imagine, some people were stunned when they discovered that something they had once regarded as a cheap piece of trash was a real treasure.

Years ago I remember reading about an elderly lady from McMinnville, Oregon, who had an old chest from back East that she had purchased for virtually nothing. It had been shipped to her with all the carelessness of an item with no special value. For some reason she was prompted to have it appraised. Lo and behold, it turned out to be furniture that had once belonged to President John Adams. A value of something like $1.4 million was placed on it. A trash box turned out to be a treasure chest.

The character of God is a legacy like that—constantly trashed by the ignorant, but a priceless treasure for those in the know. Moses speaks of God's character in Exodus 34:6–7:

> Then the Lord passed by in front of him and proclaimed, "The Lord, the Lord God, compassionate and gracious, slow to anger, and abounding in loving-kindness and truth [or faithfulness]; who keeps loving-kindness for thousands, who forgives iniquity, transgression and sin; yet he will by no means leave the guilty unpunished, visiting the iniquity of fathers on the children and grandchildren [of those who hate him—compare Exodus 20:5] to the third and fourth generations." [Brackets interpolated for clarity.]

This is the self-disclosed character of the God of Abraham, Isaac, and Jacob, and the Father of our Lord Jesus Christ. The Father, like the Son, is unchangeable in his moral and essential character—"the same yesterday, today, and forever" (Hebrews 13:8).

On that immutability of God's moral character we hang our hats. In the New Testament, this changeless God revealed himself in Jesus Christ. As Christ said to Philip, "He who has seen me has seen the Father" (John 14:9). Thus, the Savior identified himself with Yahweh, the personal, covenant name for God in the Old Testament. He is also a holy and just God who ultimately will judge the wicked who persist in despising his grace and patience.

In the mystery of affliction, our bulwark is God's moral character. Threats often come from two directions: intellectual skepticism and emotional reactions. While the main burden of this chapter is blunting the former, I must at some length also caution about the risk of allowing human feelings to distort the facts. That is, we must resist any temptation to allow perception to rule over revelation in times of confusion.

Several years ago this danger impressed itself upon me as never before. A devout lady in our church had been subjected to excruciating emotional stress over an extended period. She lapsed into such a deep depression that her doctor had to prescribe heavy doses of anti-depressants. Her life, at least in any meaningful sense, seemed over. During her emotional freefall, every "small" sin she had ever committed was dredged up and tauntingly thrown back in her face, exponentially exacerbating that residual guilt dormant in all of us sinners. In her mentally disordered state, she suddenly found herself doubting even the most fundamental issues of the faith.

Thankfully in due time, God delivered her from her burdens and "the liar's din." One lesson she took away from this black pit, however, was how crucial it is to have one's faith firmly grounded on the bedrock of God's character. What the enemy had exposed (and exploited) in this mental prison was a hairline crack in what she thought was her solid wall of faith. You see, there is usually, if not always, a little gap between our Sunday creed and our Monday convictions—between what we profess we believe and what we really believe.

In retrospect, she saw that her practical assurance of the revealed character of God had not caught up with her verbal affirmations of it, so Satan ambushed her. At some point in that awful struggle the Spirit, working through the Word, brought her back to biblical revelation and its teaching about the character of God. Retreating to the high ground of God's self-disclosure, she stationed her faith behind that solid seawall.

Friends, we believers must take refuge behind the nature and character of God. In fact, this whole business of "the life of faith" is simply trusting daily in God's sovereign power, in his infinite wisdom, in his absolute goodness, and in his constant faithfulness. Not trusting, but only talking about walking "in faith" is so much pious blather.

Why are we so vulnerable to emotional implosion? Our problem here resides in the relative incomprehensibility of a transcendent God whose inscrutable wisdom and secret workings are inaccessible to us and far too complex for our puny minds to track or decode. Our lack of total understanding is a setup for mental confusion.

When the Lord's ways do not neatly conform to our pat little paradigms of what seems (to our fallible minds) right and just, and good and faithful, it says something about human nature that usually the first thought that comes to mind is that something is wrong with God. Somehow the last thing that occurs to us is that God is simply too big for our small boxes. It is imperative at such times that we learn to be humble, not haughty. God always deserves the benefit of any doubt. And, faith always pleads with us, "Dear soul, trust God's power, trust God's wisdom, trust God's goodness, trust God's faithfulness—even though to your mixed-up, emotionally overcharged mind he doesn't seem to be living up to his résumé or promises. Just do it anyway."

Christian common sense should also remind us that divine revelation is always a far more reliable barometer of reality than our personal perceptions, distorted as they are by how we think a moral and upright God is obliged to behave in this situation or that. Friends, my advice is this: discount personal feelings—rest in the biblical facts. Don't always be awash in how things *seem;* anchor your faith on how divine revelation says they *are*. Never allow blind emotions to float you off into the open sea of doubt.

With that adjustment, one can trust his goodness even when God may not seem to be good; one can trust his wisdom even when he may not seem to be wise; one can trust he is acting in character even when he may not seem to be measuring up to his own revealed profile; one can trust his power even when it seems he is weak; one can trust his faithfulness even when it seems he is not being faithful.

Is that blind faith? No, not at all. It is humble faith. But doesn't that seem like gullibility? No, it is patience—with a biblical memory.

That was Job. Did the faith of a poor tormented soul ever look as misplaced as his stubborn faith? He was frustrated out of his mind and bewildered to the bone, yes, but in the end unyielding, "Though he slay me, yet I will trust in him!" (Job 13:15). Then, finally—after forever it must have seemed—the Lord intervened and vindicated Job's trust, restoring his fortunes greater than before. What a historical monument for any confused by the inscrutable ways of God.

Some readers, or someone they love, are slogging through a living hell on earth. They are dumbstruck that God would allow this to go on and on and on. Where is God? What is good or wise about this? Why doesn't the Lord help or intervene? Didn't God say, "I will never leave you or forsake you?" Man (you think), if this is not leaving or forsaking, you could have fooled me!

Right here, my friend, is where our faith must be firmly anchored to God's character. Otherwise swells of doubt will carry us out into the depths where we will drift farther and farther from the shorelines of hope. But how does one, especially a newer believer, who has no storehouse of personal monuments, shore up one's defenses?

Here's a crucial point: Our store of monuments need not be confined exclusively to those markers God has erected in our personal Christian experience. We can "borrow" the monuments of our contemporaries. In seminary I remember days of prayer when guys would share requests with some urgency. Time and again bare cupboards and empty wallets had fellows on the verge of dropping out of school. Then, days later, word would circulate that a certain student had gone to his box and found a substantial check that met the need. More often than not the provision came from some source with absolutely no hint of the student's plight. I used to call that phenomenon "mailbox manna."

Well, their monuments also became my monuments. I borrowed them before I had some of my own. And I will tell you, their monuments helped float my faith off many a sandbar. That is also what I am saying about biblical monuments. In the Word there is a storehouse of testimonies to God's great historical works on behalf of his ancient people. You see, their monuments are our monuments too. These are preserved by the Spirit for "our instruction, that through perseverance and the encouragement of the scriptures we might have hope" (Romans 15:4). These too the Lord expects us to store in memory banks for those bitter passages of life when the enemy may try to insinuate doubt in our minds about God's goodness, wisdom, or sufficiency.

So then, when you become overwrought emotionally and just can't figure God out, don't sink. Instead, take refuge in your biblical monuments and give God the benefit of the doubt. In the end he never leaves faith with a red face (Romans 10:11).

Now, we come to the central burden of this chapter. For some, nagging misgivings about the integrity of God arise chiefly from the intellectual front rather than from emotional turmoil. Doubts from this source in particular can defuse one's enthusiasm for the "monumental habit." First, it is always helpful to consider the source of skepticism. Insinuations against the character of God have a long and infamous history. They go back to the Garden of Eden where Satan seduced Adam and Eve by casting aspersion on the goodness and truthfulness of God (Genesis 3). Why do you suppose this episode was recorded for posterity? In part because it exposes for all time a favorite and regular satanic faith-wrecking tactic. The devil (*diabolos* – a slanderer) wants us to question God. From day one, so to speak, the enemy has always worked that angle through his various instruments.

Making matters simpler for the enemy is the fact that in these days of "happy talk," pastors, biblically illiterate parishioners, and thousands of churches that are theology-free zones, are virtual modern Marcionites. Marcion was a second century heretic who (to oversimplify a bit) embraced the "good" Redeemer God of the New Testament but rejected the (presumably) wrathful Creator God of the Old. Any discomfort with the God of the Old Testament smacks of Marcion's heresy. To view the God in the Old Testament as different from the God of the New Testament is to expose how little we understand either.

In tackling this issue, let us revisit one of the stunning actions of God in the Old Testament to clarify the moral continuity between the God who revealed himself to Moses and the God who revealed himself in our Lord Jesus Christ.

Other than the extermination of the Canaanites, the favorite passage detractors use to criticize God's character is the episode narrated in 1 Samuel 15. There, God through the prophet Samuel, directed King Saul to annihilate the Amalekite population. Once we examine the skeptics' flawed premises and put God's actions into a larger theological perspective,

I would hope that we would see that things are not as they might first appear.

Let's start with a little historical context. The Amalekites, descendants of Amalek, were a nomadic people who inhabited the area of Sinai and the Negev Desert. Amalek was apparently the grandson of Jacob's twin brother, Esau, by a pagan concubine. In time, Amalek's descendants, true to their roots, became bitter enemies of Israel.

As described in Exodus 17:8ff, Israel had just emerged from their Egyptian captivity. Reports of Yahweh's awesome signs and wonders were broadcast throughout the Middle Eastern world. We know for certain that word of his mighty deeds had reached at least as far as Jericho and Philistia and this news had struck fear into the hearts of many (see Joshua 2:10 and 1 Samuel 6:6).

The godless Amalekites were another matter, however. They were so smug that they had the audacity to launch a heartless, unprovoked attack on God's people, striking and plundering the stragglers from the rear, like a pack of hyenas. (See Deuteronomy 25:17–19, "[Amalek] did not fear God.")

This impiousness provoked divine indignation, for God saw their outrage for exactly what it was: utter contempt for himself. Though his power had just brought the mighty Egyptians to their knees, the Amalekites cruel response was to attack God's long oppressed people. In response to this gross disrespect for his holy name, God placed the whole tribe under ban—a standing extermination order. This was a signal act to all generations of the end that ultimately awaits haters of God.

So, through Moses (Exodus 17:14), the Lord directed the annihilation of the Amalekites with the proviso that this sentence would be carried out only when Israel was finally settled in the land. In this narrative, critics see proof that the God of the Bible is immoral and unworthy of our worship. Additionally, they say, this divinely directed massacre underscores the moral dissonance between the God portrayed in the Old Testament and the one proclaimed in the New Testament.

Let me rebut three specious propositions put forth by the cynics. The first is that the OT portrays God with a different moral character than the NT. The second is that the action of God in the case of the Amalekites was contrary to the law of love. The third is that such an edict was clearly unjust, because the ban included the extermination of innocent women and infants.

First, is the Old Testament image of God at odds with the New Testament image of God? Let me say at the outset that Hebrew scriptures in fact abound with teaching about the goodness of God—his mercy, grace, compassion, patience, loyalty, and faithfulness to his promises. Read Yahweh's self-disclosure in Exodus 34:6–7. That revelation was the very cornerstone of prophetic preaching and hope throughout the OT. Read Psalm 103 (or the Psalms in general) and see the goodness of God shining through like the sun at high noon. And what about the Lord's compassion and deliverance for Israel from Egypt after the children of Jacob had long since forgotten his name (Exodus 2:24 and 3:16–17). How could anyone read the tender story of Hosea and Gomer, a historical parable of God's love for Israel, and not be moved by his mercy, compassion, and patience toward his unfaithful bride? Who could fail to see those attributes on vivid display in OT chapters like Isaiah 1, 40, 53, or 55, to mention just a few?

The fact is, the OT is rich in emphasis on the love and mercy of God. Blindness to this portrait of God in the Hebrew Scriptures can only be explained by a stubborn bias that sees only what it wants to see or else by profound ignorance of the Scripture.

With respect to their presentations of God, the only real difference between the two testaments is nuance or emphasis. *The OT accents the holiness of a gracious God, whereas the NT emphasizes the grace of a holy God.* The OT prepares us for our need of redemption whereas the NT reveals its provision. In the OT we learn of the holiness of God, his moral law, and his hatred for evil. Our attention is drawn to human accountability for sin, because our moral responsibility is important.

Why would we humans seek reconciliation with God if we were never apprized of the extent of our separation from God? There is an old saying: People have to "get lost" before they can get saved. Before sinners will cast themselves on the mercy of the God of Calvary, they first must tremble before the God of Sinai. You see, no one has ever loved a gracious God who has not first feared a holy God. That is why the OT accentuates the holiness of God without slighting the grace of God.

This is not to suggest by any means that the NT downplays the judgment of God. There is a reason why the book of Revelation is called the Apocalypse. Jesus himself is by no means least among those who warn of divine judgment hanging over an unbelieving world like a sword of Damocles (Matthew 24–25).

The holy God of the OT, who recoils at sin and brings the godless to account, is very much alive and well throughout the NT. Consider passages like Matthew 23:33ff, 25:41–46; Acts 12:20–23; Romans 2:6–8; 1 Corinthians 10:6–11, 11:26–32; Galatians 6:6–7; Philippians 1:27–28, 3:17–19; 2 Thessalonians 2:6–12; 2 Timothy 4:1; Hebrews 10:26–31; 2 Peter 3:3–13; and Revelation 9:14–21, 16:1–16, 19:11–21, 20:11–15.

And don't forget those interim judgments that befell Ananias and Sapphira (Acts 5), the irreverent Corinthians who profaned the Lord's Table (1 Corinthians 11:30), and the immoral man the apostle Paul consigned to Satan on God's behalf for the destruction of the flesh (1 Corinthians 5:5). Contemplate Romans 1:18ff where the apostle Paul warns of the wrath of God *already being revealed* against those who in their unrighteousness suppress the light God has put within them.

Indeed, the theme of the indignation of God against those who take his law lightly, who persist in walking in darkness while resisting the truth and trampling on the blood of his Son, runs like a river all through the NT (see Hebrews 10:26–27). In fact, the NT proclaims the Noahic flood (Genesis 6) a foreshadowing of the far more terrifying universal judgment the world will face in the future (2 Peter 2:5).

The truth is, those who are squeamish about worshiping a God who orders the temporal annihilation of evildoers in the OT should have even greater reservations about serving the God of the NT. For in the NT, divine judgment is universal in scope, far more terrible in its sentence, and everlasting in its result.

And on this score, contrary to what our detractors allege, they cannot differentiate between the gentle, loving Jesus and the presumably cruel, wrathful actions of Yahweh of the OT.

Jesus totally identified himself as the revealer of the God of the OT. That is the motif of the whole gospel of John. (See the Prologue to John, and especially John 1:1, 14, 18.) That God is Yahweh—the God of Abraham, Isaac, and Jacob (Mark 12:26). To his disciple Philip, Jesus said, "He that has seen me has seen the Father" (John 14:9). To his enemies the Lord insisted that his message exactly represented his Father's, and that all his works mimicked those of God the Father in heaven (John 5:17ff).

Not only that, but the Lord Jesus Christ is depicted in the NT as the One who, on the Father's behalf, will personally execute the dreadful sentence of eternal punishment upon unbelievers at the Last Judgment (compare Revelation 19:11–18, 20:11–15; 2 Timothy 4:1; and especially John 5:22). In fact, Jesus himself spoke of heaven only five times, but mentioned hell eleven times.

So this image of Jesus as a saccharine-sweet rabbi who wouldn't swat a fly, step on a cockroach, ruffle anybody's feathers, hurt anybody's feelings, or most especially, cast an unbeliever into hell is quite erroneous. One reading of Matthew 23 or Revelation 19:11–21 ought to dispose of those false conceptions. Of course, it is true that our Lord Jesus was (and remains) gentle and compassionate with the weak and lowly. But with the stubbornly wicked and haughty, ah, he could take the hide off—and did.

Just ask yourself this: How did such a nice Jewish lad from Nazareth wind up on a cruel Roman cross, hissed and hooted at by the angry religious leaders? Was it because he was not the kind of person ever to offend anybody? Was it because he walked around making peace signs and assuring all and sundry that "I'm okay, you're okay, serve God however you please, but just love one another, be cool, make nice, and just sit around and think happy thoughts"? How do you suppose his "message" bent the Jews so out of shape that they fiercely demanded that Pilate crucify him?

The bottom line is, this effort to divorce the God of the OT from the God of the NT is a failure. They are one and the same God. Whoever balks at worshiping the God of the Old Testament cannot serve Jesus Christ either.

We next need to deal with the second allegation that this divine behavior is incompatible with the concept of love. There is no shared understanding of the word "love." The critics define "love" in a muddy, popular, touchy-feely way, not one based on a revelation. Hence the confusion. They judge apples by an orange standard.

Take, for example, a cup embossed with the word "coffee." Somebody fills the coffee cup with tea. Now, if the taster knew nothing about either coffee or tea, they would naturally assume from the label that the liquid content was coffee, and then would judge coffee by a tea standard. So it is with judging the moral actions of God by a non-biblical measure. It's judging coffee by a tea standard. The label may read "love" but the content does not match the label. The whole idea of "love" originates with God and nowhere else. Love is a term that encapsulates his moral nature.

In the Scriptures, for instance, we learn that "God is love" (1 John 4:16). The sum and substance of his moral being is summed up in that word. The aspects of God's moral personality cannot be atomized or separated into discrete moral particles, as it were. On the contrary, like a diamond, the love of God features many moral facets, but each facet remains part of one solid rock. Every particular face is colored by and imbued with all the other components. When my two girls were young and still in our home, my paternal love also wore different faces. At one time it manifested itself in an affectionate hug, at another time in a word of encouragement, at another with a word of correction or a measure of discipline, etc. Likewise, the love of God is multi-faceted, a "many-splendored thing." The total package is the sum that adds up to "love."

The world can write "love" on the outside of the cup and pour in any meaning, but if we are going to debate whether or not certain actions depict a God of love, we must start with the common ground of God's self-disclosure.

Let me illustrate how far we can drift when we acquiesce to street definitions of biblical virtues. It is no wonder we confuse the treasure for trash when it comes to God's ways. At a funeral we sometimes will hear folk eulogize some departed friend or loved one as a "very loving person." By way of confirmation they will often add, "I never heard Uncle Willie (or Aunt Susie) ever say a bad word about anybody!" Whereupon all the friends and family will nod or smile with affirmation, as if that were the cachet of a loving person. Certainly, as the Scriptures teach, idle gossip, malicious slander, and unjust criticism all fall outside the moral will of a God of truth (an aspect of love).

Other than that, a person who never has a "bad thing" to say about anyone, is frankly not a lover, but a bit of a louse. For the love of God in us does not allow believers the luxury of keeping silent in the face of evil. Those really possessed of the love of God do not sit by and let the wicked have their way. They condemn it, as God does. A loving person does not put on social blinders and because of cowardice or selfish interests, say in effect, "I hear no evil, see no evil, fear no evil." The love of God has moral sensibilities and does not hesitate to take sides. The God of love abhors what is evil and loves only what is good. Love then cannot be sweetly neutral and comfortably mute in the battle between right and wrong. The refusal to offend may not be a sign of Christian charity at all but rather a badge of moral deformity.

Jesus justly excoriated certain hypocrites with his words (Matthew 23). John the Baptist had harsh words for the Pharisees and Sadducees (Matthew 3:7–10). Peter solemnly confronted Ananias and Sapphira (Acts 5) as well as Simon Magnus (Acts 8:9–24) with their wickedness. John the Apostle spoke very critically of the self-serving Diotrephes (3 John 9). Paul did not mince words about bad characters in churches of Asia Minor (2 Timothy 2:17–18). And of course the same goes for all the OT prophets who constantly took the unfaithful in Israel to task for their disloyalty to God.

Now I make this particular point to illustrate how misaligned popular definitions of "love" are with biblical standards. Just imagine, for instance, a preacher taking his pulpit and torching modern hypocrites the way Jesus nailed the hypocritical scribes and Pharisees of his day. The congregation would recoil in shock and dismay at his total lack of "Christ-like spirit." The irony of that reveals just how far our modern notions of "love" have drifted from biblical conceptions.

No wonder that people today are puzzled and confused by the actions of God. All they understand is what I might call the "soft, sugary side" of love—a flat, one-dimensional view. What they fail to grasp is that the love of God, due to human wickedness, necessarily also has "severe" edges in the form of judgment and discipline. "Behold then the kindness and severity of God" (Romans 11:22). The love of God, in working out his redemptive plan in the face of demonic opposition, preserves sufficient moral order to serve his loving purposes. Today we call it "tough love."

So this brings us back now to the burning question: Was the divinely directed extermination of the Amalekites consistent with the revelation of his moral character, that is, a God of love? The answer is, yes.

Divine justice is a crucial component of divine love. A God of love does not forever ignore, wink at, or pass over evil. The devil and his cronies must get their due. Crime must not pay in the end.

That is explicit in his self-disclosure to Moses. For all his grace and compassion, patience, loving-kindness, faithfulness, and forgiveness of sin, transgression, and iniquity, God says flat-out that his moral nature (the sum of which defines love) will not allow the guilty to go unpunished but he will surely visit the sins of the fathers upon the children of those who persist in hating him unto the third and fourth generations" (see Exodus 20:5 and 34:7).

The love of God does not allow the wicked ultimate success. Those who persist in despising him, rejecting his grace, and sowing wickedness are racing headlong toward failure and defeat. Intermittent judgments are merciful acts of God that send fair warning to others on that path. In love, God makes it known that he will in the end chase down every last seed of evil and extract it.

God is the ultimate cosmic magistrate. He would be morally indifferent if the Amalekites of this world had an open-ended license to get away with murder. It is precisely because God loves that God is just; he does not wink at sin.

If anyone has the slightest doubt, just look at the cross. There we see the exacting justice he demands, but then graciously provides. Sin is capital crime against heaven. It is rebellion; it is anti-God behavior; it reflects an outlaw spirit. So, its wages are death (Romans 6:23).

Is that too severe?

Let me remind us that God is the only Judge in the universe competent to rightly weigh the enormity of sin. His justice is so uncompromising that it required his Son manifested in Jesus Christ to die on a Roman cross to pay the bill for us, that all who trust in him might be spared the extreme penalty. A loving God set, and then met, his own standard of justice.

The judgment of the Amalekites must be placed into that moral context. They, like the whole human race, were already on death row, but in their case, for aggravated sin. God chose Saul and his army as his executioners, just as he would later choose the Assyrians and the Babylonians as his unwitting instruments for the destruction of Israel and Judah respectively. So in their case the love of God was longsuffering toward their evil ways. He gave them ample time to repent. But eventually he proved that divine love is neither indulgent nor indifferent where evil is concerned. The Scriptures teach us that love abhors evil and cleaves to good (Romans 12:9), because God does.

Maybe now it is clearer to us that so long as we fall back on popular notions of love for appraising the love of God, we will be rating coffee by a tea standard. However, if we measure the love of God by his self-revealed moral nature, this problem evaporates. For those who would like a more amplified discussion of this subject, I would highly recommend D.A. Carson's monograph, *The Difficult Doctrine of the Love of God.*[2]

Now we take up the third faulty assumption of God's critics. They allege that such a terrible judgment was unjust, at least in its scope. By this they refer to the inclusion of presumably innocent children in the ban. Now on the surface that seems like a weighty objection, but let's approach the matter theologically rather than sentimentally. Only under two conditions could we judge the destruction of the Amalekites an injustice. One would be if the judgment was excessive, that is, the punishment did not fit the crime. The second would be if the innocent were punished along with the guilty.

Once again we confront a definitional issue that confuses matters. Terms like "innocent" can be misleading because they can be used in different senses. For example, if by "innocent" one means that infants played no active role in the wickedness that rendered the Amalekites odious in the sight of God, this is true. They deserved no punishment on the basis of personal involvement.

However, innocence at that level in no way exempts them (or any other human being) from a date with divine judgment. Why? Because our standing before God is not simply a matter of the bad things we do, but the bad creatures we are. That filter, my friends, catches even infants. You see, even they are fallen creatures from day one. No one, even at birth, is innocent of a sinful, pro-self, anti-God nature. The Bible teaches us that all human beings, infants included, are born in a state of moral ruination and invariably become transgressors by choice as well as by nature (Ephesians 2:3). As King David wrote in Psalm 51:5, "Surely I was sinful at birth, sinful from the time my mother conceived me."

I love little babies, but as a Christian father I personally had no illusions about the spiritual nature of those sweet girls I cradled so proudly in my loving arms. All my paternal sentiment could not obscure the truth that their childish innocence was only skin deep. All those little coos and cuddles masked fallen natures that eventually would break out, but for the redemptive grace of God, in the usual human rebelliousness toward him.

The breast of every child harbors a potential beast. Those who were once precious infants have perpetuated all the inhumanities of man on other men. The awful reality is that all human beings are bankrupt from birth; it's just that in babies that spiritual condition is temporarily latent rather than active.

So then, to speak of "innocent" people is begging the question. The fact is, in terms of moral corruption and spiritual alienation, there is no such thing as an innocent human being of any age. Consequently, there is no exemption from the penalty of sin for anyone of any age at any time anywhere on earth. All humans without exception need a Savior. All of us need the sprinkling of the atoning blood of Jesus Christ to cover our sinfulness.[1]

1. Not that I am saying that babies who die before they have the intellectual capacity or any opportunity to receive Christ are damned. No, not at all. What I

So the sum of the matter is this: Infants are not exempt from the consequences of the Fall. The notion of innocent people is a moral myth. Therefore, God did nothing unjust in destroying the Amalekite children.

Nor was the punishment of the Amalekites excessive. The truth is, we all richly deserve the fate of the Amalekites but for the mercy and grace of God. According to Romans 3:10ff, not a single inherently good person exists on the face of the earth. Not one person ever born comes into the world with a heart amicable to its Creator. We lean toward loving self instead of God and are naturally proud toward God rather than humble. Only the free gift of God, the pardon and life that God gives to those who trust in Jesus Christ, can commute the just and moral sentence of death (Romans 6:23).

In fact, friends, it is impossible for God to do any human being an injustice, for God owes no man anything. The prophet Jeremiah saw as clearly as anyone when he judged his own complaints and said, "Why should any living mortal, or any man, offer complaint in view of his sins?" (Lamentations 3:39). We are all serial sinners . . . spiritual rebels. No human being deserves anything less than everlasting punishment. "None is righteous, no, not one" (Romans 3:10).

Far from excessive, the punishment of the Amalekites was in fact symbolic of a supremely greater and more enduring punishment that awaits the whole race of men who persist in spurning the grace of God and trampling on the atoning blood of Jesus Christ.

But there is more to this matter. The reality is that God is the Creator . . . the cosmic Potter, if you please. God gives

---

am saying is this: before infants can enter the presence of God, they too need the sprinkling of the justifying blood of Jesus Christ. They too need the blood of Christ's atonement applied to them. Though they obviously cannot appropriate that atonement for themselves, still Christ has made an all-sufficient offering and God, in his sovereignty, will ultimately decide the application of its benefits in such cases.

life at his sovereign discretion and he has the inherent right to withdraw it at his sovereign discretion. He owns our life breath and he is not accountable to anyone or any law outside his own being for how he elects to spend it or use it. He can give life and he can take it as he sees fit.

> He himself gives to all life and breath and all things . . . for in him we live and move and exist . . . "For we are all his offspring" (Acts 17:25, 28).

> The Lord kills and makes alive; he brings down to Sheol and raises up (1 Samuel 2:6).

> See now that I, I am he, and there is no god besides me; It is I who put to death and give life (Deuteronomy 32:39).

God as the Creator therefore cannot by definition murder anyone any more than a potter can vandalize his own ceramics. Nor is the Lord obliged to render account to anyone or any law outside his own moral being. Who are we then to question his actions?

Hence, if God elects at intervals to impose upon some of his wayward creatures part of the punishment they deserve, or should he see fit in his eternal plan to destroy some part of his creation, what fool can claim the Creator acts unjustly? To whom is God indebted? What pot has inalienable "rights" before his Potter? Thus, at the end of the day, the ringing question is not why did God condemn some? Rather the great mystery is, why does God redeem any?

Y E A R

7

November 1, 1994

Dear Friends,

Please forgive the constant drumbeat of depressing news, but we need your prayers. This sad saga is so surreal that we all, especially Juli and Paul, feel like we've been sent into the Twilight Zone.

As you will remember, I wrote last about their dilemma of life without running water. Well, the chaos continues. It feels like we wake up every morning wondering if another of Job's servants has "risen from the dead," only to inform us that a new reign of terror has just befallen our family. What has occurred since my last writing has almost knocked us out cold. You see, Juli and Paul have been living in the dark. Many of you, with whom I've had opportunity to explain the long, drawn-out details in person, know exactly what I'm referring to; others may assume I speak figuratively. Believe me, I do not.

In my updates, I've touched on Juli's inability to tolerate the phone or furniture in the house, which includes even a TV. This begs the question, "That's so pathetic, but what's the point, Jim?"

Her inability to use a phone or a television is due to a condition known as Electromagnetic Field (EMF) Sensitivities, and it is intensifying with each passing year. This problem is not uncommon among severe MCS patients, and sometimes progresses to an intolerance of a vast array of common appliances and fixtures.

For example, in a 1991 *Journal of Bioelectricity* study conducted by Dr. Rea and other researchers, some of his patients were so tenuous in their ability to handle *any* EMF exposure that they had to be excluded due to the extreme health risk this study would pose. Many of the patients deemed strong enough to participate developed such severe responses to even weak field levels and short exposure time that they had to receive "intravenous Vitamin C, magnesium, and oxygen as a result of the prolonged and delayed reactions." The study objectively verified the existence of EMF sensitivity and proved that it "can be elicited under environmentally controlled conditions."

Thus, Juli, like many of her fellow patients, has become so "overloaded" that she has had to pull one plug after another to alleviate the progressive onslaught of symptoms. But in her case, she has become so sensitized that now, the use of anything electrical anywhere near her is absolutely *verboten*. What this means, folks, is—no electricity in the entire *house,* not even a single breaker. Oh, by the way, I guess they do have one piece of interior "décor" besides their bed: a flashlight.

Here's the real clincher. Their heat is electric too! Unlike most of us in the Pacific Northwest who have natural gas or oil heating furnaces, Juli and Paul were obligated to install electric baseboard heaters when they built their home, because she, like the majority of MCS patients, does not tolerate the more traditional heating methods. While many patients do have significant EMF sensitivities, for the most part electric heat is okay for them. We have only encountered one other patient who is unable to cope with electricity altogether.

Why not tough it out? She's tried to do just that and learned, the hard way, how that only makes things worse. This illness is like a mean dog. The more you bait it, the nastier it gets. All you can do is get away from the irritation until the body recoups its resistance.

So, to recap: the kids are in thin white clothes, bathing (when chlorine levels necessitate) in bottled water, without heat or lights. On occasion, if Juli's energy allows, they are able to escape in their truck for a while and jack up the heat in the house to knock the freeze off.

It's a chilly life at the "North Pole" in equator attire. Sometimes they just sob. At other times, the only way to survive is with a sense of humor about the whole stupid thing. So Paul tries to amuse Juli by singing the theme song from *Gilligan's Island*, "No phone, no lights, no motorcar; not a single luxury. Like Robinson Crusoe, it's primitive as can be." It works. At least God has allowed them one "luxury" that differs from that ditty, and one that so many other MCS patients lack: a "motorcar," or in their case, a truck.

However, these brief escapes have taken their toll on Juli's Chronic Fatigue Syndrome. Paul knew he had to find a medical solution to enable her to rest and stay home as much as possible. So, based on the information he gleaned from the Dallas clinic and his own research, Paul concocted a unique combination of oral amino acids to help take the edge off Juli's horrific EMF reactions. They worked—at least to the extent where she is now able to rest in bed, instead of flee the premises, while they turn up the heat for short periods of time. (Incidentally, Paul may have been a whiz at "the old ivories," but I think he could have blitzed through medical school had he been inclined to be a doctor.)

Since this approach alleviated some of her EMF sensitivities, Juli and Paul remembered that a different formula of amino acids given intravenously at the environmental hospital had helped continue her CFS improvement at the time. So, Dr. John Sandilands, one of the doctors in our church and a true angel of mercy, offered to administer them to Juli. The initial effects were positive. Hope! Then, as I've said like a broken record, the bottom dropped out. One day Juli began reacting violently to the plastic tubing used to dispense the IV. Since then things have descended, if possible, to a whole new level of Dante's Inferno. The immediate impact of this new strand in her web of sensitivities was an overwhelming sense of desperation on everyone's part and a frantic scramble to clear their space of every form of plastic that might offend her system.

Well, we finally managed to temporarily stabilize the situation to some degree and restore some order (which by any normal benchmark would be utter chaos). But now, since that plastic episode, Juli is no longer able to walk on her floors. She has become hypersensitive to many types of petrochemicals, including an ingredient in the "environmentally safe" brand of lacquer they used. When she steps on the floor, that unbearable fiery reaction starts shooting up and down her legs like she's walking on hot rocks the minute her *slippers* touch the floor! Now how do we get out of this pickle? Until Paul figured out a solution, he had to physically carry her to and from the bathroom. Finally, he came up with the idea of using custom-cut tempered glass squares, which he laid on top of the hardwood, building a narrow path.

The chain reaction continued as her sensitivity to petrochemicals extended to gasoline and vehicle exhaust. There went her last means of "escape." As a result, she has been a virtual prisoner on their bed by the French doors overlooking the back patio.

Another blow! Now she began reacting to her all-cotton clothing. Why? First, she reacted to clothing that was sewn with cotton/polyester thread. So out the door went all of her clothes and the search for 100% cotton thread replacements began. Then came the final straw. "What could possibly go wrong now?" you ask. She began reacting to her all-cotton thread clothing because it was *non-organic* (containing pesticide residues). So they both had to pitch every stitch of clothing and bedding that they owned . . . again! You talk about ripping everything up and starting all over? Well, we've done it time and time again, but this one takes the cake, and then some.

Result? We had to find *organic* replacements, and work virtually around the clock washing, along with Paul's folks, the new fabrics in soda and (new requirement!) *organic* vinegar, over and over, so that they wouldn't have to live unclothed. By the way, I can vouch for the durability of a Maytag washer.

We still have not managed (as of this writing) to come up with more than one thin organic piece of makeshift safe clothing that Juli can tolerate. The problem has been finding a seamstress who can make them under absolutely uncompromising conditions. Just one environmental mistake and all the material and effort is wasted. Her body knows and rebels immediately.

Because of the extra isolation imposed by these new developments, Juli occasionally has become so stir crazy that she feels compelled to take some chances to find relief from her confinement. Each time she ventures out into the backyard, she runs a high risk of contaminating her lone garment with perfumes and fabric softeners from the neighbors' nearby dryers. When this occurs, Juli ends up spending a couple of days literally without covering while we or Paul's parents scramble frantically to get the contaminant neutralized. Gordon and Elaine, in every respect, share a great deal of this whole burden.

This isolation is almost as unbearable as the illness. Paul has to spend much of his time out of the house going through all the incredible hoops it takes to make life work for them. He is deprived of much opportunity to spend quality time with anyone. Even when she has company, he has to seize the moment to get things done, and remember, he is not fully recovered from CFS himself yet.

Here perhaps is a good place to portray for you the caliber of man and husband Paul is. The guy is literally one in millions and I don't know a single person close to the situation who would challenge that claim. His kind today is more rare than a diamond in a dustbin. Few men would stick out a marriage—even for a few years—if they were compelled to cope with all that Paul has had to endure in the maddening course of Juli's affliction.

It's not just the monotonous twenty-four-hour care-taking; it's not just the physical exhaustion as a result; it's not just being tied down to a grinding life with never a restful holiday or a single day of unmolested rest in seven years; it's not just the denial of anything resembling a life of your own; and it's not just being deprived day in and day out of that precious commodity even the most devoted couples prize—a little personal space now and then.

116

No, it's also the endless hassles with total fools and dense and insensitive people who say or do the dumbest things. It's trying desperately days on end to drain the pond of pain while fighting off witless human alligators who neither understand nor care to. It's trying to keep twenty-five balls in the air at one time almost by yourself. It's just attempting to maintain your sanity as things lurch crazily from one unbelievable crisis to another. It's being deprived for long periods of the comforts of home that the rest of us take for granted. It's going for months without a shower or toilet because of your wife's severe allergic reaction to occasional increases in the chlorination of city water. It's being forced, every time one ventures into public, to wear a wife-safe, muslin uniform that gives the appearance of a runaway from an asylum. It's never being able to wear a warm coat outside, since the original processing chemicals in that apparel might set Juli off. It's living for years and years under semi-house arrest because of her needs. And it's living under conditions so confining that for all practical purposes one is denied the time and opportunity to form and nurture lasting friendships.

By any normal standard it's a life resigned, for the sake of his wife and for the sake of Christ, to the loss of virtually everything a typical man expects from life, including his dignity. Yet what amazes nearly everyone who has any contact with Paul is the fact that, despite all this, a smile never seems to leave his face, he seldom loses his patience, and kindness is rarely far from his lips.

Let me illustrate his extraordinary character with one vignette that has always made me shake my head. Early one winter evening when Olsie and Paul were speaking outside, what they so dreaded happened yet again. While they were conversing, a strong odor of perfume had wafted onto Paul's hair and clothes. He asked Olsie for immediate prayer, because of course, Juli's hyper-reactive body could not tolerate that for an instant. This was a *huge* problem every time it happened.

Here's their conundrum: since Juli has become virtually bed-ridden again, she depends on Paul for almost everything. Managing that is always very dicey. Because her heightened EMF sensitivities prevent use of their electric appliances, it requires Paul, rain, snow, hail, sleet, or shine, to physically cart her special glass cookware to a church member's backyard on the next street over twice a day to prepare her food. Only here can he use a cordless phone, plugged into this friend's house, to make calls, consult with doctors, or order supplements. And guess where he has to *drive* to get food from their refrigerator? To the neighborhood Friends Church several blocks away. (These dear people have become true friends to us.) Paul has to manage all these errands and hustle back home before something goes wrong (again).

The car Paul drives to the Friends Church is their second vehicle, a small Toyota parked on their property but as far away from Juli as possible. This is his "office." Here he stores everything not possible to keep in the house. From its overstuffed and sorely disheveled interior, one would have presumed his Chicago bag lady friend had taken shelter with them! But this poor guy barely has time to breathe, let alone find time to tidy up the inside of the car. No one else can do it for him without the risk of misplacing information vital to him, such as important resource addresses or phone numbers.

Now back to the perfume episode. This was one of those horrid days when everything seemed to go in the tank. It didn't matter how careful he had been, even to the point of shielding his hair with a dumb-looking knit hat. That evening the perfume smell jumped on him like fleas on a mangy dog. After asking Olsie for prayer, he opened the door, went inside, and

Juli's whole system cried "Foul!" In an understandable panic, Juli screeched at Paul to "get out, get out, get out, shut the door!"

Of course he recognized the "code" instantly. Under these circumstances that tone of greeting spelled for him another long evening of tedious and torturous decontamination protocol. Let me assure you this would not be anybody's idea of a nice way to spend a cold winter evening.

Paul made a U-turn faster than a mouse that has just bumped into the house cat. Until he could neutralize that odor, his isolation cell would be a cold, dark garage. On more "normal occasions" Paul has the luxury of proceeding directly upstairs to bathe. But in cases such as this, he immediately strips off all his contaminated clothing and stands shivering in the buff, dousing himself with vinegar until the job is done. No shortcuts present themselves. He has to be thorough, because it is simply astounding how such odors so friendly to a person in normal health can raise havoc with a person with MCS.

Here Paul confronts a classic catch-22—the poor guy couldn't be out of the house for long but now didn't dare come in any time soon. One circumstance or another had him constantly caught between a rock and a hard place. Imagine how mad that would drive you. On this particular occasion an aggravating torture was the unhappy discovery that his supply of vinegar was short. The long, drawn-out decontamination process in a garage "dungeon" was miserable enough without having to stand there chilled and idle for forty-five minutes until my wife could dash out to replenish his supplies. Thank the Lord she hadn't left the premises yet. The whole situation is reminiscent of some of the creative tortures inflicted on poor inmates of the Russian gulags just for the cruel amusement of their guards. Yet for the sake of Christ and devotion to his wife, this man shares her misery *for a few years now* with all amenities excluded from his life because her body reacts to every one of those comforts.

Imagine a situation where not only your own life is put on hold because of the round-the-clock care your spouse requires, but for her survival you must share most of the torments and imprisoning restrictions imposed by her unusual condition. You get the picture—and this is only a small part of the story. How many young men do you know who are up for that? Very, very few are. That is why I said "one in millions."

Juli's plight is no picnic either. Can you imagine lying day after day on a bed, sick and in pain, and because of your sensitivities having no newspaper, radio, TV, stereo, tapes, and for hours at a time, no company? One week of that hell would drive most of us cuckoo—especially for a type A personality like Juli's. The kid was easily bored growing up and always wanted to be on the move. Yet for years she and Paul have coped with this kind of existence. And it is not getting any easier. God knows their limits and only he can provide the longed-for relief.

It will take an unvarnished miracle for Juli to be healed. Many signals led us to believe it would be soon. Desperate people, as I told our congregation, can add up two and two and get six. I misread my cue cards about the timing, but I still feel deep down that the "fix" is in. I could have that wrong too, but I think not.

I sense that whatever God is doing in this case, his purpose transcends this family and is part of something bigger. What it is I don't know, but I can't wait to find out. I sense that the resolution, when it comes, will be far-reaching in its effects, not only in the life of this church, but spilling over into the lives of many others also.

I do not claim the spirit of prophecy. But I persist in the conviction that a blessed outcome is in store that will beggar the pain. In this confidence we endure, though we are barely surviving at times.

There is one request that would furnish some emotional relief. If well-meaning people would resist the temptation to pepper us with "solutions," that would take some of the strain off. Many are problem-solvers by nature, but in this case that mode does nothing for our stress level.

Few people, even in the medical community, comprehend this kind of illness. (Witness the stonewalling apparently chemically-exposed Desert Storm veterans are running up against.) Our communications to you provide only a hazy picture of the horror we are dealing with. After seven years in this hell, we know the terrain better than almost anyone.

Our request is simply that you pray, encourage, and assist us, but please don't badger us with suggestions for fixing it. We know what we are doing and know why one thing would be detrimental and another would be impractical. It only wears the tread off our emotional tires to have to explain and defend everything we have chosen to do.

I would ask that you pray especially for the emotional health of Olsie. This ordeal is sucking the life out of her. Signs of depression are back as she has trouble getting out of bed in the morning and facing the day, and trouble keeping focused and on top of things. She sees it all and is taking every preventive measure she can, but facing all that suffering is almost more than a devoted mother's mind and heart can bear.

So why doesn't she pull back? Because if she does, who will be there for them? Juli herself is just hanging on and Olsie knows it. Paul is stretched emotionally and is so tired that if he sits down, he sometimes falls into a dead sleep. None of

121

us knows what to do. We have no answers except to run the race until the motor gives out or God intervenes.

Thank you for caring and sharing our burdens,

Pastor Jim

Life in the Tower of Terror

At Disney World there is a structure in the MGM complex called the "Tower of Terror." Its elevator transports passengers through queasy heights and when it stops, they know something frightening is about to happen. Suddenly the bottom drops out. No sooner do you gather yourself from this initial long fall than the elevator starts to rise even higher. A brief glimpse of the sprawling park below is allowed. Then comes the thought, "I hope we don't drop from here!" As you freeze in space and time, the bottom drops out again—this time even further.

There are circumstances when life seems like one long day in the Tower of Terror. You are taken up and dropped, then taken up and dropped again. Sometimes the burdens of life seem much too heavy to bear. Things are so painful that you just wish the Lord would punch your ticket and give you an early pass into his presence.

Then again, while some people are afraid they are going to die, others hurt so bad they are afraid they won't. Losing a child, I think, has to be one of the most heart-wrenching tragedies a parent can possibly endure. If there is a close runner-up, it is seeing your child in such miserable and agonizing circumstances that you sometimes wish you could die instead and not have to watch the suffering and chaotic circumstances escalate.

With Juli's illness and the straits it imposes on her, Paul, Olsie, and me, we sometimes wonder if any of us will ever again see the light of day. It is a black, ever-descending tunnel of tribulation that seemingly worsens daily with absolutely no answers anywhere.

Our plight reminds me of the prophet Jeremiah, whose life also seemed to be crashing all around him. It matters little that this man lived in a different time and culture or spoke a different language. The fact that he never flew on a jet aircraft, used a computer, watched TV, talked on a telephone, or traveled more than six miles per hour in his entire life doesn't mean he didn't struggle with some of the same issues we wrestle with today.

Jeremiah was a prophet of God. His job, as any faithful preacher knows all too well, was pain-intensive. Prophets are almost by definition politically incorrect. Their mission is not to irritate people but, on the other hand, not to please them either. Their business is to speak for God. Like a good referee, a prophet can't be bashful about calling fouls on the home team. This does not lead to popularity. Prophets, at least the true ones, have always taken a pounding.

Prophets are human too. Throughout history these saints logged a lot of time in the dungeon of despair. That rock-like strength God gave them belied their true fragility. "Sticks and stones may break my bones," said Teddy Roosevelt, "but words will never hurt me." I don't know what planet Teddy came from, but words can break your heart and kill your spirit.

Jeremiah was a very, very human man. He was an eminently transparent man who never deviated from duty. He went to the wire in his loyalty and paid a heavy emotional price. Lamentations 3 is like an intimate page from a private diary where we are given the opportunity to feel the writer's despair, hope, confession, and relief. In passionate honesty Jeremiah bared his soul. He knew tribulation's dark passages, yet his embattled faith emerged intact. Fighting back, he testified boldly to the faithfulness of Israel's God.

He is like the psalmist David and others who are honest in telling us of troubles, deep anxieties, and even deeper felt emotions. In the end, rallied by their knowledge and past experience of the character of God, their faith lands safely and confidently on the runway of reassurance.

Does it feel as though God has taken you to the mat? Read verses 1–20 in Lamentations 3 and tell me that your story is new. Listen to this litany of utter despair from the pen of the suffering prophet. At times we may have experienced some of the same emotions and we see here that it's often a sounder spiritual therapy to take our feelings, however erroneous and confused, to the throne of grace rather than to a counselor's "couch."

Lamentations 3:

v. 1) He is intimate with affliction. "I am the man who has seen affliction because of the rod of his wrath."

v. 2) His footsteps are directed along a dark path. "He has driven me and made me walk in darkness and not in light."

v. 3) He feels God opposes him daily. "Surely against me he has turned his hand repeatedly all the day."

v. 4) His health is deteriorating. "He has caused my flesh and my skin to waste away, he has broken my bones."

v. 5) His life is difficult and unrewarding. "He has besieged and encompassed me with bitterness and hardship."

v. 6) His habitation is an emotional tomb. "In dark places he has made me dwell, like those who have been long dead."

v. 7) His prospect of escape is futile. "He has walled me in so that I cannot go out; he has made my chain heavy."

v. 8) His prayers go unanswered. "Even when I cry out and call for help, he shuts out my prayer."

v. 9) His way is barred. "He has blocked my ways with hewn stone; he has made my paths crooked."

v. 10ff) He feels his God mangles him like a wild beast and leaves him for dead. "He is to me like a bear lying in wait, like a lion in secret places. He has turned aside my ways and torn me to pieces; he has made me desolate."

v. 12ff) He concludes that his God has targeted him for injury. "He bent his bow and set me as a target for the arrow. He made the arrows of his quiver to enter into my inward parts."

v. 14) His public standing is in tatters. "I have become a laughingstock to all my people, their mocking song all the day."

v. 15) His heart is galled. "He has filled me with bitterness, and he has made me drunk with wormwood."

v. 16) His self-esteem is shot. "He has broken my teeth with gravel; he has made me cower in the dust."

v. 17) His peace and prosperity are gone. "And my soul has been rejected from peace; I have forgotten happiness."

v. 18) His dreams are dead. "So I say, 'My strength has perished, and so has my hope from the Lord.'"

v. 19ff) His painful memories are totally depressing. "Remember my affliction and my wandering," he prays, "the wormwood and the bitterness. Surely my soul remembers and is bowed down within me."

Jeremiah feels lower than a snake's belly, drier and emptier than a mud hole after a long drought, flatter than a punctured tire. Life had stripped him down to the emotional bone and robbed him of whatever peace, prosperity, or prospects of hope it once seemed to offer.

It was not just the weight of persecution nor the estrangement from his family and friends that was taking him under. It was not the animosity of his countrymen who viewed him as a Babylonian sympathizer. His oppression of spirit was derived partly from the pitiful sight of the butchery of his people and partly from the sight of the smoldering ruins of Jerusalem as he surveyed the total devastation wrought by the Babylonians. It broke his heart to see the inhabitants of Jerusalem slaughtered wholesale, and the survivors uprooted and dragged to a foreign country.

Everything that he loved on earth was in shambles. The Lord had spared his life, but for what? Whom did he have to go back to? What did he have left? This is the lament of a man who had served God faithfully, but was now in the process of feeling the weight of all the judgments he had prophesied. It gave him no pleasure to witness the havoc wrought by the enemies of God's people and the terrible suffering inflicted on his countrymen, despite their rejection of the Word of the Lord. He felt as battered by circumstances as the doors of a fort under heavy siege.

Nevertheless, one of the attributes that marks the true people of God is resiliency. We may feel as flattened as the next person when really bad things happen but we bounce back. Water comes back in the well. Nothing about becoming a Christian throws a hard shell over our humanness. Things hurt. Rejection and betrayal sting us just like the next guy. Heaven may be our future, but right now earth is where we live. Still, the Spirit of God quickens our spirits in spite of all the ugly stuff. Somehow he pumps air back in our tires and we move on. This resiliency has its foundation in convictions that go deeper than our afflictions.

As Jeremiah's story continues we see that his monument of hope is the revealed character of Yahweh, the God of his fathers.

Continuing in verses 21–23 he says, "This I recall to my mind, therefore I have hope. The Lord's lovingkindnesses indeed never cease, for his compassions never fail. They are new every morning; Great is Thy faithfulness."

Despite the distorting message from his in-the-tank emotions, his knowledge of life with God breaks through like the sun after a storm. It scatters the black clouds of doubt from the horizon. At the end of the day, Jeremiah recognizes that for all the punishment he has absorbed in God's service, he is still standing. In the final tally he sees, above all the emotional debris, clear testimony to the loving-kindness, the compassion, and the constant faithfulness of the Lord.

v. 24) If in terms of this world's standards of prosperity, the believer finds himself impoverished, let him not abandon hope. Jeremiah reminds us that he who is bankrupt is not broke. "The Lord is my portion," comes the reassuring voice. "Therefore I have hope in Him." To whatever extent the locusts of misfortune may strip our branches, let us never forget the treasure we have in reserve—the Lord himself.

In a rough way, I can illustrate the prophet's point. Throughout our daughter's illness she and her husband have been completely without means. Paul is a prisoner of her condition in more ways than one. It is impossible for him to get out of the house much of the time, much less go into the marketplace to earn a living. Yet Juli's illness eats money like a garbage disposal.

They may be busted, but they are not broke. Why? Though they have no reserves in their account, their Heavenly Father owns the bank; and though they have no "food in the pantry," God owns the farm and the cattle on a thousand hills. "The earth is the Lord's and the fullness thereof."

On one occasion our funds were exhausted. As we pondered and prayed about the situation, one day out of the blue something unexpected happened. It was a phone call from my younger brother, Bernard, which just blew me away.

First, let me give you a little context. Though he professed Christ at an early age, Bernie gradually drifted away from any pretense of Christian faith. Even so, by human standards, he remained a son and a brother to be proud of. By his own admission, co-opting many values from his Christian upbringing, he proved a steadfastly loyal husband, a remarkably attentive father, and a rigorously ethical and fair-minded businessman with whom and for whom most people enjoyed working.

But because of that inevitable spiritual wedge, our living far apart, and our intense focus on our work, we had not been real tight. At the time of this phone call, though, that passive distance had begun to close.

That background is what made this call, remarkable in any event, all the more so. Bernie had just been invited to take the top job at a national department store chain and was leaving his current position as Executive Vice President of a major electronics retail establishment.

"Jimmy, Peg and I are going to send Paul and Juli $50,000 worth of stock to help out with their situation."

You could have knocked me over with a straw. We had not asked for any assistance, and had no idea whether Bernard and Peg knew the black hole we were in. We also didn't know if they would feel generous if they did know. Yet right when there was a critical gap in our financial supply, the God of miracles touched the hearts of Bernard and Peg and built us another timely monument of divine provision to hang on to in the dark and silent passages ahead.

Yet as wonderful as this provision was, this latest monument points to a larger and more wondrous truth. In Christ we believers inherit the earth! Yes, the present may belong to others, but the future belongs to us. It belongs to all who have the Lord as their portion. In the Lord we inherit more treasure than we could ever owe, more joy than all the sufferings this world could pile on us, and glory far in excess of all the humiliation that a lifetime of shame could ever inflict upon us (Matthew 5:3–9; Romans 8:18; 2 Corinthians 4:17–18). We are in this race for the long term, not the short haul. The prize is given at the end of our life's marathon.

There are no losers among those who have the Lord as their portion. Broken, battered, deprived, disdained, defamed, and oppressed as aliens in a dark world, we may limp in pain to the finish line, but we will cross to a crown of glory and a triumphal entrance into the kingdom of God. As the late Ethel

Waters once put it, "Jesus don't sponsor no flops." Victory is guaranteed.

v. 25) At last, like a phoenix, Jeremiah's seemingly shattered faith rises boldly from the ashes of despair. "The Lord is good to those who wait for him, to the person who seeks him." Suffering has not punched all the air out of his tires after all. From deep within the furnace of affliction, he offers battered people counsel of great wisdom.

v. 26) He encourages us to wait on the outworking of God's hidden purpose. "It is good that he waits silently for the salvation of the Lord." There is a time to do the work of the Lord; and there is a time to wait on the work of the Lord. When matters are out of our hands and remedy is beyond our reach, that is the time to suffer in silence. All God's delay is strategic. He knows what's going on, why it is going on, and exactly how and when to end it.

v. 27) Jeremiah acknowledges God's wisdom in imposing our burdens, whatever the timing or season. "It is good for a man that he should bear the yoke in his youth."

We naturally think our young should be sheltered from pain. There is also the tendency for a youth-loving culture to think that when we are in our prime years, the Lord owes us an exemption from the cruelties and burdens of life. All that "heavy" stuff should be deferred closer to checkout time when everything is falling apart anyway.

One day I was having lunch with a young couple whom my wife and I were seeking to guide toward a closer relationship with the Lord. While in conversation, something came up about heaven. Suddenly the young lady laughed and blurted out, "A lot of my friends say they just wish the Lord would come and they could go to heaven. I don't want that to happen yet. I want to live and have fun. I'm not ready for that."

Her words may have carried more meaning than she knew. But, whatever her spiritual status, my thoughts as she was speaking were, "Young woman, you have been living all your life in a pain-free zone. You've been living the Mardi Gras of youth. Just wait until you see Bourbon Street in the morning. Daylight will unmask it for the seedy, smelly place it really is. In time, life with all its cuts and cruelties will make its way around to you too. Then when the shine comes off, all the glitter will disappear. At that time you will pray, 'Thy kingdom come.'"

Unburdened youth delays our rendezvous with sobering reality. It postpones spiritual maturity. The more faith visits the house of testing and pain, the more it learns to look up to the God of grace and away from the world of illusions. The sooner this maturing, refining, and clarifying process begins, the better. Youth, aflame with a faith forged under heat and tempered by severe testing, is an awesome resource in the hands of the Spirit.

The words of the prophet Jeremiah continue as he counsels us to submit to God's mysterious providence.

v. 28–39) "Let him sit alone and be silent since [God] has laid it on him. Let him put his mouth in the dust, perhaps there is hope. Let him give his cheek to the smiter; let him be filled with reproach."

Whatever burdens encumber our lives, God put them there. Knowing that should be enough for us simply to "be still and know that I am God." Part of the equation of faith is humble submission to the wisdom of an all-knowing God.

v. 31) When the mystery side of God's providence brings these things our way, what helps us to "give [our] cheek to the smiter" and "be filled with reproach"? It is knowing that God's wounds are temporary. "For the Lord will not reject forever," even though the moment when he seems to distance himself from our pains seems like rejection, it is not forever.

v. 32) We can take heart knowing that God's compassion is as sure as his affliction. "For if he causes grief, then he will have compassion according to his loving-kindness." There are cycles in the life of a believer, as surely as there are seasons in nature. Blessings always follow burdens and compassion follows grief.

Let me illustrate this last point. Remember the "allergic to clothes" saga I mentioned in the last letter? As you can well imagine, the misery and stress of that whole period was unbelievable. If someone had asked me then how the Lord could work out anything good from that experience, I would have been at a loss to tell them. It seemed like misery for misery's sake with no letup in sight. But God did use those very circumstances to bring about a surpassing blessing *indeed*.

A few months prior to the apex of the crisis, I received a call from a young woman named Lynne Mackey, an MCS patient whose condition was less severe than Juli's. In Lynne's case, her malady was precipitated by an exposure to chemical toxins at her place of employment. This assault had terrible physical consequences for her and other employees, each of whom suffered brain damage, balance disorders, chronic fatigue, and extreme sensitivities to volatile organic compounds.

The severity of Lynne's illness necessitated an extended leave of absence. After an attempt to return to work six months after that failed, her employment was terminated and she had no alternative but to pursue and receive disability compensation.

Ambitious and enormously intelligent, Lynne, like Paul, graduated co-valedictorian. She completed her Bachelor of Science degree in computer science from Indiana University in just three years, and earned her Master of Science degree from Purdue University in only one. For almost ten years, she earned positions of increased responsibility at several prestigious high tech companies, including AT&T Bell Laboratories.

Now the simple chore of whipping up instant mashed potatoes was nearly impossible due to her loss of short-term memory. Her devastating disability eventually caused her to become housebound, and her residence had to be modified to suit her particular chemical sensitivities. The physical, emotional, and financial toll on Lynne and her husband was extraordinary.

Several years later, Lynne's husband became a friend of one of our church members. After my latest update to the congregation about Juli and Paul, this fellow asked Lynne, who was faring better than Juli, to contact me in case she had any assistance or advice to offer.

We conversed like people who had been through a common traumatic experience, but it quickly became apparent that Juli's complications far surpassed Lynne's. So there appeared to be little help she could offer at that point other than prayer. However, I did promise to pass along her phone number to Paul. But, given the interminable workload and stress of his round-the-clock caretaking, I didn't give Lynne much encouragement that he would ever call.

Then the clothing crisis hit. In desperation, Paul remembered he had heard about someone a few months back who might have some clue or cure for this problem, so he dug out Lynne's phone number and called. Unfortunately, Lynne hadn't the slightest idea what to tell Paul about their dilemma. Instead, God providentially offered Juli and Paul a redemptive friendship. It was particularly wonderful for Juli. Not only did Lynne share some similar symptoms of Juli's unusual illness, but also a love of music and devotion to Christ.

The strangest thing happened at the end of her first conversation with Paul. She said, "I have to go, I have a piano lesson." Something made Paul blurt out, "Would you by any chance be studying with Don Lehmann?"

Yes, she was! And it was convenient for her to visit Juli frequently because as a fellow MCS sufferer, she "knew the drill" and posed a minimal problem for Juli. She could also identify with some of the humiliation attendant with the condition and was able to be a "sympathetic ear" rather than an uninformed "judgmental tongue." That was a godsend.

Thus, the friendship that blossomed between Lynne and Juli has far overshadowed the pain that birthed it. Like Jonathan's selfless devotion to David, Lynne's stalwart commitment to Juli in the thick of this spiritual battle is the mark of a true friend. In the process, God has given our family another powerful monument for which we all give great thanks.

v. 33–38) We can take comfort knowing that God's blows are not capricious. "For he does not afflict willingly, or grieve the sons of men. To crush under his feet all the prisoners of the land, to deprive a man of justice in the presence of the Most High, to defraud a man in his lawsuit—of these things the Lord does not approve. Who is there who speaks and it comes to pass, unless the Lord has commanded it? Is it not from the mouth of the Most High that both good and ill go forth?"

POLISHING GOD'S MONUMENTS

God takes no delight in the blows he must inflict upon us. In his secret counsels and perfect plan they are both wise and necessary.

> v. 39) In any case, be slow in resenting his supposed impositions, knowing that God's blows are not undeserved. "Why should any living mortal, or any man, offer complaint in view of his sins?" The truth is that none of us, believers included, ever have any right to complain about the hard times God allows to envelop us.

In a popular book entitled *When Bad Things Happen to Good People,* Rabbi Harold Kushner offers an explanation that limits God's power in thwarting this supposed injustice.[3] The title assumes that in the eyes of God, natively good and deserving people actually exist, a fallacy we exploded in the last chapter. Had the rabbi been more in touch with Hebrew Scriptures and the prophet Jeremiah he might well instead have pondered a riddle like *When Good Things Happen to Bad People.*

Of course few folk would rush to buy that volume, but that is the right question that nobody asks. None of us, however virtuous we (or others) may think we are, has any right, based on our moral résumé, to expect any favors of God. Innately we are lost sinners, natively ungrateful and hostile to God. We are focused on self, supremely worthy of everlasting damnation. We humans have no margin for complaint, no matter what hits us.

Some people want to point the finger accusingly at God and rail, "Where is God?" God could point the finger back at them and ask, "And where have *you* been? All your life you have brushed me off and now you demand that I, like your personal valet, be at your beck and call? Get real, my friend!"

God is not impotent or handicapped by circumstances. He is omnipotent, that is, all powerful. He is also omniscient (all knowing), and has no need for any man to make lame excuses for him. In reality, God owes no man anything. Let us imprint on our minds Jeremiah's words, "Why should any living mortal, or any man, offer complaint in view of his sins?"

A couple of years ago, a dear friend of ours became acquainted with a young Christian woman who was battling brain cancer. It was this lady's second brush with the dread disease. Seven years previous she survived radical brain surgery that necessitated the removal of her entire left hemisphere along with the cancerous tumor. Tragically, the cancer was now back, treatment options were exhausted, and she was facing a painful and undignified death, completely bedridden and dependent upon others for life's basic needs. Racked with pain, and through clenched teeth, she uttered these unforgettable words, "When I became a Christian, I surrendered all my rights to Jesus to do with as he chooses. If it's his good pleasure to slice me into pieces and barbecue me on a skewer, that is none of my business. The Lord is good; his ways are perfect and I have no complaints." She died a couple of months later. Her epitaph reads, "Through it all . . . I've learned to trust in Jesus," and is a shining testimony to the faith of one who rightly understood God's character and her own moral bankruptcy apart from Christ. This knowledge gave her comfort and strength to face her tough circumstances and finish well.

"Mercy" is a term that says God withholds from us the punishment we truly deserve. God is gracious. In bestowing his benefits upon us, God showers us with undeserved blessing. "Why me?" is a question born of human conceit. Jeremiah proposes that the real question ought to be, "Why not me?"

No man in his sufferings ever has cause to raise his fist to God and say, "How dare you treat me this way." If we could see our rap sheet in heaven, we would quit our brooding in self-pity and just blush and bear it. The prophet concludes in Lamentations 3:40 that we should take stock and cast ourselves upon God's mercy: "Let us examine and probe our ways, and let us return to the Lord." There is no place for those who plead their own merit as a ground of exemption. By far the wisest course is for us who are being scoured by suffering and sand-blasted by trauma to "examine ourselves and probe our ways."

Hard times bring out hard places in our hearts. Pressure exposes the cracks in our spiritual walls. Fire consumes the hay, wood, and stubble in our work. Instead of thinking about how God is lacking, Jeremiah redirects our focus and reminds us that we are the ones who are falling short. Let trials do their perfect work (James 1:2–4).

This is why the Bible speaks of the troubles believers experience in terms of "discipline," and in being "reproved by him." It also says, "He scourges every son whom he receives" (Hebrews 12:5–6). This is not to say that we believers bring down afflictions on ourselves because we are knowingly transgressing the boundaries of his will. No, sometimes it is because, however sincere we may be, like an old house, there are always areas in need of maintenance and repair. Nothing exposes our spiritual dry rot like a scourge of pain and suffering.

I am reminded of a modern-day neglect that may relate to polishing monuments. It happened a few years ago when I was working on my computer. A dreaded message appeared on the computer screen informing me that my hard drive had just died and was now in electronic hell. I had been remiss in backing up my computer files and was about to pay the price of neglect. Years of invaluable data were lost.

In the Christian life we often make the same mistake because we neglect to back up our spiritual files. Throughout this book, I've called this exercise "polishing our monuments." Like Israel's monuments, these are personal markers of God's faithfulness to his revealed character. These works from our past bear silent but eloquent witness in the present that God will perform as advertised in our future. If I will just be patient, God will ultimately live up to his biblical billing.

My monuments reassure me that no matter how current experience may seem to contradict his revealed character, God remains the same yesterday, today, and forever. When circumstances shout that God may not be who he claims to be, my monuments speak up and say, "Just you hang in there. Be faithful and you will see that he remains faithful. He is everything his Word declares him to be—all powerful, all wise, wholly good, always faithful to his promises, and consistent with the inner laws of his own moral being."

Right there is where Satan will challenge our faith. Remember in the Garden of Eden how the devil seduced Eve by impugning the character of God (Genesis 3:4–5)? When Moses recorded that primeval dialogue he gave us a clue to the devil's favorite device. Note how he insinuated to Eve that God was a self-serving liar and a moral hypocrite by withholding something really beneficial from them. Bottom line, God wasn't really good after all.

This account serves prophetic notice that Satan is on a mission to smear God's good name. When we too begin to question his character, then victory is his. No opportunity is overlooked by this deceiver to seed a confused or reeling mind with doubts about God's character. The last thing the devil wants you to believe is that God is to be trusted mindfully, emotionally, and completely.

Sometimes in the mysteries of his wise providence, our heavenly Father finds it necessary to expose us to prickly hedges of disappointment, disaster, and despair. Whenever you find yourself among those thorns, expect the enemy to jump into your thinking like a dog on a bone.

The devil, you see, is the ultimate slanderer. Our media and politicians haven't caught up with this news yet, but Satan is the father of spin-doctors. He was the first to spin reality to reflect badly on God. Whenever we Christians take our place on the field of faith, we would be wise to prepare ourselves for this onslaught. Satan's subversive activity pursues our faith like a relentless knight. Expect a battle and remember to polish those monuments into bright, shining fortresses.

In war, it is as important to know your weapons and resources as it is to know your enemy. Because Satan has been around the block, he knows that God, in the mystery of his purposes, will at intervals prescribe heavy burdens for his servants. During these times faith may stagger under the load. Did he not seize the moment to tempt our Lord when, after a prolonged fast, he hungered in the wilderness (Matthew 4:1–11)? Our adversary regularly waits in ambush for convenient crises that offer him the opportunity to invade our thinking.

This is why it is imperative that we learn the habit of polishing our monuments. It is imperative because there will be days, weeks, months, or yes, perhaps even years when God appears to be an absentee father. There will be times when heaven is as silent as the calm before a cyclone. At such times, prayer seems futile. Life can be so tempestuous that emotionally we seem ravished by hell rather than refreshed by heaven. There will be those times when God seems to go on vacation and leaves us stranded in distress and despair without relief or prospect of deliverance. This, my friend, is the mystery side of God.

A "monumental faith" is the best way to develop a higher threshold for perseverance. Unless we learn the habit of polishing our monuments today, we may find ourselves at spiritual risk tomorrow. Harsh experiences and heavy emotions are the devil's favorite playground. Blending emotional distress with a seasoning of intellectual doubts will be used by the devil to attempt to stagger our faith and loosen our hold on the Word of God.

Jeremiah starts in shadows of deep despair, but as he polishes the monument of God's character, dark thoughts recede and the sunshine of his holiness, wisdom, justice, and love beams brighter and brighter. There Jeremiah's faith finds a place to rest. At the same time, he sheds any remnant of human conceit that says, "Hey, I deserve better than this." He accepts his nation's sorrow in profound humility and says in effect, "Take the heat, stay the course, and trust in the Lord and his tender mercy." Only then does a tower of terror become the tower of triumph.

On occasion, when we have asked Juli if she ever feels abandoned by God, her answer is "yes" and "no." Emotionally, she admits she often has *felt* abandoned. But then she remembers the flight training principle of trusting one's instruments in inclement weather.

She recounts the story of a tragic plane crash I relayed to her many years ago. What made this event a double calamity was the lethal convergence of two factors: bad weather and pilot error. The investigative report of the incident indicated that the unfortunate pilot was flying in heavy fog. It went on to explain that when a pilot is flying in those conditions, it is vital that he rely solely on his instruments as opposed to flying by the "seat of his pants." This is because without a visual point of reverence, one's senses can be easily fooled into thinking the plane is doing the *exact opposite*.

Though the pilot in this story was apparently quite experienced, he was notorious among his peers for having one fatal flaw: he tended to rely predominantly on the feel of the plane and his visual reference, rather than to trust the guidance of his instruments. In the report, his colleagues remarked that they could never understand why such a well-trained pilot was so disposed to this grievous error, though they warned that for a new pilot, it's not an easy skill to master.

Neither is it an easy spiritual lesson to learn. But, when one is living in adversity, trusting in the revealed Word of God is as essential as relying on instruments when flying airplanes into fog. In fact, it has been this very discipline that has sustained my daughter during her own seasons of dark despair. She tells herself, "Juli, as hard as that is, no matter what your feelings tell you, trust your instruments!"

That is the difference between walking by faith and walking by feelings—trusting our instruments rather than our sight or instincts. In the fog of life our feelings will mock our faith and fairly scream at us that God has walked out on us, but our instruments will always reassure us that he is still there, walking right beside us.

Y E A R
8

July 15, 1995

Dear Friends,

It has been a longer interval than usual since I last updated you on Juli's condition and the circumstances surrounding it. Let me first express our profound appreciation for your continued prayers and concern for Juli and Paul. We owe a special debt of gratitude to our "Young at Heart" Sunday school class for reaching out to them, planting flowers in their backyard, and holding a special day of prayer on their behalf. Perhaps what has meant the most to us personally, however, is the class's determined faith that Juli and Paul will someday be in their midst. For the last year they have exhibited this confidence by designating two empty front row chairs with their names attached. But I'm asking for the prayers of our entire church body now more than ever. Juli's life currently hangs in the balance.

We have recently learned that on top of everything else, Juli has ovarian cancer. She has a whopping tumor in her lower abdomen. We have been in great crisis and distress knowing how to deal with it, given her special health issues.

Dr. Sandilands from our church became concerned about her abdominal mass when he made a house call three months ago (in the backyard). Ironically, around that same time, Dr. Corrine Allen, their Ph.D. Nutritionist from California, came to see them as well. Because she suspected that Juli and Paul had picked up parasites on their overseas mission trips, she brought along a book by Dr. Hulda Clark about anti-parasitic treatment. Even though the book primarily contained her theories about the relationship between cancer and parasites, Dr. Allen thought that parasites could be a factor in their CFS and that they might benefit from Dr. Clark's anti-parasite treatment.[4]

Like Dr. Sandilands, however, Dr. Allen was shocked at the sight of Juli's abdomen and decided personally to take her lab work to Dr. Clark for analysis. Two weeks later, the doctor called with the results. She had found the presence of a cancer hormone known as orthophosphotyrosine and concluded that whatever was growing was cancerous. Recently, Dr. Sandilands made a return visit and estimated that the mass had grown 25% in the interim. He also took a blood sample, which revealed several abnormalities that fit the cancer profile.

Dealing with this looming danger using the traditional medical approach poses an awful quandary, since the only way to determine definitively what we are dealing with is to have ultrasound followed by surgical removal. The question is, to diagnose the problem, should we expose her to a chemical-intensive hospital environment and conventional treatments that could so aggravate her MCS that *these* end up killing her first? Or, worse than that, would these exposures and treatments create a torrent of fresh complications and new layers of misery with her MCS so that cancer would seem like an easy way out? It's always a catch-22 . . . pick your poison.

The only other option, a trek to see Dr. Clark in Mexico, also entails serious risks. But, believe it or not, it would be less hazardous than chemotherapy for her highly weakened immune system, or a hospital environment would be for her acute chemical sensitivities.

So about the time we were discussing whether or not to "bet the house" on taking Juli to Dr. Clark's clinic, I was engaged to speak for a week at a conference in Sandy Cove, Maryland. While it was Paul and Juli's decision to make, I was unalterably opposed to them going to Mexico—opposed because almost every time they took a risk with Juli's environmental safety zone, it was chaos. This was an extreme risk. As many of you are aware, about one and a half years ago Juli's sensitivity spectrum expanded, without warning, to petrochemicals in all forms including gasoline and vehicle exhaust. This development, among other complications, literally locked her out of their truck and left her pretty much homebound. Therefore, just *getting her to the airport* entailed exposing Juli to chemical substances that she could not tolerate.

And *now* what were they considering—flying by private plane from Hillsboro airport to San Diego at the exorbitant sum of $10,000? Imagine the environmental challenges she would face in San Diego, then again at the border, and who knows what in Mexico. Oh, it was just too much! Besides, can any good thing come out of Nazareth? I mean, if medical help was hard to come by here in the U.S., what chance was there to find help in Mexico, for crying out loud?

But Paul and Juli believed it was a risk they had to take. What I didn't know, they figured wouldn't hurt me. So while this Big Cat was away, all the mice played, including both moms. Paul had already been making arrangements for the private plane, clinic appointments, and hotel. Meanwhile, Dr. Sandilands pulled some major strings at the hospital and arranged for the ultrasound machine to be brought out to the hospital *parking lot*! So on the way to the airport Juli underwent the ultrasound procedure. The radiologist told Juli that he observed the probability of a low malignant ovarian cancer. He explained that this term meant not a lower likelihood of malignancy, but rather a slow-growing kind of cancer. That was the good news. The bad news, of course, is that ovarian cancer is one of the most deadly forms of the disease. He offered to send the ultrasound images and his report to Dr. Clark.

(His final report read "bilateral large cystic masses, most likely of ovarian origin. Diagnostic considerations include dermoid cysts, endometriomas, cystadenoma, or cystadeno-carcinoma of low malignant potential. The low level echogenic material within the cyst would certainly go along with endometriomas, but these are usually smaller than in the present case. Additionally, the thick septum between the cysts and its vascularity [albeit, high resistance] is worrisome for a more active process. Similarly, the presence of a small peripheral solid nodule in the larger cyst is also worrisome.")

Thus, Juli and Paul took wing for Mexico via Brown Field in San Diego, along with Olsie, Elaine, and a nurse from our church to monitor Juli in flight. The moms were an integral part of this travel team, as Juli and Paul would need their constant assistance to run errands in Tijuana and back and forth across the border into San Diego.

To our great relief, Juli withstood the transition from her safe environment to one laced with many hazards. Previous

146

bad experiences had primed me for calamity. You can't appreciate my intense apprehension unless you've endured again and again the catastrophic fallout of the simplest environmental miscalculations. Trust me, this was a near miracle—not a term that I am given to using loosely.

But, praise God, I am happy to report that as of this moment Juli is not only surviving the perils down there, but (by her benchmark) almost thriving in it. Amazingly, she has even gathered enough strength to take short beach walks with Paul, as their motel accommodations are only three blocks from the Gulf of California. I should insert here that Juli actually began some of Dr. Clark's treatments about two weeks before their exit to Mexico. She attributes the relatively smooth travel transition, her recent surge in energy, and the further assuagement of her sensitivities to the liver detoxification procedures prescribed by the good doctor.

Even so, other sensitivities persist and life for them remains incredibly challenging. So what are their accommodations down there? During the day their "home" is the clinic where she receives her treatments. When they finally return to base, with permission from the motel manager, they literally camp out (sleeping, cooking, eating, fending off insects, etc.) on the veranda in just their light clothing! Though the night time temperatures in this season are reasonably comfortable, any discomfort from the weather or the ubiquitous mosquitoes are relatively minor nuisances for a pair who have had to become inured to all those privations (and worse) right here in Tigard, Oregon. Overall, however, we are encouraged by the good news. So Olsie, Elaine, and I felt secure enough leaving Juli in Dr. Clark's hands.

Now for a more recent update, July 28, 1995. Happily we report that Juli's reactions are sufficiently tamed to the point where Paul has time during the hours she is in the clinic to cross the border and go for supplies in public places. Previously he was unable to risk the contamination. This part of our letter is a great monument of God's wondrous and timely provisions when we needed them most. With immeasurable relief, I now report what appears to be a testimony of much answered prayer and landmark intervention by our God.

First off, you will be delighted to learn that Dr. Clark's tests now indicate that Juli's malignancy does not fall in the active category. Furthermore, Juli's blood work has returned to normal, though one cancer marker (while now within normal range) still needs to be lowered another 20 points for the doctor's comfort level, to ensure that Juli is completely in the clear. Additionally, the latest ultrasound results indicate that the cysts have shrunk slightly. Dr. Murphy believes that if Juli follows her protocol diligently, the cysts will remain benign and continue to shrink further on their own. Since Juli's immune system is so weakened by her CFS, the doctor is advising against surgery, "because the benign cysts would probably grow back anyway and there is a risk of infection."

I cannot speak for Dr. Clark's medical approach and theories, but at the end of the day, it's the results that matter. And so far the results have been most encouraging. Not only have her treatments succeeded in changing the status of her ultrasounds and blood work, but they also have alleviated some of Juli's most tenacious and troublesome chemical sensitivities! Dr. Clark believes that Juli's MCS and the toxicity of her liver were integrally connected to her cancer development, which is why the treatment for one is the "cure" for the other.

But please don't rush to judgment here. The MCS side of the problem is not yet history. That came home to me forcibly the day we left for home, when I looked down from the fourth floor of the hotel for the last time and saw them camping out on the complex patio. No, Juli is not close to being "fixed" yet, but at last God seems to have directed them to someone who understands at least part of what is going on in her body and offers helpful treatment. We are very hopeful of better things to come.

Another amazing piece of progress is her renewed ability to travel the highways without ill effects. We are so heartened that down here she has been able to commute to the clinic through relatively heavy traffic without reacting. In addition, her physical strength, though nowhere near what it used to be or ought to be, has picked up dramatically. But then one has to remember that she has been at least semi-bedridden for the better part of the last eight years. It's a wonder that the parts still work.

The marvel is how God prepared her body in a timely fashion and watched out for them every step of the way, from "baby's first steps" at Hillsboro airport, to their ability to withstand and even flourish under the elements in Mexico. The probability of missteps was enormous with almost no fallback options void of unthinkable consequences. Frankly, I wonder at it every day. It reminds us that when God decides, then all the objections of hell cannot prevail against it.

God seems to have raised up this medically gifted and enlightened woman when concern, care, knowledge, and relief were lacking in the traditional medical venues. Since Juli notices incremental steps of improvement each week, she and Paul have decided to stay several more months for the following reasons:

1) They want to obtain as much help and information from Dr. Clark as possible. Paul is receiving anti-parasite treatment as well to accelerate his CFS recovery and is more energetic than ever.

2) And now people, GET THIS! Juli has improved enough so that they are able to reside in their (carpeted) hotel room. They know that flying home commercially is still a long shot, but they are hoping that if Juli recoups enough, she can withstand the close quarters near perfume and save the family some money (for once).

3) This may seem hard to believe, but this cancer clinic has turned out to be an emotional and spiritual tonic for a couple who has suffered such social isolation for the better part of eight years. The Lord has sent numerous Christians to its corridors, including my brother's dear friends from the Navigators, Warren and Ruth Meyers, authors of seven books between them. Every evening, the Meyers spend time with Juli and Paul praying and encouraging them. To be quite honest, Juli and Paul are having a jolly good time down there, just cutting up and fellowshipping with Christians and witnessing to non-Christians as well.

Please ask God for continued care over every step of their way. We want to thank all of our friends, congregation, and family for being there for us through all these difficult years. Your support has been monumental. Without your prayers and assistance, we would have dropped in our tracks years ago. Your love, labor, prayer, and generosity have been so sustaining. We have often felt near the end of our string, but you have never allowed us to feel alone in our pain. To us you are a church where people really care and truth matters. Olsie and I bear witness to that.

In Christian love,

Pastor Jim

December 29, 1995

Dear Friends,

Last Sunday many of you experienced with us a monument of such proportion that none of us will soon forget. As you may know, I announced from the pulpit during our Christmas Eve morning service that we had special guests in our midst. "God has sufficiently healed my daughter Juli so that she and her husband Paul are able to attend church for the first time in six and one-half years." Our entire congregation broke into joyous applause. Allow me to share with you the poignant events that preceded this spectacular moment.

First, Juli and Paul flew back to Portland on Southwest Airlines on December 22, just as they had prayed God would allow them to do. In spite of sitting amidst "all the perfume I could inhale" (Juli's own words), the flight went smoothly. They came off that plane decked out in Spiegel clothes they had ordered in Mexico and I literally had to do a double take; my eyes couldn't believe it was really them.

These adjustments take time, for it happened again on Sunday morning when they both walked through the church doors in their Sunday best. I said to Juli, "You look beautiful, honey; how are you faring in here?"

"The vasculitis is a little rough because of the new carpeting, but don't worry, Dad. Things don't work the way they used to. It'll get better. Paul and I want to go into our 'Young at Heart' Sunday school class to thank them for all their prayers."

So the kids walked in and sat on the back row because the announcements were already underway. They couldn't help but notice those two empty chairs on the front row with their names still on them. The class president, Billy, who'd spoken to

151

Paul several times face to face when the class planted flowers at their home, interrupted his announcements and projected to the back of the room, "Are you guests?"

Paul hesitated for a minute, a bit bewildered, and then realized the problem. "We're Paul and Juli." Everyone in the room was in shock. They had only seen Paul outside, bearded, with that dumb-looking hat and his "asylum" uniform and Juli behind French doors in undyed, hand-sewn clothes. They let out a collective gasp and in one fell swoop descended on a clean-cut Paul and a primped-up Juli with tears of joy.

We are so grateful to our God, for though he came to our daughter and son-in-law through this cancer ordeal in the form of a frightening ghost, his rescue in "the fourth watch of the night" has enabled us all to share not only Christmas lights together again, but more importantly, *the* Christmas Light of the World.

Thank you for all your prayers,

Pastor Jim

Anatomy of a Spiritual Break-in

Twice intruders have bashed in our doors and trashed our place in search of valuables. In the second instance my wife apparently surprised the burglar, who managed to beat a hasty retreat out the back door just before she walked in from the garage. A break-in experience, whether or not one encounters the intruder, challenges our sense of security in that little civilian fortress we call "home." The dread is magnified by the knowledge that whoever violates our domain without our welcome or permission has entered our domicile to help himself—not us. To take—not give.

There is another kind of intrusion into our life space that produces high anxiety. But unlike a burglar, it comes as a friend. I am talking about a spiritual break-in.

What is a spiritual break-in? And how do you recognize when this is happening? A spiritual break-in occurs whenever Christ breaks into our experience in some new or unfamiliar way. It may also happen in some familiar, but more challenging way. Either approach comes with the intention of extending within our hearts and minds the kingdom of God to new frontiers of reverence and obedience.

It is wise to raise our consciousness to monuments of this kind, as we have this almost reflexive tendency to treat these intrusions like foes rather than friends. If we are to learn anything from biblical precedents, it would be that when grace comes calling, it can sometimes appear as frightening and disrupting as an unearthly ghost.

In chapter fourteen, Matthew recounts one of these break-in experiences, the feeding of the five thousand. I believe as he reflected upon the disciples' experiences with Jesus during his earthly ministry, this one struck him as possessing something of a typical quality. That is, he saw in the unfolding events a virtual metaphor of Christian experience in general.

True, he did record this miracle to explain how he and others came to understand the magnitude of the person of Christ. But this explanation alone is too narrow to account for all the detail. Biblical narrators are notorious for their literary economy. They write with a purpose and spare us details that do not serve their intentions. When they throw in what may seem like extraneous details, it is not because they are garrulous. We just need to be better readers. So I personally feel quite certain that Matthew saw more in this event than the solitary message that Jesus is the Son of God, as centrally as that truth is communicated.

There are some timeless principles embedded in these time-bound details. Today, I think Matthew, if he could speak for himself, would concur that Christ still trains his disciples in much the same way as in the past and for exactly the same purposes. That is, he breaks them out of little mental prisons of weak faith, confining conceptions, binding prejudices, and narrow obedience.

Before looking at this specific narrative, it is instructive to observe the circumstances leading up to it. Note in passing that it is not uncommon for the Lord to balance times of blessing with times of testing, and elevated experiences with humbling ones. Can it be said, without too much exaggeration, that behind every hilltop of exultation in the Christian life there is a valley of confusion on the other side? In our walk with Christ miracles meet mysteries as regularly as blessings meet burdens. On this occasion that is exactly what happened to Jesus' first disciples.

It had been a landmark day in the ministry of Jesus. He had just performed a sign of staggering magnitude. Over five thousand hungry men (plus women and children) somehow feasted on a Jesus-blessed boy's lunch of only five loaves and two small fish—with twelve basket loads to spare! The crowd was so amazed at his unearthly power of provision that they were ready to take Jesus by force and, in defiance of Rome, proclaim him as their king.

Jesus saw this for what it was and rejected their carnal enthusiasm. He was not impressed by their "faith." He knew full well that these folk did not recognize him for who he was. They weren't owning him as One who had come to save them from their sins and restore them to a right relationship with the God of their fathers.

No, their sights and perceptions were much lower. Seeing this incredible supernatural demonstration of material provision, all they saw was a free lunch and a political messiah with a big "S" on his chest. With his cooperation those supernatural powers might be exploited to throw off the irksome yoke of the Romans, their political masters. Politics, not spiritual redemption, was the zenith of their withered vision. Sound familiar? The farthest thing from their sense of need was a Redeemer who could set them free from the shackles of sin and Satan.

Now bear in mind that Jesus' disciples were, no less than we, children of their culture. Because it's virtually impossible to walk in the cultural rain without getting our heads wet, one can see why Jesus would not want his disciples dallying in that politically charged atmosphere. They were susceptible to those same carnal aspirations.

So it is no surprise that when Jesus detected a popular momentum gathering to declare him king, and thus revolt against Roman authority, he quickly pre-empted it. His disciples were already waiting for Jesus to make his move, set up an earthly kingdom, and elevate them to positions of authority. Jesus promptly compelled his disciples to get in their boat and head for the other side of the lake. They needed to be shielded from this wave of political innovation.

It must have felt much like when your team wins the Super Bowl. The fans of the winning team always want to hang around after the game and bask in the afterglow. No doubt the disciples warmed to the reception that greeted Jesus after the feeding of the five thousand. They weren't anxious to leave the scene. Yet for them it was a dangerous place to be, one where they might become infected with wrong notions concerning the purpose of his miracle. So Jesus promptly dispatched them. Then he dismissed the crowd before impulse could find a plan, and retired to a mountain spot overlooking the Sea of Galilee.

Perhaps this is a good place to observe that God's purposes in ordering and superintending the currents of Christian experience are complex. Often people inquire, "Why, Lord, why?" as if there were a single explanation. The truth is, our God is not a simple God. He may have many reasons for what he does.

In this case, one reason the disciples found themselves out on the Sea of Galilee, battling in a boat against an onslaught of raging wind and billowing waves, was the need to be removed from carnal influences that would do their hearts no good. Surely they didn't have the slightest understanding at the time for Jesus' sense of urgency in herding them into their boat and sending them away. When the winds came up, they probably thought they would have been far better off to have stayed where they were. And it would have done little good for the Lord to have pulled them aside on the shoreline and explained that this was a situation where exposure to the winds of worldly ideas posed a greater danger to their souls than the winds on the sea.

Returning again to this point: We have to raise our threshold for the mystery-side of God. Remember—we don't have to know why. Our business as disciples is simply to get into the boat and go wherever Jesus directs us. If his commands take us into the approaching storm, we can be assured that our souls are better off there than in whatever situation we left behind. Thus, we note here as always, the Lord leaves many things unexplained. This calls for the "walk of faith." It is not a blind faith, as blind faith has no basis. Christian faith rests on the knowledge of a Person and the reliability of his time-tested Word.

Whatever God's purposes, the harbinger of a spiritual break-in is often some set of threatening circumstances. Note how the disciples found themselves "in the eye of the storm." We are told that Jesus

> . . . made the disciples get into the boat, and go ahead of him to the other side, while he sent the multitudes away. And after he had sent the multitudes away, he went up to the mountain by

himself to pray; and when it was evening, he was there alone. But the boat was already many stadia away from the land, battered by the waves; for the wind was contrary.

(Matthew 14:22–24)

Now Jesus knew in advance what would happen. For the disciples to find themselves all seized up in a tempest of wild waves was no accident. That was precisely where he wanted them. As much as the Lord wanted to get them *away* from one thing, he also designed to get them *into* another.

This time the break-in of a seemingly threatening windstorm would furnish a window of opportunity for another spiritual *break-out*—out of a small faith, shallow conceptions, and spotty obedience. Rough waters would set up a learning situation which would stretch their faith, elevate again their conception of the magnitude of Jesus Christ, and bend their wills more and more in the direction of unconditional obedience. He has the same program for us.

Notice also that in spiritual break-ins it is so typical for relief not to show up until the eleventh hour. "And in the fourth watch of the night he came to them, walking on the water."

In that era the Jews marked time in three-hour blocks. Since "night" began at 6:00 p.m., "the fourth watch of the night" means Jesus came to them between 3:00 and 6:00 a.m. Prior to that, as Mark's parallel account informs us, Jesus had eluded the confused multitude by taking a hike into the surrounding hills where he sought privacy for prayer. From a mountainside overlooking the basin Jesus observed them, even through the darkness, doing combat with the wind-driven waves and making little headway:

And after bidding them farewell, He left for the mountain to pray. And when it was evening, [that is, just getting dark] the boat was in the middle of the sea, and He was alone on the land. And seeing them straining at the oars, [from the mountain top] . . . at about the fourth watch of the night, he came to them, walking on the sea (Mark 6:46–48).

Note how Jesus responded to their plight. At first he didn't lift a finger. But evidently the Lord was interceding for them with his Father while they were contending with the elements. At last, when his purpose was fully served and the timing was right, he came to them in the fourth watch of the night.

I don't know why it is, but it seems more often than not the Lord's deliverances do not arrive early. He seldom saves the bacon before it is crisp! That is, for reasons sealed up in the mysteries of God's providence, the Lord often sees fit to hold our fat to the fire, as it were. Typically divine interventions come down to the wire . . . arrive just in the nick of time . . . right before our boat capsizes, one might say. Such works showcase his greatness, boggle our minds, bolster our faith, and enrich our always too impoverished sense of the glory of God.

One of our church monuments is a story like that. For some years the congregation had been meeting in temporary quarters at a junior high school. Remodeling was scheduled so we had to find a place to relocate. Although everybody knew that we had to move by mid-June, it was already March and little had been done to lock in a new location. For me, as interim pastor, this was a huge concern. Although we were a much smaller church at that juncture, it was not easy to find a suitable meeting place for 375 people. No options were readily available. Frankly, though I wasn't saying it out loud, we were in real trouble. The waves were rising and a storm appeared to be approaching on the horizon.

As time passed, we still weren't coming up with a viable alternative. With just fourteen days to go and counting, almost simultaneously two of our men, totally independent of each other, came to me with knowledge of a vacant building eight miles south, just off Interstate 5. Quickly we checked it out. The facility once had been a lumber brokerage, had ample parking space and amazingly enough, was so designed that it almost appeared to have had a church in mind as a secondary use. With time running out, we immediately explored the possibility of leasing the building for a reasonable sum and getting a conditional use permit from the city. The answer was "yes" on both counts and just in time the storm calmed and our ship stabilized.

Not long thereafter we faced another threatening wind. In 1984, the congregation purchased a prime parcel in our city. Though they owned the land, the church had been unable to start construction. By the late spring of 1991, about a year after I came aboard, the church was into its third building permit renewal and it was due to expire in a few months. Another extension was unlikely to be granted, at least not without a major battle with the city. Every attempt to find financing had hit a dead end. Things looked bleak. We continued to spend much time in prayer. Then out of the blue one of our men called to say that he had a lead on a "possible" source. It was simply unaccountable to us how quickly things came together after that. As I recall, around mid-summer our financing was approved and boom! We were negotiating a building contract, etc. But the meter was running and it was going to be a close call to move dirt before our permit expired. We beat the clock by only two days and were once again reminded that our God will not fit into our neat little boxes that we sometimes impose on his revelation.

Are we always to expect confusion when encountering God? No, as some of the mystery is cleared up through the boundaries he has set for himself. There are many truths we take to the bank. We can be assured that God will not lie. He will not void his promises nor violate his own moral character. The Lord may need to break into some of our mental houses in order to break us out of notions that leave us with a God much too small.

Let us come to terms with the reality that he can and will act as he pleases, our stifling preconceptions notwithstanding. God can deliver us sooner . . . or later. He can deliver us through a storm, in the midst of it, or send us around one altogether. So ride it out and wait on God to do what is best and trust that he knows better than you what "best" is.

Another very common aspect of these spiritual dramas is exemplified in this narrative. Namely, when the Lord comes to meet us in the midst of our afflictions, *he often shows up in totally unexpected ways*. Notice that when Jesus finally did come to them in the wee hours of the night, he didn't come in a rowboat, the orthodox conveyance. No, he came to them "walking on the water."

Whoa! Who would have expected that? He could have simply stilled the waters with a sovereign word. He had done that before. But here, in the middle of their distress, Jesus comes walking on the water like a brave tourist out for a late stroll on a stormy night. This extraordinary scene alone should seal to our minds the fact that his ways are not our ways (Isaiah 55:8). Yet we see this principle illustrated again and again in the course of biblical history. The Lord loves to humble those who know too much. He blows the minds of those who persist in reducing him to the conventional.

To Hosea (1:7) the Lord once said, "But I will have compassion on the house of Judah and deliver them by the Lord their God, and will not deliver them by bow, sword, battle, horses, or horsemen [that is, in any of the usual or conventional ways one might expect]."

The Jews of that era expected their Messiah to come conquering the world by a sword; instead he came conquering by the cross.

The Lord taught Elijah this lesson as well because he too was a proponent of the "big bang" approach to get the attention of stubborn sinners. We read in 1 Kings 19:11–12, "the Lord was passing by! And a great and strong wind was rending the mountains and breaking in pieces the rocks before the Lord; but the Lord was not in the wind. And after the wind, an earthquake, but God was not in the earthquake. And after the earthquake a fire, but the Lord was not in the fire; and after the fire a sound of a gentle blowing." Where was God? Not in force, noise, and flame. The touch of the Lord was in the gentle breeze.

So when Christ breaks in, don't always presume that you know which door he is coming through. He may meet you in circumstances you never imagined. Here Jesus took his disciples by complete surprise. Not the first time either. He had astounded them before when, by a simple command, he turned a surly storm into a pussycat.

But this was really out of the box—coming to their rescue walking on water during a wild wind deep in the night? Even today God stretches our faith and imagination. Events that seemingly form a conspiracy to bury us, happenings that seem to spell impending disaster, just might prove to be the Lord coming to help us in some unorthodox, unimagined way.

Indeed, Christ may break in through the storm door of disease, bankruptcy, failure, broken dreams, death of a loved one, disability, divorce, accidents, or any number of traumas that befall people during this life here on earth. The Lord knows how to snatch eternal profit from the jaws of temporal pain in ways we never imagined. This is the very reason Jesus' word to us is precisely the same as his word to his shaken disciples when they encountered the unidentified figure walking calmly on the water, "Take courage. It is I. Don't be afraid."

When life seems to pin a bull's eye on us, and shots are heard all around, our poise is dependent upon knowing that *Christ is in the crisis and he is master of it.*

As you know, the first stage of our daughter's horrifying and multi-layered illness appeared in the spring of 1987. Little did we dream at that time that she (and we) were embarking on a terrible odyssey (not over yet) to a health hell, one that would carry us through dark and dreadful passages that we could scarcely imagine.

Yet this experience has been break-in intensive. Time and again the Lord has come to us walking on the water, so to speak. What we have seen is as terrifying as a ghost—an ominous, threatening specter. We didn't expect him to visit us that way. But time and again in this ordeal it has indeed been Jesus breaking in and showing his glory in unconventional fashion.

For the longest time it seemed more like Satan breaking us down than the Lord breaking in. The Lord and Satan often use the same doors but for different purposes. Somehow the purpose and will of God is always bound up in the events of our lives. At times grace wears a fearful face.

I don't mind admitting that when we learned about Juli's cancer diagnosis I thought we had reached the end. Unless the Lord intervened and miraculously healed her, it seemed our daughter would soon lose her long and hard-fought battle with disease. We were fresh out of options, or so I thought. But as Maria in *The Sound of Music* asserted, "When God closes a door, somewhere he opens a window."

Our particular "window" led us in a direction that I personally would never have looked for nor expected help from. We will thank him even when his methods embarrass our

163

pride of human wisdom. After all, who would have expected the champion of the Philistines, Goliath, to be cut down by a ruddy-cheeked teenager with only a simple sling and a few smooth stones (1 Samuel 17)?

How like God to take a young woman, devastated with one of the most severe cases of CFS and MCS ever encountered, along with the deadly ovarian cancer and direct her to a place where conventional wisdom would least expect relief. Then, in Mexico, to place her in living conditions that ought to have quenched any hope of a good outcome, and bingo! There is a simultaneous, dramatic improvement in her CFS and cancer, and, a significant lessening of the MCS. In fact, a mere six months after she arrived in Mexico, we found her back inside our church building, fraught with all its environmental hazards, wearing normal clothes, walking around freely socializing and worshiping God.

Who would have thought after eight years of almost indescribable weakness, pain, and miseries galore, that the answers would be found in Mexico? After eight years of hitting a stone wall everywhere we turned, reaching out desperately in all directions for help, including the wacky, the weird, and the unorthodox, I am now convinced that neither conventional nor alternative medicine have a corner on fools. Both have some answers, both also have their limitations, and neither is too fond of confessing them.

Somewhat like the parents of the blind man in the ninth chapter of John, all we know for sure is that nine months ago God led our daughter, in a surpassingly miserable state, to Mexico and now he has returned her to us in a remarkably livable condition. Should someone be disposed to attribute the reversal to the Pygmalion principle, that is, the effect of changed expectations, try to explain this: Why for eight previous years did we throw tens of thousands of dollars (literally) at high hopes and great expectations and everything kept on going south? Sorry. That theory won't fly. No, the reality is that God sent her there for some reason. Why he didn't provide understanding and treatment for her condition in the United States is a mystery.

In the ordinary course or nature of things, miracles are happenings or results that one would have no reason to expect or predict. In them the power and wisdom of God is more intimately and irregularly involved than in the predictable rhythms of nature which he has set in motion. Miracles stick out as happenings that suggest divine intervention and beg for a more transcendent explanation.

Whether what has happened to Juli qualifies as miraculous is then a matter of definition. If we consider it a "wonder" when one finds significant healing of Juli's MCS, a condition that so far has been impervious to the understanding and methods of conventional medicine, then I would say we have a candidate for "miracle" here.

If God directs one to employ means to some end that most human experts would consider madness and folly, one which human wisdom or expertise would neither use nor accredit for that purpose, then I think we have the essence of a miracle. I am reminded of Gideon in his daring midnight rout of the Midianite horde, accompanied only by a corporal's guard of 300 chosen men. Only a fool would have attempted the ruse God directed and it tripped nobody's wires more than Gideon's. The Pentagon would never have approved that military strategy.

What more can we say? How God surprises us! The proud Syrian general and chief-of-staff Naaman was mortified and indignant when the Israelite prophet Elisha, by divine direction, prescribed washing in the humbling Jordan River as a cure for his leprosy. God's way required Naaman to accommodate himself to God's ways and submit to a regimen that challenged his paradigms, injured his pride, and violated his sense of dignity (2 Kings 5).

That is how God worked on me at least through this. As I have mentioned to many, I for one was opposed when Paul and Juli entertained the idea of going to Mexico. Had anything ever worked? Not a lot. Hadn't almost every desperate move only magnified the problem? We needed a miracle all right, but my preference was not to rock the boat. My vote was just to sit tight and wait for God to act right here.

People had stood by us all this time and I feared, among other dreadful outcomes, that by taking her problems to Mexico, especially with a disease so deadly as ovarian cancer, we would risk losing credibility by treating her there. Who cares to look so foolish?

That particular prospect, among others, raised my anxiety level immensely. One of the most wrenching collateral agonies of victims with this affliction is the cruel innuendo that the problem is in their heads rather than in their body. I dreaded any move that might feed that heartless, uninformed notion. As much as that appraisal insulted our intelligence, given our vastly superior knowledge of both our daughter and experience with the disease, the worse effect is that it trivializes the mighty work of God.

He is the One who has so unbelievably sustained and even enriched our faith in this incredible ordeal, the One who has kept us all afloat financially under the burden of overwhelming expenses that should have sunk us three times over, and he is the One who finally provided relief and understanding from an unusual source at a time when none was available elsewhere.

Now a word of warning. After the crisis has passed, be cautious of post-break-in backfire. There are times, just after a spiritual break-in, when we get swept up in a wave of spiritual enthusiasm. In a spirit of emotionally unanchored radicalism we may dive boldly into things over the head of our present faith. Emotions outrun our minds and feelings run way ahead of faith.

Peter's response in Mathew 14:28–30 to the strange appearance of Jesus in such alien circumstances is a good example of break-in backfire. It is instructive for us all to understand this potential danger anytime we have a close brush with the supernatural. Peter, at least at this stage of his spiritual development, was no cool hand Luke. He seems to have been a strong, emotional, perhaps excitable personality. In this case his spiritual exuberance was running ahead of his faith.

Yet, there is also something positive about Peter's response. He had a newfound vision of the possibility of the impossible and discerned the Lord's enabling potential. Whatever impelled Peter to want to emulate Jesus in walking on the surging water, at least Peter gained from the Lord's actions a vision of the unearthly power available in him. He was bold enough in his faith to ask the Lord to help him do the impossible. It is good for us all to think in those terms.

Still, no sooner had Peter taken a few steps than the winds blew away his confidence in the Lord's power to keep him afloat on that murky water. Taking his eyes off Jesus, he focused on the danger posed by fearsome winds and churning waters about him. Doubt seized him and "he became afraid, and beginning to sink, he cried out, saying, 'Lord, save me!'"

To "walk on water" and stand up against the strong winds of worldly opposition, or withstand the battering ram of devilish circumstances, takes more than a burst of mere religious excitement. Religious enthusiasm cranked up by emotionalism or even set afire, as here, by real brushes with the power of God always flames out as quickly as a Fourth of July sparkler.

The secret of spiritual staying power resides in that bold faith that looks to Jesus for strength to overcome any and every threatening circumstance.

Peter's experience teaches us that a faltering faith is not a failed faith. In the final analysis his faith, like all genuine trust, proved deeper than his doubt. As he began to sink into the depths, Peter turned back to Jesus for rescue and the Lord delivered him.

Jesus is forever coaxing and challenging our brittle faith. As here, he may allow us to be surrounded with threatening circumstances, let us experience our troubles for the longest time, or visit us in ways we least expect. This can draw out of us good things along with the bad, strengthening the one and weakening the other, and bring us again and again to the point of gentle reproof, "O child of little faith, why did you doubt?" Note that when the lesson was finished, so was the trial. "When they got into the boat, the wind stopped."

"When will it end?" the heart cries. When God is finished. Not one minute sooner. Not one minute later.

The capstone of the whole break-in experience for these disciples was the confession, "You certainly are God's Son." All of a sudden he was seen for who he is and was magnified in their eyes.

Let's understand something: God's agenda is not to make us happy (in terms of temporal bliss). He came to make us holy. This only happens as we begin to understand who he is. The bigger Christ becomes in our eyes, the smaller we become in our own. The ground a redeemed sinner stands on is not purchased with play money or cheap trinkets. It is blood-bought and won by the Spirit over the bitterest opposition of the flesh. That is why so many doors to our hearts and minds have to be forced open by rough break-ins. These things shake us up, but it is the only way to shape us into conformity to Christ.

Real worship breaks out where Christ has broken in. Expect God in his providence from time to time to hold your faith hostage to threatening circumstances. And don't be surprised when deliverance comes late and in totally unexpected ways. Prize and polish these monuments lest you become forgetful.

Y E A R S

9–11

November 1, 1996

Dear Friends,

I know that those of you who've labored intensely for us in prayer and aided our harried existence these last several years were exuberant at the marvelous display of God's handiwork in allowing Juli and Paul to worship with us for the first time last Christmas Eve. The impression was almost as stunning as seeing them raised from the dead!

Before I give you the latest, I want to relay an intriguing sidebar to that remarkable turnaround, a conversation I had with a lady in our congregation shortly before Juli and Paul's trip to Mexico. One Sunday after the second service, Gigi, a very stylish, vivacious, and godly-minded New Yorker approached me. On this particular Sunday she had hung around on the edges waiting for the right moment to pull me aside after most of the people had exited the building.

She expressed some ambivalence about sharing with me what was on her heart, fearing for one thing that it might stir up false hopes in two anxious parents, and worrying also, she admitted, that I might take her for one of those flaky, unstable types always seeking to draw attention to themselves by posturing as latter day oracles of God.

But Gigi had my attention, not only because I knew she prayed a lot for us, but also because she had enough on her own plate of affliction. She was stricken with terminal cancer. I knew Gigi had no hidden agenda. Her concern was totally genuine.

"Pastor," she ventured as we sat down on a soft bench, "I hesitate to share this with you, but somehow I just feel compelled to do it. The other night I had a dream. In it I saw your daughter, a dark-haired young woman, sitting at the piano on the platform and playing for the church. I really don't know what it means, but I just felt the Lord wanted me to share that with you."

Sensing this was from the Lord, I almost cried right there. In fact just as I started revisiting this conversation, tears again surprised my resistant eyes. For, as I recall, that was the last time dear Gigi was ever in church. Shortly thereafter, her cancer took her all too soon.

The thing is, Gigi had never laid eyes on Juli, knew nothing of her appearance or the color of her hair and, for that matter, may not even have known that Juli was a pianist. Mostly what she knew was that Juli was her pastor's very sick daughter and that she and Paul, as well as Olsie and I, were going through a living hell and she cared. That Sunday I sensed in my spirit that her dream probably had some deep significance.

171

Sure enough, the Christmas Eve Sunday after Juli's return from Mexico, what a sight to see our petite, dark-haired girl *inside*, sitting with Paul in the narthex of our church on the very bench where Gigi had shared her dream!

So now for the latest. How is life in the real world treating them? As for Juli, I've mentioned to many of you that the progress she's made with her maladies is nothing short of miraculous—especially when you consider she started off down deep in the Mariana Trench. As I've explained, CFS, which ironically carries the most innocuous label of all her conditions, is the most sluggish in bouncing back.

Nevertheless, like first-time parents, Olsie and I have been tickled pink watching Juli experience "novelties" that have been off-limits for so many years. Just to be able to watch TV together and hear her contagious laughter at Barney Fife is a precious gift. Recently she's gained enough strength to begin practicing piano, a little bit at a time. In her native pianistic perfectionism, she insists she still feels a little wobbly on the keys, but it's music to our ears.

Now she can sit up all day, pray, practice on a limited basis, read books, and take care of her own needs. Paul, with his own health up to par, is free to go back to business. This is one of the most exciting headlines of this year. We've just passed a major milestone, which last year was beyond reachable. This September, Paul has returned to his previous profession and resumed piano instruction. He eventually will work out of their home once they have remodeled a back room into a music studio, but for now, he is teaching at a piano store.

It will take time for him to build up a clientele of students again, but at least for once there will be a trickle of cash flowing in instead of a flood gushing out. I can't tell you what a relief this will be to our hip pockets. Previously, we were so used to getting soaked by their medical expenses we became virtually numb to it . . . so much so that we just reached mechanically into our wallets, didn't ask questions, shelled out the dough like human ATMs, and wrote off the robbery as the price of survival in a defenseless situation where the muggers have the drop on you.

It's also gratifying to hear Paul play again. With his health on the mend, he hopes to perform again soon. They are both chafing at the bit to resume study with their master teacher, Don Lehmann, but Juli needs to become a tad stronger first.

You've all said what a pleasure it is to finally be able to fellowship with Juli and Paul after praying your hearts out for so many years. One dear church member even remarked, "Who could imagine that two souls who've lived in the doldrums for so long could be so delightful?" For their part, Juli and Paul love our Sunday evening service because it lends itself to building relationships with many of you. To sum up, they thank God for church body life and normal American comforts like never before.

These newfound joys, however, were rudely interrupted late one night last month when Juli exclaimed to Paul, "I can't open my eyelids!"

"You mean you're sleepy?" he replied.

"No, I mean they're half-open and I can't open or close them."

He came in to look.

"Paul, I'm having a really difficult time breathing, too."

She ran outside to get fresh air. Once outside, she kept heading toward the truck, but just before she got to the driveway, she lost all motor control, her knees buckled in, her arms folded uncontrollably, and adding to the horror, she lost complete control of her bowels right there. The normally imperturbable Paul lost it, screaming on the front lawn at 1:00 a.m., "Oh, honey, oh honey, oh honey!" One thing Juli knew by this point—no air was coming in or out. Moreover, she realized she'd lost all speech control as well. She desperately wanted to scream, "Take me to the hospital! I'm suffocating!"

She feebly tried to open the truck door but to no avail, because she couldn't control her arms, let alone her hands. She then passed out cold, hitting her head hard on the pavement as she fell. Reacting like a New York City firefighter, Paul grabbed her up and tossed her limp body into their Ford Ranger pickup. Somehow in the chaos of the moment he still had the presence of mind to buckle her seatbelt—a detail guy all the way. He jumped behind the wheel and raced with her as fast as that Ford would fly to the nearest hospital.

Fortunately traffic at that indecent hour was negligible and the cops, who certainly would have given fatal chase, were conveniently occupied elsewhere as Paul blazed his way to the hospital through one stoplight after another with Juli slumped against the door panel turning blue. With every passing minute she was fast approaching the point of irreversible brain damage or death.

Thank the Lord, from the moment she stopped breathing to medical intervention it took only seven to eight minutes! After the doctors revived her, they told Paul that just another minute or so and Juli would have been an obituary item. Saved by a whisker!

In God's mysterious purposes, he had allowed her two prior brushes with death, and this night he had refused to let her go again. But our fear was that this time she had been spared a quick death only to suffer a torturously slow one, or to remain permanently brain-damaged for the rest of her life. For two terrorizing days, our minds were left worrying about which horrifying scenario would be ours to face. She was still flailing her limbs, her speech remained severely slurred, and her eyes stayed weirdly fixed in that half-open position.

If that agony weren't enough, the lead physician on her case, a neurologist, after reviewing Juli's 1995 blood work and "parking lot" ultrasound (with its diagnostic possibility of "cystadenomacarcinoma of low malignant potential"), initially speculated that cancer had spread to her brain and lungs.

Later that Tuesday morning, Juli was rolled down to the radiology department where she underwent a CT scan of the abdomen and pelvis. To our great relief, the report came back with good news, "the cysts appear to be 2 to 3 cm smaller in mean diameter when compared to the ultrasound exam dated 6/95. At this point, the likely diagnosis is bilateral endometriomas or cyst adenomas."

"Excuse me, but is something missing here? What happened to the 'worrisome, solid nodule on the right cyst' and the diagnostic option of 'cystadenocarcinoma of low malignant potential'?" you ask. Stay tuned.

Within a few more days, Juli rallied and all of her neurological abnormalities, including her eye problem, cleared up while she was still undergoing diagnostic testing to determine what was causing them in the first place. The doctors never were able to determine exactly what caused her to stop breathing along with the subsequent symptoms, nor could they understand why she had recovered just four days after her arrival. Since Juli suffered no ill effects from the whole ordeal, she and Paul believed that God had led them to the hospital to have the cysts surgically removed in case they were weighing her system down.

When the surgery was completed, it was confirmed that the cysts were benign endometriomas, though the right ovary (where the solid nodule once was) had been completely engulfed by the cyst and consequently destroyed. The surgeons were able, however, to remove the left cyst while leaving most of that ovary.

Juli and Paul left the hospital late last week, and we are all overjoyed that she's alive and certified cancer-free . . . but a bit befuddled that after all those batteries of tests, there are no answers whatsoever as to what caused this incident. We praise God for giving Juli her latest lease on life and we are hopeful of better things in the years to come.

With gratitude to God,

Pastor Jim

November 26, 1998

Dear Friends,

This Thanksgiving season, we have much to be thankful for, beginning with our salvation in the Lord Jesus Christ. We want to thank you for your persistent prayers for Juli and Paul. We are especially grateful to their siblings and spouses for their many visits, financial gifts, and prayers over the years. We are also thankful for extended family: grandparents, aunts, uncles, and cousins, who've come out to see them and given monetarily to help meet their needs. In addition, we deeply appreciate the unwavering love and support for Juli shown by Paul's folks.

We want also to give thanks to our faithful God for his merciful answers to your previous intercession. While there's no doubt Juli and Paul continue to need your prayers, there is also little question the Lord has finally granted them substantial reprieve and blessing in their lives.

Olsie relayed to me an enlightening insight regarding their amazing metamorphosis just last week. A month ago, Paul began to teach lessons out of their *home* in the room they remodeled as a music studio. Paul's grandparents recently bought him a grand piano for his practicing and teaching. Paul and Juli also took out a loan to complete construction on their unfinished second floor and to buy Juli her own grand piano.

So when Olsie drove over to help Juli recently, she took in this scene as one who experiences a dream come true. Juli and Paul had just driven into the garage after their two-hour study session with their master instructor, Don Lehmann. Paul, in a breathless hurry, told Olsie about Juli's performance for Don that day, "Juli was playing her Beethoven Pastorale Sonata this afternoon and Don was just sitting behind her, swaying with the music, smiling every minute. When she ended, he gave her a rave review, 'That, my dear, is a feather in your cap . . . great tempo, beautiful tone, exquisite lines, and perfect pedaling. You know it's such a joy to see you come back like this.'"

Paul rushed into the music studio. A new student and her mother had just arrived. In front of their Cape Cod style house, adorned with lace curtains in every window, a pink glow from the family heirloom Victorian lamp lighted the front bay window. The duo proceeded to the back French doors, shook Paul's hand, and watched his stupendous demonstration of the Leschetizsky technique while he performed Rachmaninoff's Liebesfreud. Then boom, they heard another grand piano playing in the living room and asked Paul, "Who's that playing?"

"Oh, that's my wife," he replied.

The transformation was reminiscent of a dramatic conversion . . . or of a caterpillar metamorphosed into a butterfly. As you can imagine, the bizarre occurrences at their home over the years had not escaped their neighbors' notice. Now wafting into the street from that house of strangeness came the most divine music! One baffled neighbor, who came by when Olsie was out working in the yard, inquired about the source.

"Wow, they're both pianists? My goodness, it sounds like a concert in there!" she exclaimed.

But as for this new student, she never knew what a house of horrors their place had been or how they previously had to live. All she saw was a nice-looking piano teacher who lived in a pretty house and played beautiful music.

So I encourage Juli, "You've come a long way, baby." I also ask you, our church body, for your continued prayers. She indeed has come a long way, but she's still not completely "fixed." Juli is thrilled that she can be active at last, but the malaise with her CFS is still quite pronounced and she must pace herself carefully. Often during these performances for her teacher, for example, she has to stop in mid-piece to rest.

But we know from the Scriptures that our Lord Jesus is the God who has the creative power to effect change, be it water into wine (John 2:1–11), diseased bodies into healthy ones (Mark 8:22–26), or wretched lives into regenerate ones (John 8:1–11). We can use these accounts in our spiritual bank. God has his own time and reason for everything.

Thank you for all your faithful prayers,

Pastor Jim

Everything for a Reason

Big earth-moving construction projects always fascinate me, as in the end a hundred-and-one seemingly confusing, separate activities finally come together as a planned result.

One summer, in the distant past, I briefly operated an air track drill on an interstate road construction project. Heavy equipment for miles around bedecked the mountainous terrain of my native West Virginia. Bulldozers, scrapers, graders, front-end loaders, drills, shovels, trucks, and cranes ripped and tore like hungry vultures at the innards of the wounded landscape. An army of men and their machines filled the rural air with a cacophony of mechanized sound.

Everything everywhere seemed to be waging all-out war on the land with no obvious scheme for constructive transformation. Men and machinery crawled about like a colony of ants, with no clear purpose or plan to the casual observer. Initially, big construction seems like little more than an exercise in affording bored men an opportunity to act like boys and play recklessly with giant, dangerous toys in the vacant countryside.

Although I personally didn't have a clue as to how it was all working together for a good outcome, it was evident that there was a master plan as the managers and engineers on site kept everything moving toward some sort of pre-ordained result. My faith was not blind, since a company truck, driven by a project superintendent in an official white hard hat, would daily show up at the construction site. A foreman would usually greet him, and then they would often unroll a set of construction plans on the hood of his orange truck. Consulting the blueprints, they would point knowingly to features of the drawings and then to the site. After a brief chat, the "super" would speed off to some other area in a cloud of dust. It was pretty clear that they knew exactly what to do, when to do it, where to do it, why to do it, and how to do it.

That summer nobody ever asked me to understand the plan. My job, you see, was not to understand, but to move the air track drill to a designated site, drill out a pattern of deep holes for the placement of dynamite, help fuse it, place it in the ground, and then let the powder man detonate the explosives. The only result I saw, whenever my particular job was done, was an upheaval of rocks and convulsed earth. Seventeen years later on a trip through central West Virginia I had the opportunity to see the finished project. Now I could see what my small temporary part had accomplished in the overall scheme of things. It had not been clear to me back then.

This experience is analogous to the operation of God's providence. Apart from biblical revelation, life doesn't always make sense. People without the benefit of this objective perspective often respond in despair. They turn to destructive crutches for relief from what seems at times like a comedy of the absurd. Alcohol, drugs, illicit sex, gratuitous shopping, mindless buying, pleasure seeking, and risk-taking are some of the ways people choose to help themselves cope with, or numb their pain. Some go over the edge and resort to suicide to escape from a life that seems to have nothing better than torture for our souls and mockery for our existence.

From our very limited vantage point life can appear to be undirected events and accidental circumstances leading to nowhere in particular. Without divine revelation to enlighten us, it may be easy to conclude that nothing has a reason, everything is random, and life is quirky. We all stand at the mercy of blind fate. There is no designer and no design. Stuff happens.

This hopeless perception is a false conclusion. Christians know—or should know—that what makes no sense to us makes all the sense in the world to God. Hidden in the little things of life that seem to be nothing more than the "filler material" of everyday existence are sometimes significant occurrences directed by the sovereign hand of God. These may change the whole course of life.

We live in an intentional world where the providence of God reigns. The hand of God is in all things, not usually perceptibly or loudly, but silently, mysteriously, and so effectively that he maintains control of the course of history. We can think of history as the working out of his promises.

With God everything is for a reason. No matter how small, each circumstance has a unique place in the divine blueprint of history. God does not approve of the wrong I do, but he makes even evil the servant of his righteous purposes. Events in our lives have sometimes subtle, often inscrutable connections to other events and circumstances. Chains of causes and effects are produced that we would never in ten lifetimes be able to fathom, predict, or imagine.

Why do we believe this? Because we believe in the fact of supernatural revelation. "God is there and he is not silent." He has spoken through the prophets and apostles of old who, moved and superintended by him, conveyed to man what he wanted to reveal. The Bible is the repository and preserve of what God has chosen to make known about himself. Thus what the Bible teaches, God teaches. And that for us is the end of all confusion and hopelessness. We have his Word on it.

The isolated, individual, day-to-day events of my life, some of which cause pain and anguish, are perfectly coordinated with and adapted to, his eternal plan for a new heaven and a new earth.

Job, of the Old Testament, understood this when he said, "I know that you can do all things, And that no purpose of Yours can be thwarted" (42:2). The Preacher wrote in Ecclesiastes 7:13, "Consider the work of God, For who is able to straighten what He has bent?" In Proverbs we read: "Many are the plans in a man's heart, but the counsel of the Lord, it will stand" (19:21), and "The plans of the heart belong to man, but the answer of the tongue is from the Lord" (16:1). God is sovereign in such a way that his purposes—not man's—prevail.

Time and again the Lord speaks of "plan" and "planned." In Isaiah we learn, "The Lord Almighty has sworn, 'Surely, as I have planned, so it will be, and as I have purposed, so it will stand'" (14:24), and "This is the plan determined for the whole world; this is the hand stretched out over all the nations. For the Lord Almighty has purposed and who can thwart him? His hand is stretched out, and who can turn it back?" (14:26–27).

These are only a few such passages from which this perspective is gleaned. Plans involve details, times, sequences, coordination, and effects. We serve a God who takes care of details, right down to "clothing the lilies of the field." Our confidence in God directing the details of history and experience is not a matter of human speculation. It is a premise of divine revelation.

This truth is part of what makes the Christian life such an exhilarating adventure for those of us who have submitted ourselves to follow Christ wherever he leads. There is a reason for everything, even when we would least expect it. God's unseen hand of providence holds no accidents.

What do we mean by providence? Louis Berkhof defined it as "that continued exercise of the divine energy whereby the Creator preserves all his creatures, is operative in all that comes to pass in the world, and directs all things to their appointed end." God thereby causes all things, even the little things that seem trivial and unimportant to our limited vision, to work together so as to produce a result that is for our good and for the accomplishment of his purposes.[5]

We can see in the narrative of 1 Samuel 9:1–17 how the Lord coordinates and converges the most routine and seemingly random circumstances. It is an example of how he can accomplish his purposes and redirect our lives to suit his plan. Even the small and most unsuspecting details of life lead toward a rendezvous with his sometimes secret, but always wise and just result. This phenomenon in theological terms is what is called *concurrence,* where God mysteriously acts in the free actions of men.

In 1 Samuel 8, we see that Israel is characteristically faithless toward God, clamoring for a king. They wanted a visible, human ruler. After all, the surrounding nations had theirs. They wanted to catch up with their neighbors. The problem with this is not the idea in itself. Sin, while not always found in the

185

substance of our proposals or practices, can exist concealed in the motives. So it was in this case.

Although it was actually God's time for that change, as Moses earlier had predicted, their motive was all wrong and it drew divine fire. The nation was not rejecting the prophet Samuel's leadership. It only appeared that way. In the final analysis they were rejecting the One for whom Samuel spoke and acted. The truth of the matter was that Israel did not feel safe in the hands of her unseen Monarch. They wanted to replace their invisible ruler in heaven with a visible human king in an earthly palace. They preferred a protector they could see to one they couldn't. It was unbelief, pure and simple. God knew this and judged their insistence accordingly.

Israel felt her future would be more secure with a human guardian backed by a standing army. Without this visibility she felt exposed to the aggressive whims of every hostile neighbor who came along, especially the expansionist-minded Philistines who had been oppressing them for years.

There was also a pride issue tangled up in the motivations of her leaders when they wanted to be like the other nations. They wanted "to be conformed to the world" or they were caught up in "pride of life." It's an image thing. Israel figured that to be taken seriously as a political entity, she needed royal hype. You know, a king, a throne, a court, courtiers, pomp and circumstance, and a big standing army that spelled "Whoa!" to any potential aggressor.

The worldly mind always prefers its methods to God's. To the unspiritual Israelites, this new political arrangement represented better security and, in modern athletic parlance, "more respect." Israel forgot to remember that, despite the absence of a human monarchy in the long march of their national history, their unseen king in heaven had always taken marvelously good care of them. As long as they trusted him, he faithfully thwarted and roundly thrashed their enemies. Somehow they missed the connection that it was only at the times when they turned their backs on God, broke their covenant promises, and trampled rebelliously on his law that the national fortunes became misfortunes. He let them reap the consequences of their choice and allowed enemies to dominate events. But such is the nature of man in blaming God for his misfortunes instead of taking responsibility for his own lawless ways.

As Proverbs 19:3 puts it so well, "The foolishness of man subverts his way and his heart rages against God." Blind to both their disease and its cure, they sought a home remedy in an earthly king rather than continuing to depend upon their heavenly ruler. Observe that this move of men on earth did not catch the Lord unawares in heaven or subvert his plan.

And, we see in 1 Samuel 9:16–17, because the time was right, that the Lord acceded to their request. Their plan fit his plan, regardless of the thoughts and intentions of their hearts.

God never relinquishes control of his purposes to human whim or contradictions. Israel would receive the king she longed for, as God intended even before they thought to ask. He allowed them to say what they wanted but reserved for himself the prerogative of who they would get. The man he would give them was not a man after God's own heart, but one they well deserved. He was also a king who would, with free moral choice, accomplish God's ends.

Saul was one who showed no more confidence in God than the people he represented. He was innately as rebellious as they and his love for God's law was as shallow as theirs. In the end he would bomb in a failure reflecting their own.

This narrative, like the book of Esther, is a study in the subtle ways of the providential hand of God. It can serve as a historical monument reminding us that God is also in the details of our lives, directing or allowing circumstances and events. His invisible hand is superintending and coordinating them to effect his plan in history corporately and individually. Nothing defeats his purposes. Nothing frustrates God. Everything, including evil, is part of his eternal purpose. Saul, as the first king of Israel, is a lesson in how God weaves together little things in causing a plan to come together. We are reminded to never despise or underestimate the place of the small experiences.

Kings don't have to look like Tarzan, but subjects aren't too keen on crowning a toad either. People tend to be hung up on appearances. They prefer, if they have a choice, a monarch who has a royal bearing. Kings ought to be kingly, and presidents presidential. The Lord, providentially, had such a man in waiting for this very moment. Saul had a royal stature and, it appears, something of an aristocratic pedigree as he belonged to a tribe with a great military tradition. In physical terms, at least, Israel literally had to look up to him since Saul was a good head taller than anyone in Israel. Now how was he brought into the plan?

One day it just so happened, providentially, that some donkeys got wanderlust, spooked, or who knows what. The point is that they turned up missing at the Kish spread in Gibeah. Not a major event to record in one's diary. But the stock was a family asset of some value, like a rancher's cattle, and naturally Kish wanted to find them. A man like that had plenty of servants who could take on this duty but for some reason (Kish had his reasons, God had his) he elected to send Saul, his son. Ordered to accompany Saul was a certain unnamed servant whose character, as events turned out, played a crucial role in the eventual outcome. God was in charge of that detail also.

These lost animals were no big deal in the grander scheme of human events or even in determining the well-being of Kish's family. But God used their disappearance to set in motion the shaping of a nation. So Saul and this obscure servant set out on a Rand McNally adventure to search for those long-eared donkeys throughout the hills and valleys of Benjamin and adjacent Ephraim.

After a length of time with no success, Saul expressed concern that his father would now be more worried about him than about the lost animals. Saul's readiness to pull the plug on his search and rescue mission at this point might (in the human way of seeing reality) have foiled God's providential plan right there. But not to fear. This is where the character of this particular servant comes into play as he turned out to be a more persistent kind of fellow.

One would naturally figure that if Saul was ready to throw in the towel, it would be no skin off this servant's back. "Not my animals. If the master wants to pack it in, fine with me." But not this guy. For this very situation, if for no other reason, the hidden providence of God had nurtured in his character a resourceful and timely "gift" of obstinacy about finishing what he started. Before aborting the search, this servant offered an idea that might save the day. Like most of Israel, he was aware of the celebrity of the prophet Samuel. Today it would be like most Americans are aware of Billy Graham, even if they are not religious. This man didn't seem to recognize Samuel as much more than a person with paranormal skills who might "see" (hence the name see-r) things not visible to normal people. He knew Samuel had a reputation for always hitting the future on the nose and was also aware that they presently were in the vicinity of this prophet's hometown. If the seer was home, he just might be able to tell them where to find the donkeys. It is a telling silent commentary on the spiritual condition of Saul that this king-to-be seemed oblivious to the towering figure of Samuel.

But there was a tiny, very awkward obstacle with the plan. Saul at least was aware of social conventions where seers were concerned. Since seers had no regular income and depended on the appreciation of the people to sustain them, Saul would need to give Samuel something for his trouble. The problem was, he was broke. Left home without his wallet. This of course would have been no obstacle for Samuel, but Saul didn't know that.

Again in the providence of God, this servant was prepared. Just happened to have some coin in his purse, enough to save embarrassment, at least. Humanly speaking, a crown could have been lost for lack of a little coin. God had provided even the foresight of the servant. So, stripped of any further excuses, Saul and his trusty servant pressed on.

All these little things with their twists and turns remind us again of this biblical truth: Man proposes, but God disposes. A little thing here, a little twist there and his plan comes together.

As they were making their way to the town where Samuel was supposed to be, their encounter with the prophet was sovereignly facilitated when, in the evening, they came upon young maidens drawing water. In the Orient, only reasons of modesty would bring maidens out in the evening. The timing was perfect. When inquiring about Samuel, the two men were told that at that very moment Samuel was ahead, making his way up a height for some religious festivities. If they hurried, they could catch up to him.

In the plan of God, each little event conspired two very important personalities to cross paths at just the right time. God also prepared Samuel to identify Saul. Just the day before, the Lord had communicated to Samuel that "about this time tomorrow I will send you a man from the tribe of Benjamin."

When they met, the Lord spoke to Samuel and confirmed the identity of his chosen man.

Saul did not have the slightest idea what he was chosen for when he set out on a thankless pedestrian trek to find some lost asses. If a cattleman in Pennsylvania went looking for some stray cows as far as suburban Maryland only to return home a few days later as President-elect of the United States, it would scarcely be less amazing than what happened to Saul. How true are the comments of Alexander Maclaren when he says:

> And behind all these, and working through them, the will and hand of God, thrusting this man, all unconscious, along a path which he knew not. Our own purposes we may know, but God's we do not know. There is something awful in the thought of the issues that may spring from the smallest affairs, and we shall be bewildered and paralyzed if once we get a glimpse of the complicated web which is ever being woven in the loom of time, unless we, too, can, by faith, see the Weaver, and then we shall be at rest. Call nothing trivial, and seek to be conscious of his guiding hand.[6]

This consciousness helps in understanding other Biblical events. In the book of Esther there is the moving account of the providential deliverance of the Jews from the malignant designs of the wicked Haman. Some people puzzle over the fact that the name of God is never mentioned. This is deliberate, for it teaches "by indirection," to use Dr. Leland Ryken's apt phrase,[7] the typical hiddenness of God's providential hand as he works concurrently and unobtrusively with human actions to accomplish his purposes.

This same providence was at work in the timing of the birth of Christ. In Galatians 4:4, Paul speaks of Christ appearing "in the fullness of time." He also says in Romans 5:6 that at "the right time" Christ died for the ungodly. To the average person, things just happen. There is no guiding hand behind the forces that shape history. Yet from a biblical perspective, this is God's world and what he doesn't make necessary, he makes certain, a distinction that Millard J. Erickson makes in his book *Christian Theology*.[8] So it was when God became flesh. The course of history intersected with the Incarnation when the cup was full.

At that time in history the civilized world was the original beneficiary of something resembling a common language. The far-reaching conquests of Macedonia's Alexander the Great, more than 300 years preceding the birth of Christ, and Hellenization (Greek-izing) of those countries and territories by his political heirs, spread the Greek language everywhere. This language furnished a vehicle that greatly expedited the preaching of the Gospel to this Roman world.

Also, for the first time, there was something in the ancient world that resembled our modern interstate road system. The Romans were masterful engineers and always mindful of military necessities. Because it was so critical to the defense of her far-flung territorial conquests to be able to move men, weapons, and supplies quickly, the Romans built a "rapid transit" road system, mileposts and all, still in evidence to this day. Here is the law of unintended effect in action. The Roman road system greatly facilitated the spread of the Gospel and Christianity.

Providentially there was Roman justice with its love of order. Christians suffered enough as it was, but without that Roman insistence on order and due process, at least for citizens, the hysterical mob opposition might have stopped the spread of the gospel and the preaching of Paul.

At this particular juncture in history, the Roman world was blessed with a turbulence-free window known as the Pax

Romana (Roman Peace). This lengthy period of relative tranquility was brought about under Caesar Augustus. Ordinarily, wartime conditions are not favorable to evangelization—too much distraction, confusion, and upheaval. It is a time for survival and not a climate very conducive for sober reflection. Had the Roman world been in the state of constant convulsion, as it was the century before the appearance of Christ, it would have impeded greatly the spread of the gospel.

By the time Christ was born, the Jewish people and their synagogues were established in virtually every corner of the Roman world. These synagogues numbered many Gentile proselytes and served as incubators and launch pads for the preaching of the gospel.

It is a well-known fact that at this particular period in the ancient world the old traditional religions, for a variety of reasons, had begun to lose hold on their adherents. Pagan religion had ceased to satisfy and there was unprecedented openness to a better hope. God in his sovereign providence caused all these influences and circumstances to converge and produce a stream of forces that shaped the very face of history.

God hasn't changed. He is still the sovereign superintendent of history and experience. Our comfort here resides not simply in the fact that God is sovereign in all our affairs, but in the corollary truth that this sovereign God "causes all things to work together for [eternal] good to those who love God, to those who are called according to his purpose" (Romans 8:28). [The brackets are my interpolation for the sense.]

Our sovereign God is not a capricious controller who is alternately merciful or mean as the mood strikes. His moral nature is unchanging. Whatever comes down from his sovereign hand, whether we can see it or not, is never at variance with these bedrock attributes the LORD revealed to Moses, "The Lord, the Lord God, [is] compassionate and gracious, slow to anger, and abounding in loving-kindness and truth [i.e. faithfulness]" (Exodus 34:6). [Brackets by the author.]

Mercy sometimes masks compassion behind a severe face. One day when my older daughter, Kristi, was about three years old I took a break from the office and walked up to the parsonage to visit Olsie. As we talked in the kitchen, I was standing near the outside doorway watching Kristi racing around recklessly on her trike in our neighbor's driveway when suddenly she jackknifed. The tricycle went south and Kristi vaulted headlong in the other direction, her little chin bouncing ominously off the concrete surface. Not good.

I immediately bolted out the door across the yard to Gothard's driveway where I picked up a crying little girl to inspect the damage. As I feared, a gaping wound. Looked like a three-stitcher to me at least. "Oh, no," I thought, "this little thing is hurt bad enough. I don't want to put her through stitches too. Maybe a clean-up and butterfly bandage might work? No, this is a little girl's face you're dealing with Dad. Don't wimp out. Do the right thing. Take her to the doctor."

So I promptly carted her off to the doctor's office and took a seat in the waiting room where I could stick my head in the sand while the doctor and his nurse dealt with the tears and the dirty work. I just sat there hoping I didn't have to hear her cry when shortly the nurse popped in and beckoned me to the "operating room." Could have killed her! What was I paying them for?

"Mr. Andrews, we need you to hold her down while we stitch her up."

"Oh, no," I protested inwardly, "now I have to watch the little tike suffer through the ordeal. I don't know if I can stand this."

It got worse.

"I'm not going to numb it," the doctor explained, "that will hurt as bad as stitches, so I just need you to help me hold her down."

"Hold her down!" I exclaimed to myself. "Hold the baby down! Oh, man, how did I draw this duty anyway? What are doctors and nurses for? Since when do dads and moms have to pin their little ones to the mat while others hurt them?" I was thinking to myself.

As the doctor started his painful work, I grasped Kristi's tiny shoulders and held them down firmly. Never in my life will I forget those confused little eyes looking up at the daddy she trusted to protect her from bad things.

"Daddy, make him stop! Make him stop!" she cried again and again, and wiggled and writhed in pain as her loving and compassionate father kept her pinned down in the face of that nine-foot needle.

That restraint on my part was a severe mercy. I could hardly stand it. But as her father I had the foresight to know she would not appreciate looking in the mirror at sixteen and seeing a female prizefighter staring back at her, all because of my short-sighted "compassion" when she was three.

Had I tried to explain all that to her then, Kristi would have rejected out of hand my reason for subjecting her to that brief pain. You can hear it now. She would have insisted, "Daddy, it will be all right. I won't mind." But I knew better. My adult wisdom was far superior to her myopic childish perspective. Today there is no scar and she looks like a woman rather than a veteran of foreign wars. Mercy briefly wore a mean mien but the other compassion would have been deceptively cruel.

So it is with our sovereign God as he manages the traffic of detail in our lives. Some harsh things don't mean what they appear to and small things often mean a lot more than we ever imagined. Don't despise the small stuff. You have heard the saying that the devil is in the details? Maybe, but our God is *in charge* of the details. Much may happen mysteriously, but nothing happens aimlessly. With God there are no messes, no misses, no mistakes.

One time during my Colorado days I was invited to speak at a retreat in the Rockies. Well up in these mountains, I was driving down into a sort of swale. The two-lane road ran downhill from both directions, so I approached with some uncertainty the left turn where my instructions indicated I should turn off.

My misgivings caused me to hesitate slightly. I turned my wheels as if to turn in front of an oncoming Porsche. Sensing my indecision, the driver of the fast-moving sports car braked to give me space just in case I was dumb enough to go for it. Meanwhile I was unaware of a vehicle bearing down on me from the rear, speeding recklessly. Electing what he presumed to be the better of three options (flying off the side of the mountain, sending me into eternity, or playing chicken with the Porsche approaching us in the oncoming lane), the nut went for it, careening out of control around me, just missing the Porsche and crashing up ahead.

The state police took the teenage driver, who had a suspended license, into custody. The Porsche driver, still shaken by his narrow miss with eternity, came up and thanked me profusely. "If you hadn't turned your wheels and prompted me to hit my brakes," he said, "I would have collided with that guy head on. You didn't know it, but you saved my life! Thanks."

The turn of a wheel and a life saved. In a split second a fellow human being lives to see another sunset. Life is full of such trivial events and circumstances that have the most consequential impacts.

This very thing happened to our daughter in 1996 on the day of her fateful flight to the emergency room when she stopped breathing. What you don't know is how the Lord orchestrated events in advance to make that wild ride to the hospital even possible—thereby enabling her life to be saved.

You see, at this point Paul and Juli's mode of transportation remained a yellow 1983 Ford Ranger donated to them several years back by an older couple in our church, who knew of Juli's previous sensitivities to formaldehyde in newer cars. One of their financial goals was to eventually purchase a new, more reliable vehicle, but since Paul had just begun teaching two months prior, funds were insufficient. As you may recall, another priority was to remodel a back room in their home into a music studio for Paul's piano students. That too would have to wait. So for the time being, Paul had to drive to a nearby music store in their chariot, "Old Yellar," as they affectionately dubbed the pickup.

Paul's first student for the week was scheduled for Monday afternoon. On this particular Monday, when Paul climbed into "Old Yellar" and turned the key, the truck wouldn't start. Juli has always bragged that given time, Paul could figure out anything. But Paul is no mechanic and besides he didn't have time. Fortunately, he remembered we had a church member who worked out of his home down their street. Paul called, hoping the neighbor would be home that day. Our friend knew exactly what to do, and cleaned the corrosion off the battery terminals and corresponding cables. The car was inadvertently ready for an emergency run. Had this been a non-work day, Paul and Juli may have been unaware that the truck wasn't running and she would have died waiting for an ambulance to come.

How many other people have been saved from a fiery death in some horrific plane crash because of a late connection, a delay in traffic, a misplaced ticket, or some other seemingly trivial happening? The media and historians remark with great irony and no little curiosity about these fortunate coincidences when they occur. Still the impact of most of these small details is hidden in the purposes of God.

The bottom line is that we live in a purposeful world with a linear movement to a grand climax. Thousands of sub-plots unfold enroute to the great finale. Behind *your* life is an unseen and unfathomed blueprint where every experience is purposeful. Within this divine plan we are not robots, but responsible moral agents. We make choices and we are responsible for these choices. But God, in a way that you and I will never fathom, integrates into his plan our choices long before they are ever made.

For example, an interesting sub-plot to Juli's story concerns Lynne, Juli and Paul's dear friend and fellow MCS sufferer. After Juli and Paul returned from Mexico, Lynne's illness continued to nosedive over the following year, so they urged her to undertake Dr. Clark's anti-parasite treatment. Lynne was understandably hesitant, knowing that a wrong move could forever worsen her situation, but since Juli had gone before her as a "scientific rat" and had come out alive and well, in desperation, she finally agreed. Within six months, Lynne's MCS had improved to the point where she could venture out more to limited places without ill effects. Within a year, she was able to handle our relatively new building and join our congregation. Ironically, at the beginning it was Lynne who called to help us. So God blessed this concerned young lady, for in the end it was Juli and Paul who saved her from her languishing circumstances. In the final analysis, they've been there for each other in too many ways to count.

Thus, we can be thankful that God is not in a perpetual state of having to react to human whimsy. He is in control of events, not at the mercy of them. And he never goes back to the drawing table. Not that I can fathom it all. But then, I don't need to understand electricity to turn on the lights. That is why we should in all things give thanks. I repeat, "For God causes all things to work together for good to those who love him and are called according to his purpose" (Romans 8:28).

This may seem like a strange connection, but recipes always remind me of this great promise about the providence of God. Like my dad, I enjoy cooking, though I am no master chef by any stretch. On holidays when our grandchildren come to visit, they will never settle for any bread but grandpa's special rolls. Not every ingredient in my roll recipe, for example, qualifies as "good" in the sense that one would find it appetizing by itself.

For example, my recipe calls for 1/3 to 1/2 cup of shortening. Try that for breakfast! Ugh. How about 4 1/2 cups of flour for dinner? Or two raw eggs for lunch? You get the picture. Most of the ingredients in my recipe would not delight the palate. Yet when they are blended together in a certain measure under certain conditions, they yield a most delectable culinary product.

So it is with the providence of God in the lives of his people. Not all the ingredients of experience the Lord provides for us delight our experiential taste. Some are downright nasty, painful, and distasteful. But mixed up in a certain measure at certain times under certain conditions by the providential hand of an all-wise God, it "works together" for our good.

Now "good" in this context means "good" in the sense that everything God brings into our lives is calculated by him to bring us into conformity with Christ, to render us holy, to bring us into more intimate communion with God, and fit us for the presence of God. "Good" is defined then in terms of God's eternal, redemptive purposes. It does not mean "good" in the sense of bringing about results that will make us happier in the present temporal life. Just the opposite.

To return to our initial construction analogy, life can wear a very confusing face. Things that happen seem more designed to tear us apart than to build us up, but it is not my business as a Christian to understand the details of God's plan. Frankly I do not need to know what his purpose is in this or that. My job is to live the Christian life . . . to walk with God . . . to be a disciple of the Lord Jesus Christ at all times and under all conditions and let things play out.

All I need to know is that God is sovereign and behind all these events, both great and small. The hidden hand of God is blending everything together for his glory and our eternal good. Standing on those promises is what we call the walk of faith. God said it, we believe it, and we act upon it.

Remember, we are talking about a God of mysteries as much as a God of miracles. As Isaiah says, "Thou art a God who hides himself" (45:15). We Christians must develop a higher threshold for the mystery aspect and march on in the confidence that God is guiding our experience in all of its dimensions for the very best in the long-term.

One thing we all experience is change. With most changes, especially the unpleasant ones, comes the question, "Why?" W. Glyn Evans in his book *Daily with the King* talks about the possible fear and upset of change. He points to the cross of Jesus and says, "The basic difference between a natural and a spiritual man is that the natural man demands to *know*, while the spiritual man is content to *obey*."[9]

Evans reminds us that much of our lives are lived in the dark and in mystery. He reminds us that an understanding of God's involvement usually comes with, or after, the experience. In trying to fathom God's actions, Christians place themselves under unneeded stress. The key to peace is found "in my relationship with him. In the hands of a changeless God, I need fear no change."

Polishing the monuments of God's love, wisdom, and sovereignty can turn mystery into a sense of adventure and help us see that adversity is for our eternal advantage.

YEARS

12-15

April 15, 2002

Dear Friends,

Early last Monday morning we received a phone call from Paul. He had taken Juli to the hospital in the middle of the night. She almost died there again.

As you are aware, I've asked for prayer from the pulpit for nearly two years now. It's taken all the strength I could muster just to get up and report that Juli's CFS has returned with a vengeance, without breaking down in front of all of you.

As the Psalmist says, "You number my wanderings and put my tears in your bottle. Are they not in your book when I cry out to you?" (Psalm 56:8–9a, NKJV). Well, that's pretty much my sentiment as tears descend on these computer keys. Like an old country tune, this will be a sad tale.

It all began just over two years ago when Juli came down with an atypical flu-like illness that lasted two weeks. We haven't the foggiest idea what on earth it was. In fact, you may be surprised to know that, besides mono which began our fifteen-year nightmare, Juli has never caught a substantial bug since then, despite her severely weakened immune system.

Prior to this incident, while she still had to carefully pace herself, she had improved to the point where she began exercising on the treadmill. Her doctors had previously advised her against achieving an aerobic level, but even so, she was walking at a pretty fast clip. She also continued Dr. Clark's regimen and Dr. Corrine Allen's nutritional program, which excluded sugar and white flour and included healthy portions of vegetables, fruits, grains, and low-fat proteins.

When she began putting on weight, initially we were all thrilled; this had been on our prayer list for many years since. Like so many other CFS patients, she remained underweight. But suddenly it just kept coming.

This baffled us for two reasons. Number one, her diet couldn't have put weight on Tweety Bird. Number two, she was the second coming of her grandmother, not only in her passion for the Lord and love for life, but also down to the woman's very mannerisms and tiny frame. I always told my dad that if he missed Mom, "Come out here to Oregon, because as long as Juli lives, Mom will never die."

So after Juli's bout with this bug, she tried to resume her normal activity level for a period of several months, but quickly discovered that her energy was declining like air leaking out of a tire. She had to eliminate cherished activities one after another, from church to piano studies, and our hearts sank with each loss. Meanwhile, whenever Paul wasn't teaching, he researched on the internet to find a knowledgeable specialist out of state before she became too ill to travel. (They had seen every so-called CFS doctor in this one.) Their local GP had already made it clear that she was unable to render aid.

Furthermore, Juli and Paul were reluctant to "roll the dice" and try just *any* doctor because they knew that CFS patients are notorious for responding exactly opposite to a given drug's designed purpose. The negative consequences of this very scenario had occurred both early on and often during Juli's bout with CFS.

As time passed, the situation was getting ever more bizarre. Not only had she become increasingly bedridden, but also about nine months before, the weight she gained had morphed into a disproportionate body mass distribution. Her tiny shoulders, thin oval face, and trim figure ballooned into an upper body like the Hunchback of Notre Dame. She had a head as swollen as a basketball, while at the same time, her legs shriveled up into thin sticks.

Juli and Paul began to pray, "Lord, we don't know which way you want us to go. We've had one positive experience with a non-conventional method; otherwise we've been burned by both medical perspectives. We feel like we are in a unique situation where you are telling us, like Ahaz in Isaiah 7:1–14 'Don't be afraid. Hands off! Ask for my clear-cut guidance'" (paraphrased). Then Juli began to pray, "Lord, I want this like a hole in the head, but if I need traditional medicine, leave me no alternative. Send me back to the emergency room with breathing problems."

So a week ago Saturday, Juli began violently throwing up. It reminded her of a twenty-four-hour stomach flu she had in college, when even shots from the health center failed to stop the vomiting. Then, last Sunday evening, it began. She started having extreme difficulty breathing; only this time it wasn't a sudden onset of respiratory arrest. Her breathing became extremely rapid as the rate of inhale/exhale grew wildly out of control.

They arrived at the hospital emergency room, Paul got a wheelchair and rolled her in, and Juli said, in between gasps for air, "Well, God has sent me back here again; let's hope this time they have some answers."

The doctor promptly began treatment; everyone there could see she was in a bad way. Blood drawn immediately. By this point, Juli was beginning to become delirious, but she tried to answer the doctor's questions after the blood work came back. "Ma'am, does anyone in your family have diabetes?"

"Oh Lord," she prayed, "I know what this question means— do I really need one more disease to add to my résumé?"

As the night wore on, she kept crying out, "I can't breathe, I can't breathe." She went further into delirium, as she begged Paul to slip her some water. She didn't care how much she threw it back up, the thirst of a camel in the desert (a classic diabetic symptom) drove her to drink water or die! The doctor finally relented and let her have her fill, which she kept upchucking by the gallon.

So around 7:00 a.m. Paul called with the grim news. We drove as fast as we could to the hospital where the doctor told us that her blood sugar had reached an astounding 650, she had an acute onset of Diabetic Ketoacidosis, and had barely survived the night.

The doctor had also noticed her odd appearance and informed us that she possibly had Cushing's disease. Only later did we learn from a specialist how insightful this particular emergency room doctor was. He told us that it was not uncommon for patients to be given the "You're overeating" rap from other MD's, while they desperately search for answers until they find a doctor familiar with the symptoms of a serious brain-related condition such as this.

Oh, by the way, as an extra "bonus" Juli's previously low blood pressure of 110/70 had skyrocketed to 200/110! After the nurses checked her blood pressure for the umpteenth time, they decided it was time to weigh her "deformed" body on the bed scale. This was a dreaded moment. Juli had given up weighing herself or looking in the mirror. She even asked Paul not to reveal what size was indicated on her clothing tags. Once, she caught a glimpse, saw "XL" and nearly lost it. "One sixty," one nurse announced. After they left the room, Juli sobbed.

When we returned to the hospital for our daily waiting-room vigil early the next afternoon, however, Juli was laughing her head off. After events unfolded throughout that day, she insisted I relay this "medical debacle" story to our church members because it was just too hilarious to pass up.

The previous evening, Juli was having difficulty falling asleep and Paul came up with the bright idea of brushing her hair. So with her round brush in hand, he began to soothe Juli's frazzled nerves. Paul was really bored and asked, "Can I curl it?"

"Sure, anything," she said, half-awake. After a few minutes of this routine, she heard a soft "Oops."

"What's wrong?" she asked.

"Uhh . . . uhh, nothing—let me see here." Well, the brush was stuck, and stuck but good!

Juli told him to go to bed (they only permitted him to sleep in the waiting area lounge) and she tried to sleep on one side. As a few of you know, Juli has always bragged truthfully that Paul could figure out anything: medical, electrical, mechanical—you name it.

Hair dressing was the one exception. The times Juli needed to go someplace looking nice and her arms wore out, Paul would offer to "help" with the curling iron. According to Juli, she always ended up looking worse than some mishandled version of Shirley Temple headed for a freak show.

So when the nurse came into the room in the morning with her "up and at 'em" at 7:00 a.m. she added laughingly, "You have a brush stuck to the side of your head." Anyway, poor Paul proceeded with all his intellect and tenacity to take a bottle of conditioner and dump it on her hair, trying to wiggle the brush out—to no avail.

Can you believe this was the one day she had to be wheeled from floor to floor for various ultrasounds and tests? Ironically, this was also the one time in Juli's life when everyone in that hospital who saw her wanted to help! They all took a crack at that brush, but with no success. Even the coldest technician in the place was in stitches. So were the people in the halls.

Juli called her best friend, Lynne Mackey, and explained her latest predicament. Lynne, with her great mind for detail, got busy thinking of a solution. She arrived at the hospital later that afternoon armed with wire cutters and crochet needles, and Juli, after a humiliating total of seven hours in front of every kind of hospital staff and patient imaginable, was desperate enough to submit her head to Lynne's form of "surgery."

Lynne slowly snipped away each bristle as she inched out tiny pieces of hair in succession (while deftly hiding the strands she accidentally cut) and the grueling procedure literally took four hours. But finally, her efforts were rewarded when, "voila," the brush was out! Now, not only had Juli's life been saved here, but her hair as well. She looked at Lynne and Paul who were standing on both sides of her bed, smiling triumphantly, as if the whole thing had been a team effort. "Well, it took a valedictorian to get the brush in and it took a valedictorian to get it out!" she exclaimed in relief and gratitude.

We were disheartened later that evening to learn that Juli's left ovarian cyst had grown back, just as Dr. Clark had predicted it would, though it was smaller than in the 1995 and 1996 exams. The same radiologist who performed the "parking lot" ultrasound did this one as well, and said to Juli, "Of course, there's no way to prove the status unless it's surgically removed, but I can say with ninety-nine percent certainty that it's benign, probably an endometrioma based on your 1996 surgery report."

Well, what should Juli do about the surgery? We didn't find out their decision until the day before she left the hospital. It took the doctor assigned to her case *that* long to visit the room and update us on her condition!

In the meantime, another maddening situation occurred when a male nurse barged into Juli's room at 4:00 a.m., after she and Paul had finally managed to get their first hour of shut-eye. At this point Paul was sleeping upright in a chair in her room.

"You're smuggling in food and fruit juice for Juli aren't you?" he bellowed. "Don't you realize how dangerous that is? It's keeping her blood sugar levels way too high! They certainly weren't this high on my last shift!"

Paul, more awake by now, calmly tried to explain that on this guy's previous shift (Juli's first day in the hospital), she wasn't allowed to eat at all! Now that she was permitted food (a highly restricted diabetic diet, of course), certainly her levels would be higher. But he remained unconvinced and left angrily in disbelief.

When Juli phoned us early that morning and told us about the exchange, something in me snapped. After fifteen years, it was just one accusation too many. You would never meet two more disciplined, perfectionist kids in your life—it's part of who they are. I did remain calm, but I was going to find that male nurse if it was the last thing I did and let him know what kind of people Juli and Paul are, how hard they'd toiled for a decade and a half to get Juli well, and how they wouldn't jeopardize her health like irresponsible teenagers, for goodness sake.

After I found the nurse and had a word with him, I spent the rest of the day pacing the halls, muttering to Olsie, "Where's that doctor? Why won't he come?"

Finally, Friday afternoon, he strolled into Juli's room and remarked, "You're very lucky to be alive. A Diabetic Ketoacidosis attack is fatal about thirty percent of the time, especially in such an acute case such as yours. But I think you'll survive."

"Gee, thanks for informing me after five days, Doc!" Juli thought.

"The dietician will visit soon to instruct you on the diabetic diet, and the nurses will show you how to give yourself insulin shots and time your pharmaceuticals."

"Well, what do I do about this possible Cushing's matter and my cyst?"

"We'll have to wait on the Cushing's test for a month and the cyst is benign—just leave it there." (Seems like we'd heard that advice before!)

They pleaded with the doctor to order Juli's release for Saturday because they were both so sleep deprived. He doubted that would be possible because Juli's blood sugar numbers needed to stabilize further and it would be next to impossible for them to catch on to the intricacies of the diabetic protocol/lifestyle in that amount of time.

As for the blood sugar levels, that was up to the Lord; but as for the latter, he didn't know who he was dealing with. As the day progressed, Paul succeeded in scheduling the dietician to come Saturday afternoon, and by the next morning, Juli's numbers were coming down steadily. Only a few more obstacles remained before they could gain their "freedom": insulin injection instructions and the okay from the doctor.

So they implored the nurses one last time to ask the doctor to release her. The doctor's partner arrived in his stead at 7:00 a.m. and wryly said, "I hear you want out of here."

"Yes doctor, please, we need sleep!"

He told Paul, "Okay, I think we can do it. Listen closely. This is how you control her blood sugar."

Lynne arrived later that morning and watched Paul take the "diabetic course" like a pro. The nurse then showed Paul how to draw up the shots and give the injections. She warned them, "This is very complicated; you'll probably make a lot of mistakes and I expect to see you in the ER in a few weeks."

Whether this nurse's prediction will prove true, we'll soon find out. I sure hope not. But we can take solace in our Sovereign Lord who holds his design for their lives in his omnipotent hands.

Thanks as always for your prayers,

Pastor Jim

A God Who
Wrings His Hands?

One anxiety that has sometimes tormented my daughter is the nagging fear that her health miseries are consequences of her own bad judgment rather than a sickness, "that the works of God might be displayed" in her (and Paul) as in the case of the man born blind (John 9). Take, for example, the way she apparently contracted mono, the catalyst that seemed to set in motion the whole avalanche of health horror that has plagued her life for these long years.

If you recall, Juli was participating one evening in a communion service where a common cup of grape juice was used. Unfortunately, two young women seated near her were unknowingly on the cusp of coming down with mono and Juli drank after them. Shortly thereafter, she left for her Wheaton College Concert Choir annual spring tour, during which the symptoms struck Juli herself and she returned to campus quite ill.

The reason Juli beats herself up for that innocent mistake is that her mother, always extremely finicky about courting germs, had always inveighed against such things (as drinking after other people, etc.). So knowing better, but not wanting to be a spoiler in a religious environment, she gave in against her better judgment.

Worse damage resulted from another decision around 1990. As mentioned previously, CFS sufferers could find little help and even less sympathy in the traditional medical community. As foul times are often the inspiration for desperate measures, she and Paul had gambled on the only game in town, a naturopathic physician who had his own allergy-based theory about the cause and cure of CFS. His "treatment" was a health train wreck. She has never been the same.

Down through these dark years, she has occasionally wondered, "Did I run ahead of God? Should I have waited on the Lord to guide me instead of firing up desperate petitions and grasping frantically at the first medical mercenary (an apt description of this character) who came along? Am I now paying the price of my impatience or was this choice also interwoven into an overarching plan of God to glorify himself through all this?"

It's natural to ponder our human culpability in innocent mistakes (as well as willful transgressions) and to wonder how much differently life might have been had we chosen to go right instead of left. But for those of us whose faith is firmly anchored in the sovereignty of an all-powerful, all-wise, and wholly benevolent God, those thoughts are a pretty fruitless exercise. For our rock of security in the troubles of life is the assurance that we serve a sovereign God who *"works all things [not some] after the counsel of his will"* (Ephesians 1:11).

Thus his plan, we are confident, comprehends every choice we will make. In his sovereign counsel, and through his infinite wisdom and almighty power, we inhabit a flow of historical events and experiences, confident that God himself stands at the headwaters of that flow, calculating its causes and effects and finely calibrating every part to the whole.

In God we see the Prime Mover in creation and the Ultimate Actor in human events, not the Great Reactor to them. History is moving inexorably "in accordance with the eternal purpose which [God] carried out in Christ Jesus our Lord" (Ephesians 3:11) and that includes all the forms and mysteries of human pain and suffering.

As obvious as the biblical teaching of the sovereignty of God seems to most whom we associate with Christian orthodoxy, and as comforting as that truth is to those enduring life on the rough side, there is an alarming new viewpoint gaining some attention in influential circles, called *open theism*, which trashes the whole idea.

Take my daughter's intermittent fretting about whether her troubles are of her own making or part of a larger divine plan. The proponents of this so-called "doctrine" would say that such unfortunate personal actions are just the price of doing business in a free will economy. God gave us latitude as fallible, free agents but if we fail—oops! "I'm so sorry," says God, "but now you'll just have to buck up and live with it, I can't really help you."

Far from the all-knowing, all-wise sovereign administrator of human events most of us have always believed him to be, in reality [they say] God does not know in advance what choices we free moral agents will make. He has denied himself the luxury of that knowledge just to protect the "integrity" of our free will.

God may know what is possible or even probable, but even he does not know for certain what choices we will make. God learns after the fact just as we do. He reacts in history as much as he acts and even then, not very sure-footedly. Remember, he doesn't know what's coming next! Worse yet, God sometimes miscalculates as he tries to anticipate what choices his unpredictable creatures will make. He flat-out blunders and lives to regret his own mistakes.

"You've got to be kidding!" someone says. Unfortunately, I'm not. These folk are deadly serious—and, I might add, seriously deadly.

In his excellent book *God's Lesser Glory: The Diminished God of Open Theism*, Bruce Ware writes:

> Many readers may be surprised to learn that this very view (namely, that God does not know much of the future and has to learn what happens as the future unfolds) is being advocated by a growing number of biblical scholars, theologians, and philosophers who identify themselves as evangelicals, some of whom teach at highly respected evangelical colleges and seminaries. These scholars call the position they advocate 'open theism' because they like to make central the notion that, for God as well as us, much of the future is 'open' and hence not known or foreordained (p. 18).[10]

Couched in theological jargon, views like these can be seductive—that is, their academic texture makes their ideas sound more intelligent than they really are.

Between sterile academics who study God, not on their knees, but more or less like a microbe, and the chronically bored who are always chasing after the latest theological fad, combined with the growing mass of biblically untaught believers who scarcely know God from the jolly green giant, it is no surprise that such notions find a hearing. They gain even more traction when their adherents promise (with the help of allegedly misconstrued biblical data) to absolve God of his (supposed) moral culpability for allowing human suffering. This latter bonus is especially appealing to nervous Christians who fear God is morally vulnerable to his critics. They welcome any theological solution that might shield our Creator from the unfair expectation that he ought to be able to manage his fallen creation less messily.

The reason I address this subject is because, if ignored, some sufferers who encounter this false doctrine may find themselves awash with hopelessness. It is a viewpoint not only unworthy of God, but most unhelpful to believers in long, drawn-out agony who cry daily to God for help.

The scriptures assure us we *can* dwell in the shelter of the Most High and rest in the shadow of the Almighty (Psalm 91:1). Let's cruise quickly through the Word of God, noting en route how his will is accomplished even at the hands of the wicked. Let's observe also just how wide is the shadow of his wings around the circumstances of his saints.

Consider first, for example, "The Lord works out everything for his own ends—even the wicked for a day of disaster" (Proverbs 16:4). Does that sound like a God making his plans on the fly? On the contrary, our sovereign God makes even the wicked unwittingly serve his own purposes at the very time they think they are controlling their own destiny. For example, in his prayer after meeting with the Sanhedrin, Peter said, "Indeed Herod and Pontius Pilate met together with the Gentiles and the people of Israel in this city to conspire against [God's] holy servant, whom you anointed. They did what your power and will had decided beforehand should happen" (Acts 4:27–28, NIV; see also Isaiah 46:10–11).

No human contingencies, we are told, can thwart him. God has a plan and it will prevail. He will make certain it all comes together. The bottom line is that in heaven and on earth God rules and overrules. We see this in Isaiah 8:10, "Devise a plan but it will be thwarted; state a proposal, but it will not stand, for God is with us." (See also Job 42:2; Psalm 33:11; Nehemiah 4:15; Job 5:12; Proverbs 19:21; Isaiah 19:3b; Daniel 4:35.)

Though God always checkmates man according to God's own design, man is never in any position to checkmate God. As the Lord once warned rebellious Judah, whose leaders imagined they could by their own devices circumvent the impending disaster, "even if you had defeated the entire army of the Chaldeans who were fighting against you, and there were only wounded men left among them, each man in his tent, they [the few wounded] would rise up and burn this city with fire" (Jeremiah 37:10). Moreover, none of the actions of our God is ever at the mercy of human choices that may force him to adjust or abandon his plan. He knows our minds before we know them; the Lord told Judah, "But I know your sitting down, and your going out and your coming in" (Isaiah 37:28; see also Amos 4:13).

Finally, the ultimate example of God's sovereign control of human events is the redemptive work of Jesus Christ. Everything went exactly according to plan. "This man," the apostle Peter proclaimed on Pentecost, "delivered up by the predetermined plan and foreknowledge of God, you nailed to a cross" (Acts 2:23).

Not only that, but our choosing Christ was itself the result of a divine initiative in which he first chose us before we were ever born:

[God the Father] chose us in [Christ] before the foundation of the world . . . He predestined us to adoption as sons through

216

Jesus Christ to himself, according to the kind intention of his will (Ephesians 1:4–5).

For whom God foreknew, he also predestined to be conformed to the image of his Son . . . and whom he predestined, these he also called, and whom he called, these he also justified, and whom he justified, these he also glorified (Romans 8:29–30).

So whatever mystery our pain and suffering may involve, there is consolation and encouragement to any saint of God living in a valley of the shadow of despair that somehow this is comprehended in the plan of a sovereign God. It is a big help to just know that God has said,

> I am the Lord, and there is no other, the One forming light and creating darkness, causing well-being and creating calamity [sometimes a mystery]; I am the Lord who does all these things [at my sovereign discretion] [brackets mine for clarity].
>
> (Isaiah 45:6–7)

So how can these scriptures blunt the edge of our suffering? Well, if God uses even evil for his own ends, we rest assured that any hardship we encounter will be woven by God into the fabric of our lives for our eternal good.

As far back as Genesis, this motif is enshrined as the providential backdrop to the whole affair about the fall and rise of Joseph. Joseph's brothers, acting as free moral agents, made their own wicked choices; God did not compel them in any way to try to rid themselves of their half-brother. Yet in the end, their voluntary evil was comprehended in God's predetermined plan for his people. As Joseph told his chastened brothers,

> And as for you, you meant evil against me, but God meant it for good in order to bring about this present result, to preserve many people alive (Genesis 50:20; see also 1 Kings 12:15).

But someone may ask, "Is there any comfort here for a repentant believer who once sinned in a great moment of weakness?" Yes, certainly. Consider, for example, the Lord's anticipation of Peter's denial and the other disciples' desertion of him on the eve of his crucifixion:

> You will all fall away because of me this night, for it is written, "I will strike down the shepherd, and the sheep of the flock shall be scattered." But after I have been raised, I will go before you to Galilee. But Peter answered and said to him, "Even though all may fall away because of you, I will never fall away." And Jesus said to him, "Truly I say to you that this very night, before a cock crows, you shall deny me three times" (Matthew 26:31–34).

Clearly predicted by the prophet Zechariah (13:7b) through the Spirit some 400 years previously, one can fairly infer that these cowardly lapses on the part of Peter and his fellow disciples were from long ago planned by God. Not that God compelled Peter and his fellow disciples, contrary to their own desires, to temporarily fail. Not at all. God did not approve of their sin, nor make them sin apart from their own desire to do what they did.

And why was that important in God's plan? In retrospect, their shame and humiliation that night would serve them well later as sympathetic shepherds of the sheep and remind them forcibly of the meaning of Jesus' words, "Keep watching and praying, that you may not enter into temptation. The spirit is willing, but the flesh is weak" (Matthew 26:41).

Still others may inquire, "What if I *deliberately* disobeyed as a believer and repented; furthermore, I'm humbly submitting to the consequences of my sin. May I still assume the Lord is in control of my present and future circumstances?"

Dear reader, if this is your status, let me assure you there are even monuments for muddlers. Let the experience of King David be your comfort. Yes, David endured for the rest of his life the repercussions of his outrageous sin—his adultery with Bathsheba aggravated by setting up her husband, Uriah, for a battlefield death to cover it up (2 Samuel 11). Confronted by the Lord, he profoundly repented (Psalm 32 most likely speaks of that) and thereafter humbly submitted to the discipline of the Lord in its sad and serial consequences, beginning with the death of the love child born from their illicit union (2 Samuel 12). (See also 2 Samuel 15; 16:5–11.)

Yet—note this—God reassured David of his love through the prophet Nathan, when their second son, Solomon, was born, telling him to name the child Jedidiah, which means loved by the Lord. What is so astounding (as we know from Matthew 1:6–7) is that Bathsheba and Solomon found a place in the lineage of the Messiah. Does anybody imagine that stroke was a divine afterthought, a plan made up on the spur of the moment by God? You see, my friends, these sinful events, ugly and despicable, condemned as they were, remained under God's sovereign control and were comprehended in his plan from the beginning of time.

God by no means approves all our choices nor does he always shelter us from their fallout. But whether it is our stupidity or our sins, our God is neither surprised by our actions, nor does he have to scramble the powers of heaven to adjust to new realities, nor are the purposes of our Creator ever thwarted by his creatures. Rather, in our trials and troubles, self-made or providentially inflicted, we take comfort in the conviction that from eternity, God's plan was settled in heaven to the last critical detail and the whole human experience was all present to the mind of God. In his infinite knowledge and inscrutable wisdom, he superintends and correlates every element of his plan perfectly and flawlessly to ensure that his purposes for us prevail.

It is not as though God made our actions *necessary* (compulsory), but, as needful, he did make human actions *certain*—a crucial distinction. One makes choices necessary when one compels them. One makes them certain when one orchestrates circumstances that produce them without compelling them. God did not force Pharaoh to harden his heart by opposing God (Exodus 7:13). Yet God orchestrated events to ensure that the wicked Pharaoh would act precisely according to his godless disposition and gain the exact result the Lord planned (Exodus 11:9–10).

I am nonplussed that anyone could read the Bible and gainsay God's knowledge of the future, as open theists do. The Psalmist declares the intimacy of God's knowledge of us when he says:

> O LORD, You have searched me and known me.
> You know when I sit down and when I rise up;
>   You understand my thought from afar.
> You scrutinize my path and my lying down,
>   And are intimately acquainted with all my ways.
> Even before there is a word on my tongue,
>   Behold, O LORD, You know it all.
> You have enclosed me behind and before,
>   And laid Your hand upon me.
>
> (Psalm 139:1–5)

So this confidence of ours in a sovereign God, whose providence secretly and subtly directs all history and human events, derives not from our intuition or aspiration, but from objective revelation. Because we are firmly persuaded that God knows all things and has worked everything, good, bad, and ugly, into the intricate fabric of his eternal plan, we hang tough in thick and thin. We draw every breath in the crisp, fresh air of God's uplifting promise that he "causes all things to work together for the eternal good of those who love him and are called according to his purpose" (Romans 8:28). This is something he obviously could not promise if he were ignorant of the future and human freedom was such that everything was contingent.

Given such clear statements, it's hard to imagine how those who subscribe to *open theism* arrive at their conclusions biblically. As a teacher of biblical hermeneutics (the science and art of Biblical interpretation) for many years, I always emphasized to my seminary students this principle: *the best solution to any difficult text is the interpretation that answers the most questions and leaves one with the fewest problems.*

Open theism does not meet this test. Are there biblical texts or statements about God that a person could reasonably construe in such a fashion as to lend plausibility to open theism? Yes. However, when it comes to biblical interpretation, one cannot take texts in isolation. The context of any given text is the totality of biblical teaching.

You see, at the end of the day, if we believe in the inspiration and inerrant authority of the Scriptures as the repository of divine revelation, then it follows that one cannot cite one strain of passages against another, but is logically compelled (by the nature of the Bible) to arrive at an interpretation that ties them all together in the most coherent and harmonious doctrine. A commonplace interpretative canon passed down through church history is that Scripture is best interpreted by Scripture.

In this chapter my chief interest is more to spread the light than to condemn the darkness. Yet this error is so serious, potentially deflating to sufferers, and so undermining of the principle of monumental faith, I must make certain the reader is sufficiently apprised of its absurdity. For I personally find it a blatant contradiction of core biblical theology as well as a wasteland of practical comfort for the believer.

In his masterful rebuttal of the tenets of Open Theism, Ware lists (p. 60) these facets as important features of the approach of proponents' of Open Theism:

1. God does not know in advance the future free actions of his moral creatures.
2. God cannot control the future free actions of his moral creatures.
3. Tragic events occur over which God has no control.
4. When such tragedies occur, God should not be blamed, because he was not able to prevent them from occurring, and he certainly did not will or cause them to occur.
5. When such tragic events occur, God feels the pain of those who endure its suffering.
6. God is love, and he may be trusted always to do his best to offer guidance that is intended to serve the well-being of others.
7. At times, God realizes that the guidance he gave may have inadvertently and unexpectedly led to unwanted hardship and suffering.
8. At times, God may repent of his own past actions, realizing that his own choices have not worked out well and may have led to unexpected hardship (e.g., 1 Samuel 15:11).
9. Some suffering is gratuitous and pointless, i.e., some suffering has no positive or redeeming quality at all, so that not even God is able to bring any good from it.
10. Regardless of whether our suffering was gratuitous, or whether God may have contributed inadvertently to our suffering, God always stands ready to help rebuild our

lives and offers us further grace, strength, direction, and counsel.

That, my friends, is not a God of monuments; that is a God of well-intentioned futility.

During my college years I was always struck by the way technical language or fine scholarly cadences lent respectability, if not credibility, to ridiculous ideas. Stripped down to their bare essences, it was so often apparent that notions hailed as gourmet fare turned out to be just another serving of greasy-spoon hamburgers disguised with a little academic garnish. In my opinion, open theism fits into that category.

To illustrate the bankruptcy of its proposal as a source of help and comfort to God's afflicted servants and its uselessness as a serious apologetic for God in allowing pain and suffering into his world, let me drag it down from the ivory tower and trot it out in unpolished shoe leather.

What kind of answer would the God of open theism give, were he so inclined, to his servants like my daughter and others in great crisis? By the way, if the language I have chosen in the following imaginary response seems unfit for God, it is because the diminished God of open theism is an unfit God who wrings his hands, not a God who has things in hand.

If the God of open theism actually existed and he were to respond to the pleas of Juli and Paul for answers, here is about all he could say:

> *Juli, I know you and Paul are in a world of hurt and I deeply sympathize with your plight. But I must correct you. Never imagine I had any hand in directing these problems your way. Remember, I made you two totally free moral agents. In that respect, I'm just a bystander. You folks make the choices and the choices make you, if you know what I mean.*

223

You see, although I am God, I'm deliberately flying somewhat blind here. Contrary to what you may have been taught, the truth is, even I, the Lord God, am never certain what choices you (or anyone else) are going to make. I can only guess along with everyone else, though I can guess better than others.

So, the best I can promise in your plight is, like a trusty paramedic or loving parent, to try to help you pick up the pieces when you mess things up, however innocently. But even here, let me add, I am more limited than usually thought. Since I myself don't know the future, I obviously cannot prevent nor always fix things when they go wrong. I never have any certainty about what future choices my people (or relevant others) might make that will complicate or impede my moves to fix things.

And that is important for you to understand. You see, it is entirely conceivable that my well-intentioned interventions would actually wind up hurting you more than helping you, strange as that may sound. True freedom of action has its price. That's one big drawback in the scheme of creation, my not knowing the future. Still, those are the rules of the game—you got your untrammeled freedom and I got blinders. Obviously, with that limitation, even I, God, can occasionally miscalculate and with the best of intentions, flat-out err.

I hope this explanation brings you solace in your long term of suffering. Maybe now you can understand that when I haven't seemed to be there for you, it isn't because I'm heartless, my children. I'm just helpless. By the rules of engagement, that is. But just know I really care for you and will do what I can.

What a God, this deity of *open theism*! What a shelter in times of trouble, what a source of "hope" in days of darkness. This is not a God who directs the traffic of history, but a God who is caught up in it. This is not a God who acts, but one who merely reacts—not always in the most prudent ways at that.

For the open theists, if God's ways are sometimes hard to explain to his detractors, their answer is not to point out the immeasurable ignorance of small minds, but for small minds to dumb down the inexhaustible greatness of God. To get God off his critics' hook, their answer is to shrink God, not his critics. Just brilliant.

It baffles me that any thinking person would offer this sort of God as a source of help to believers in the valleys of discouragement, despair, defeat, disease, and death. For me, to think that God was like that would reduce me to a feeling of unparalleled futility and hopelessness.

Such a grotesque theology may explain, to the satisfaction of some, why God allows gratuitous pain and suffering. If the best God has to offer us is sympathy, I'm sorry, I have more than enough of that for myself, thank you. I don't need a God with a hanky; I need a God who can and will help.

When I first shared this latest theological novelty with my daughter and told her it was put forward as a serious effort to vindicate the inaction of God in human suffering and to explain why the Lord was not rushing in to set things in order in her life, she virtually gasped, as did my wife. The question of both was the same: Can anyone, especially theologians, possibly think this "helps" the image of God or offers the least comfort to those in despair and distress?

Now, do I pretend to fathom all the interplay between the sovereign government of God and its interaction with human choices? Do I think I have a perfect handle on how it all works? Can I answer all the natural questions any thoughtful person may have about how the sovereignty of God interfaces with the moral free agency of man? Certainly not.

You see, here we are confronting the limited scope of divine revelation. God has revealed all we need to know, not everything we would like to know. We piece and patch together the strands of self-disclosure God has given us. We allow ourselves a high threshold for mystery. Our subject is way too deep for frail human understanding to plumb his depths. So we need not blush that we don't have all the answers and are unable to fill in all the theological blanks. If natural scientists, for all their study, still cannot fully understand a tornado, why should we be embarrassed if we can't explain all about God? As the Psalmist and the Preacher of Ecclesiastes marveled, "Such knowledge is too wonderful for me; it is too high, I cannot attain to it" (Psalm 139:6), and "Just as you do not know the path of the wind and how the bones are formed in the womb of the pregnant woman, so you do not know the activity of God who makes all things" (Ecclesiastes 11:5).

What we have revealed to us is fully true, but that revelation is not truly full. Now "we see in a mirror dimly, but then face to face," the apostle Paul reminded us. All the mysteries will evaporate in greater light. We must be content to take the incomplete picture God gives us, process it, link the pieces of the puzzle and infer from them what we safely can, and leave the rest for later.

If at the end of the day we can't comprehend and compute all that in a tidy self-consistency, it's OK. It's not because it's illogical; it's because God is transcendent and not fully comprehensible. Our information is partial. God just asks us to believe all that he has revealed, not explain everything he hasn't. It's called "walking by faith." If we can't figure out how all the pieces fit together, we simply chalk those parts up to "mysteries to be explained later."

It's like the doctrines of the Trinity or the hypostatic union (the divine-human nature of Christ). We believe and teach them because we see those truths in the Word and because the Christian church as a whole has confirmed and held from ancient times that the Bible indeed teaches those doctrines. Yet both dogmas entail inscrutable aspects that no one can fully penetrate or explain—not because they are irrational, but because they are supra-rational. That is, they are not accessible to unaided reason alone, but involve realities that transcend all human experience or analogy or knowledge.

We comfort ourselves with this truth: We do not worship a God who wrings his hands. We serve a God who works his plan. Otherwise, there would be no rational basis for the monuments on which we hang our faith in times of storm.

Y E A R

15

December 31, 2002

Dear Friends,

So much has transpired since my last communiqué, it's hard to believe only nine months have passed. We have two items of extremely encouraging news and one pressing prayer request.

First, let me give you the play-by-play account of what led to these astounding developments, which will yet again illustrate God's guiding and protective hand on Juli and Paul.

The day Juli was released from the hospital last April, the nurses instructed her to check in with her GP within four days. Furthermore, the attending Internal Medicine physician who managed her care implied that he would be overseeing her diabetes and possible Cushing's diagnosis on an outpatient basis.

But when Paul called on Monday morning, the doctor refused to take her case. We were all shocked because Juli's health was in such dire straits. Next Paul called their GP. She told him that she felt unqualified, not only to manage Juli's CFS but her routine diabetes as well. When Paul explained to her that the attending physician at the hospital refused to see Juli, their GP insisted, "He is obligated to take you as a patient; you've already established care with him!"

So Paul called his office, and again he refused, giving only a list of referrals. At this point, they took it from the Lord that this man was not the doctor for Juli. Then, Paul started calling the referrals. So far, everyone was booked—what on earth were they going to do? After many frantic phone calls, Paul finally found a physician, but after two visits with her, it soon became apparent why this doctor had "openings" for patients.

The first visit got off to an ominous start when Paul explained to the receptionist that Juli had severe CFS, and the week prior had suffered a near-fatal Diabetic ketoacidosis attack in the hospital. She was running a temperature from an acute bladder infection (a typical condition that accompanies the onset of this kind of diabetes) besides having significant difficulty walking.

"Can she please lie down in a back room while she waits for her appointment?"

"No," the receptionist said coldly, "she'll have to sit up and wait like everyone else."

Once inside the exam room, Juli collapsed onto the small table until the doctor arrived. When the Internal Medicine doctor walked swiftly in the door, Juli immediately sat up, a reaction she'd learned from years of conditioning when dealing with many doctors. "Do it or die," she has previously told me, "otherwise you'll be treated like a malingerer."

The doctor's office had not asked Paul to fill out any medical history forms, only insurance ones, and this doctor didn't even ask Juli for any medical background! She commented curtly, "You're going to have to watch your diet very closely and start exercising to get this weight off you." As the doctor rattled on, Juli began to get the impression that this woman had pegged her as a couch potato who had ended up overweight and consequently diabetic.

While Juli wanted to give her the benefit of the doubt, she decided to dispel any hint of that notion just in case. "Doctor," she said, "I know I am overweight right now, but I can assure you I'm a very disciplined person who has been eating a healthy diet for many years and exercising faithfully up until this latest health crisis prevented me from doing so. Because of my healthy lifestyle and disproportionate body mass distribution, the doctor at the emergency room thought I may have Cushing's disease . . . will you run this test for me?" She made no promises, just simply emphasized that Juli needed to start exercising. When Juli returned for her next visit, she informed the doctor that she had begun walking two laps around the outside of the house (with Paul's help).

"Good," she said condescendingly, "I didn't think you were the type we could get to exercise at all."

At this point, I can only imagine the ire emanating from Juli's dark brown eyes. "I told you in our last visit, doctor, that I'm disciplined and a fighter; you're thinking of the wrong person."

Later in the appointment, she finally took down Juli's medical history. She asked at one point how long Juli had CFS. When Juli said "Fifteen years," there was literally no response—just a blank stare—what I call the "glazed donut look." Then she persisted in pressuring Juli to cut more calories, to which Juli replied helplessly, "But I'm eating like a bird as it is!"

As Juli went for subsequent visits, the doctor continued the same mantra. Even in the early summer when Juli wore shorts to show the doctor her ultra thin legs, the physician refused to do any Cushing's tests or refer her to an endocrinologist. She remained as blind as a bat. Even a medical idiot such as myself could see this wasn't a normal weight gain scenario.

It took only five days of laissez-faire treatment from the attending physician in the hospital and one visit with this new doctor to realize that the "train" they had boarded was headed nowhere! This "ride" so far had only brought back painful memories of the mistreatment they received in their early days of CFS. Paul desperately wanted to get off this train, and was determined to find the next "station" on the internet as soon as possible. But as I've said many times before, Paul is a detail guy all the way, a man devoted to prayer, and he knew from years of experience that he needed to avoid a hasty decision.

So they were unsure whether the Lord would move this doctor's heart to refer Juli to a local endocrinologist or whether he would eventually lead them out of state. Paul believed that they should follow the example of Nehemiah, so to speak, "Those who carried the materials did their work with one hand and held a weapon with the other, and each of the builders wore his sword at his side as he worked" (Nehemiah 4:17–18). Thus, Paul and Juli would work both tracks at the same time and ask God for his direction.

Paul also looked back over his notes from Juli's 1995 appointments with her cancer specialist, Dr. Clark. During their stay in Mexico, she had taken a special liking to Paul because she sensed his enormous intellect and innate medical instincts. Dr. Clark had shared with Paul her new theories regarding diabetes. She believed that a specific parasite might be involved with that disease process, and when it was killed, patients could markedly improve.

Now Paul began to theorize that perhaps because of the brain trauma from Juli's horse riding accident, her system might have been more impaired than others in eliminating this parasite. To find out if this stone had been left unturned, Paul proceeded to administer a different phase of anti-parasite treatment. Wouldn't you know it, one by one, the dead parasites came out through her urinary system—Olsie even saw them on numerous occasions. With each one, Juli's blood sugar numbers started to drop steadily and a little bit of weight did as well.

We were further encouraged by comments made by their pharmacist when Paul told him about Juli's cancer and diabetes history, and the headway she'd made under the guidance of a naturopathic physician. He interrupted Paul and asked, "Would this person by any chance be Dr. Hulda Clark?"

"Yes it was. Why do you ask?"

"Because I've had about thirty customers with different health crises, ten of whom had cancer, tell me that they've been extremely helped or cured due to her treatments."

Anyway, when it came time for her next appointment with the Internal Medicine doctor, Juli brought along a picture of herself, taken right here in our church narthex after a Sunday evening service. "Oh, then you've been tiny before!" the doctor exclaimed.

"Yes," Juli replied, "I've been trying to tell you that. I've been tiny all my life."

After three months of delay the doctor finally agreed to order a screening test for Cushing's disease, a twenty-four-hour urine collection for the adrenal hormone cortisol.

Ten days later, she called with the news, "Juli's cortisol is elevated and I'm going to refer her to an endocrinologist at OHSU. She needs to be very careful. I've reconsidered my recommendations about exercise and lifting weights; with Cushing's disease that's not wise."

In mid-August, Juli finally got in to see the endocrinologist at OHSU. He walked in the door, smiled, shook their hands, opened up Juli's file—staring at it for a minute or two—and then said, shaking his head, "You don't have Cushing's."

Juli was dumbfounded, "But the Internal Medicine doctor said . . ."

"She read the test results wrong."

"But I'm overweight."

"I know," he said, "I can tell this much just from your appearance—the way you've put on weight in your upper body and abdomen and not in your legs is an endocrine problem stemming from brain dysfunction. It is not your fault and is not caused by caloric intake. There are many conditions that can cause a Cushing-like appearance. Unfortunately, if you don't have Cushing's, there are no available treatments for you on the horizon."

Thankfully, back in July while Juli's doctor had been dragging her feet to refer Juli locally, Paul got busy locating "Plan B": a UCLA endocrinologist who specialized in Cushing's and other pituitary diseases. Moreover, he had experience with many CFS patients. This MD/PhD put many of his research articles on his website, which Paul absorbed like a sponge. He found that a number of CFS patients had growth hormone deficiency and explained how this deficit can cause a Cushing-like appearance, high blood pressure, etc. When Paul read that, he began making preliminary arrangements for them to fly to LA in the event Juli's doctor refused a referral. Now that this OHSU doctor said there was little he could do for Juli except run a few tests for other rare conditions, Paul proceeded to finalize the arrangements for their trip to LA.

Paul and Juli knew they needed an MD who had extensive understanding of all her conditions: diabetes, her unknown endocrine problem *and* CFS, because the CFS was always the monkey wrench in the mix. For example, in July, Juli was beginning to experience side effects from one of her diabetic drugs. When Paul checked on the internet, sure enough, CFS patients didn't fare well with that pharmaceutical.

Interestingly, however, there were promising developments at this very juncture. By this point, Juli was able to discontinue insulin injections after her body began ejecting the parasites. By mid-August, even more parasites came out. But now she was having increasing trouble tolerating her only remaining diabetic drug. Was this because she was getting better or experiencing the typical CFS intolerance to medications? They weren't sure.

At her last OHSU appointment in mid-September, before her trip to LA, she asked the endocrinologist if there was any way she could discontinue the problematic drug Glucophage. He smiled kindly at her, laughed a little and said, "I don't think so."

But the side effects soon became so intolerable, Juli decided to chuck the Glucophage and hey, those blood sugar numbers remained "A-OK." She also continued to drop about three to four pounds a month.

As it so happened, Paul's mom Elaine was in LA in early September helping his sister Jennifer prepare to move to NYC. Elaine was able to make reservations at the nearest hotel to the doctor's office and become familiar with the surroundings. In late September, she went a day ahead of the entourage to make all the final arrangements.

So when Juli, Paul, and Olsie arrived in LA at about 1:00 a.m. at a charming hotel decorated in the Lucille Ball/Desi Arnaz 50's style, everything was all set. Beautiful hotel location. Only one problem: a high-power line ran literally just a few feet outside the windows of the rooms where they all were to stay.

Now Juli's MCS has remained remarkably stable through all the medical crises she's endured since Mexico. If her energy level allows (which is rare these days), she goes wherever she wants, environmentally speaking, including to the beauty shop. But because her EMF sensitivities were previously so extreme, exposing herself for five days to something of this nature was unwise. (Dr. Rea advised Paul about this risk during phone consultations a decade before.)

In the middle of the night, the four of them went looking for a "room at the inn." The closest hotel with openings, to Juli's great delight, was the Hotel Sofitel, one of the ritziest in LA, and after tears of exhaustion, she began singing, "Oh well we're movin' on up, to the top, to the deluxe apartment in the sky." Perhaps this was the Lord's way of giving them a reprieve.

On the following day, the two-hour appointment with the UCLA endocrinologist was highly instructive. He ordered tests to be performed locally and said he would discuss Juli's results and continue consultation by email.

After Juli and Paul returned to Portland, further tests were done that finally ensured that she did not have even a rare form of Cushing's. When the blood work came back to the endocrinologist, he diagnosed Juli with partial lipodystrophy (disproportionate body mass distribution) and Leptin deficiency (a brain hormone which regulates fat cells). Based on the results of Juli's screening test for growth hormone deficiency, he did not believe Juli had this condition. But the more Paul read about it, the more he realized that nearly every symptom fit this pattern. He asked the doctor to order more extensive tests. The doctor hesitated, but agreed.

The first growth hormone stimulation test had to be performed at the hospital for two hours in early November. To the endocrinologist's great surprise, the test came back positive! He emailed back to them, "This is very exciting; this would explain a lot of Juli's symptoms."

Now, she just needed one more GH stimulation test to confirm the diagnosis. The doctor scheduled it for early December and it required a five-hour hospital outpatient stay. After an agonizing two-week wait, the test results came back negative. Adding to their profound disappointment, the endocrinologist sent them his final bill, told them there was little more he could do for Juli, and advised her to go back to the OHSU endocrinologist to pursue a research-stage drug to correct the leptin deficiency. He explained that this was the OHSU doctor's specialty. Funny, the Oregon doctor had never told Juli and Paul this was his specialty before, and had been emphatic that there was little he could do for her if she didn't have Cushing's.

So where does this leave us? Despite the dearth of "doctoral" assistance provided for Juli over the last nine months, we've been delighted this Thanksgiving and Christmas to see her splurge for once and eat all the carbs and pecan pie she wanted—without any medications—while all blood sugar levels remained well within normal. Though she has not returned to her small frame yet and needs to put more fat and muscle mass in her legs, those clothing tags now read "M" on the back instead of "XL." All of her doctors are at a loss to explain the amazing rapid turnaround in Juli's diabetes. And the endocrinologists in particular are a bit befuddled by her weight loss, since both know that the brain dysfunction she's been diagnosed with requires drug intervention to reverse the condition.

But she's not out of the woods yet, not by a long shot. Her CFS remains a formidable Goliath. Paul believes he's found one more lead on the internet, but who knows. Even still, he prays, "Many times during Juli's life, you have delivered her 'from the paw of the lion and the paw of the bear'; if it is your will, by means or by miracle, deliver her 'from the hand of this Philistine' and help us slay this spiritual giant. No matter what, Lord, we are your servants. Help us do the next right thing."

Thanks so much for caring,

Pastor Jim

The Next Right Thing

Over the years I have preached around the country and even a little in Canada. Of all the messages I have ever preached, no theme has ever struck a chord so consistently as the subject of monumental faith.

A well-known preacher in Southern California, who heard it when we were co-speakers at a summer conference in Wisconsin, later passed word through a friend about how much it had meant to him and said, "Tell Jim I've preached that message several times." Some who've heard my message in one version or another have inadvertently adopted its theme in their sermons. This foundational truth resonates with the human spirit at a deeply personal level. One guest speaker, oblivious to its provenance, even preached it in my own church in a little different form!

Because it registers with believers in pain, every few years I recycle it for our congregation. The impact never seems to diminish. The need for renewal of hope and a way of snatching victory from the jaws of despair remains a constant in the walk of faith.

Yet there is still, I believe, a missing link or two in this coping strategy. Whenever one offers spiritual counsel and people pick it up like a drumbeat, one knows there is a sensitive nerve. As much as this habit of monument polishing has sustained my wife and me over the years, for her a couple of nagging problems remained. She in particular struggles with pent-up anger and we both are numb with battle fatigue. "A broken spirit dries up the bones" (Proverbs 17:22b) and "hope long deferred makes the heart sick" (Proverbs 13:12). Eventually the will to push on weakens.

So I decided to garnish our theme by two more condiments of counsel I hope will season the whole platter just right.

When I finished a rough draft of this chapter, it couldn't have been timelier. Just yesterday Olsie found herself again on the verge of emotional implosion. Early warning bells had gone off a week ago when she mentioned in passing her on-going battle with bottled-up anger. I knew for sure her emotional rivets were loose when last Saturday she feared to be left home alone, worried that she might lose it.

So yesterday when I finished the first draft, she was very anxious to read it since earlier I had given her a heads up. In the afternoon when she was headed over to the high school where she plays piano for the choir, she took the manuscript to read during breaks.

When Olsie returned a couple of hours later, she wanted to go for a walk. Along the way she told me, "Somebody must be praying for us. Earlier today I was just about to fall apart. During breaks I read your chapter. Suddenly it all went away." If the Lord used this counsel to bail water out of Olsie's emotional boat, it encouraged me that it might help other embattled believers wrestling with the same things.

Let me set the scene in living color. Let's say you practice polishing your monuments and hope revives. You've been in a dark tunnel and suddenly way off you see a light.

"Ah, at last . . . light at the end of the tunnel. God has not abandoned me after all! He hasn't changed. He's just working off a different plan. Wait on the Lord, O my soul. Wait! He'll show up—in *His* time."

But here's where we may still find ourselves in a spiritual squeeze. A prolonged battle with adversity, especially when we just keep hitting one pothole after another, can wear our faith wheels flat. Frankly it's hard when we've called again and again for "emergency road service" to be put on hold, even if we do believe the Lord will eventually "pick up the phone." This is not to blame God for strategic delays in our deliverance, but simply to admit the frailty of faith.

How do we spring up and keep moving *today* when even the brightest mornings wear a dull, gray face, the flowers seem never to bloom anymore and the cheery birds refuse to sing? Trust me, we've been there and done that.

Clearly I am exaggerating for effect. Like the psalmists, though obviously minus their depth and poetic elevation, I am only expressing here the way we sometimes *feel* things are as opposed to the way things really are. No need to flagellate ourselves unduly. All but the most saintly sufferers tend to be myopic. We have trouble occasionally seeing the forest of God's grace for the trees of God's routine discipline (Hebrews 12:5–6).

How do we deal with this? Well, here's the drill. When your burdens get so heavy you feel you can't take another step, *put one foot in front of the other and just do the next right thing.*

Don't obsess too much about the future. Don't drain your energy craning your spiritual neck to see whether or not your deliverance is on the distant horizon. Just tackle today—step by step. Jesus cautioned us about fretting too much about tomorrow, for the evils and temptations of today are ample to occupy us (Matthew 6:25–34). So *today* just put one foot in front of the other and do the next right thing.

Sometimes the heat of the battle sucks all the vitality right out of us; disappointments beat vision to a pulp. We find ourselves so weary it seems easier just to lie down and die. As a former melancholic associate used to say to "cheer" everybody up when things were in the tank, "Life is tough and then we die!"

Well, at times everything does seem to dump on us. We pray and pray, yet nothing seems to happen. We go to the Word for a little spiritual bounce, but still everything seems stuck in the same ol' miserable rut.

How do we keep it going *today* until the Lord comes to the rescue some down-the-road tomorrow? There have been times as a pastor when I felt my emotional reserves were so stretched I could barely help others in their crises because I could hardly help myself. *Tomorrow* God may send joy unending, but *today* I am virtually paralyzed by unforgiving pain.

What do we do while we hold the phone? Do we just go into idle, take a seat and wait passively for the Lord to finally answer and create all things new? No. Passivity is no solution except in those rare cases of divine prescription. As one of my dear friends put it, "When we get depressed, the first thing to go is *action*. And inaction only makes the hole deeper."

Our Christian calling does not afford disciples the luxury of sitting out the battle until the Lord shows up with the supplies.

Our orders are to keep holding the fort. But how? My strength is depleted, my vision is shot. Just put one foot of faith in front of the other and do the next right thing—whatever it is.

If it's to pray when God seems deaf to our petitions, pray anyway. Pray the best you can; don't give in to despair. If it's to feed on the Word, go to dinner. Don't despise or neglect God's means of grace just because at the moment all his promises seem far, far off. Follow the program. If it's going to church and maintaining an accountable relationship with God's people when attending doesn't light you up anymore, go anyway. Give the Spirit of God a chance. You never know where his lightening will strike. If it's obedience that never seems to be rewarded, obey anyway. Put one foot in front of the other and just do the next right thing.

Be faithful even if it doesn't seem to be fruitful. Outcomes are not for you and me to decide. Waiting on the Lord is not sitting down on the Lord. The Lord's blessing, when it strikes, always favors a moving target.

So, when the serving heart is heavy, when the helping hands are weary, when the obedient feet are dead, when the godly mind is clouded with confusion, and the human spirit is numb with despair, don't go to the sideline. Put one foot in front of the other and do the next right thing.

Now let's talk about anger. How do we defuse that? Most of us somewhere along the line (usually more than once) have lost something dear to us—perhaps a dream, maybe a companion, a child, a parent, a relationship, a business, a livelihood, or our health. Not all those things are losses on the same level of importance, but any of them are emotionally devastating.

An emotionally detached person could sit down with us and explain why, however bad the loss, this grief was not the end of the world, life would go on and we would heal. Rationally we could hear it, even know it was true, but emotionally we just could not receive it.

Perhaps we could not, in part, because we don't want to. For at the time, especially if the loss involved a loved one (either through death or just a broken relationship), we feel overwhelmingly sad and empty. No matter how much we still have to be thankful for, the loss of what we value is so crushing and the relative value of everything else is so diminished by the price we put on what is gone, that nothing could offset our pain enough to alleviate it.

Once we had the little world we wanted and now it is gone. Thereafter nothing would satisfy but to have things back the way they were. Our emotions balk at any relief less than a return to the status quo. No talk therapy, however compelling, could appease or quiet them.

I remember once back in high school losing a girlfriend. My heart was crushed flatter than a bug under a big man's boot. The next morning was an exquisite summer day. It struck me so, because, as I rode in the back of a Board of Education maintenance truck to my summer job, that radiant sky so bright to others was strangely black as night to me. The sun could have been an optical illusion. Joy was an empty word . . . an emotion as remote from me as Nepal.

Oh, other girls were everywhere. Pretty ones, too. Didn't matter. They may as well have been lifeless mannequins or images on a wall. No attribute they possessed could fill the awful void. They had nothing I desired. The vacuum could not be filled nor the bleeding stanched. The sorrow could not be suppressed or assuaged. The ache was just there, defiantly there, and it would neither be denied nor contradicted by any amount of reason. No distraction could be contrived to mollify my woundedness. I just wanted the world my way . . . the way it was . . . the way I loved . . . Here is where we Christians in

244

our sin and brokenness often aggravate our suffering and let our fevered feelings get the upper hand. When our emotions riot, biblical prescriptions often hit a wall of resistance. It's hard to talk mad feelings down from their protesting perch. We don't want to hear about divine cures for sick and suffering souls.

When our emotional water gets tipped, that normally impacts our spiritual balance as well. God has so integrated our being that when the emotions sink, they almost invariably, by a kind of internal gravity, pull down our spiritual life as well.

Certainly I am no expert on all these emotional dynamics. However, having been through tough and painful times, seeing my wife suffer as we struggle through our daughter's illness, plus being a pastor and walking through so many heartbreaking situations over the years, I know the gravitational tug of anger. When God's plan seems to take our lives apart piece by piece and he seems in no hurry about putting us back together again, festering anger can take root.

So how do we uproot or bridle it? Though I possess a fierce, quick-strike temper (which as an adult I rarely display), I am not usually the simmering type, though I did visit that territory some in the mid-90s. The emotion most familiar to me personally in these dark passages is just profound hurt. However, like the branches on a tree, both these emotions, anger and hurt, really have the same roots but grow in different directions. And from that vantage point, I can relate and to some degree diagnose the problem and the fix.

Those of us who are more transparent tend to pre-empt the buildup of inner rage. We ventilate our emotions just enough that they dissipate. As one clears smoke from a closed room, airing our feelings through proper vents disperses anger before it settles in.

The more close-to-the-vest types, however, may become "anger traps." Like an overheated hot water tank with a bad pressure valve, their anger has nowhere to go. As the pressure builds, the need for relief is irrepressible. Eventually the strain will take its toll and the "containers" will either explode or implode. This "diagnosis," I know, is not exactly professional, but experience tells me it's not too far off the mark.

I have seen how this pressure gathers firsthand, particularly through my wife's experience and my totally inadequate response to her needs. Olsie is by nature a very calm, cool-under-stress, even-tempered woman. Roiling anger is as uncharacteristic of her as a heat wave in Maine. Still, during the years of our daughter's illness with all its frustrations and near impossible complications, Olsie confided to me with some worry that she struggled with anger.

Humanly speaking, one can totally understand why an empathetic mother might wrestle with that emotion. She struggles especially when she sees other young women Juli's age enjoying life, living their dreams, bearing children, and rearing families while Juli and Paul scramble every day just to survive. A good day is just a day with *less* pain.

In Olsie's case a large part of the problem has been that, to protect myself and preserve my own functionality, I shut her down. By this I mean, when it comes to my hearing about the "crisis of the day" in Juli's life, I seemed to lack the emotional strength to listen patiently to her and help her deal with the pain of the moment without losing my grip on my own sanity or my other responsibilities. I'm trying hard to fix that, but sometimes my shoulders don't seem big enough. Yet this is where, I have had to remind myself, God can and will give grace if I will just do the next right thing and trust him for it.

This particular emotion needs "fresh air" before it goes absolutely toxic. Anger is the methane gas of the soul. Any of us with loved ones in this fix must recognize their need for "talk therapy." They absolutely need to ventilate . . . to let it out in good ways before it goes sour.

But what if no other "ear" is there for us? Do we forget that God's ear is always open to us? "Cast all your anxiety upon him, because he cares for you" (1 Peter 5:7). "Let us therefore draw near with confidence to the throne of grace, that we may receive mercy and find grace to help in time of need" (Hebrews 4:16).

In fact that is how the psalmists "vented." As was Job, they were honest emotionally and poured out their feelings, good and bad, before God. The Lord already knows what's at the bottom of our buckets; we may as well spill it. No point in hiding it under ten gallons of frothy piety. If it's down there, take it to the one person we know who truly understands our vexation and exhaustion even better than we do.

> Just as a father has compassion on his children, so the Lord has compassion on those who fear him. For he himself knows our frame; he is mindful that we are but dust.
>
> (Psalm 103:13–14)

Far from impious, it is imperative to tell God how we *feel* so long as we confess our base emotions without approving them. We need to clear our inner decks of toxic emotional waste. Otherwise this debris will poison our spirits.

No one should ever complain that there is *no one* to whom we can talk. No man is an island where God is. Who understands our infirmities better than he does? Who has more power to alter our circumstances and restore order than God Almighty?

When anger sprouts in the soul, one can usually trace the roots to two errors. The first error is the insinuation that God is unfair. In reality God owes us nothing. The human race is bankrupt before him. No exceptions. Hence God cannot be unfair to people who by definition are condemned and undeserving. There is no logical way that a God who makes a world of spiritual and moral outlaws the undeserving beneficiaries of his manifold grace can be charged with being inequitable to them. No, the truth is, in our worst predicaments, it is we who are unfair to God.

As Jeremiah remarked in Lamentations 3, given our sinfulness, how can any person complain even if life does drop the hammer on us? When we get right down to it, perhaps the real sticking point is either that our creed is firmer than our convictions, thus feeling we are more deserving of God's favor than we admit. Or else we feel entitled to kinder gentler treatment than many of those "yahoos" out there who are having a good go of it.

There is no instant cure for these hang-ups. Human conceit blinds us all to some extent. The Lord just has to show us our nakedness so that eventually we wonder at his grace rather than chafe at his discipline. A good place to start is asking him to unmask our sinfulness and strip us of our self-righteousness. Once we discover we are not as "good" as we think we are, we are less prone to obsess about "Why me?"

Something else we need to understand is that we Christians are God's family, not Pavlov's dogs. The program is not to reward God's children with happy, comfortable lives for good behavior. God's plan is that we may partake of his holiness, not dine on the fleeting happiness of this world. To that end rigorous discipline goes with the turf (Hebrews 12:8–11).

Shaping up requires chipping away. The whole idea of the Christian life is for us to be conformed to Christ, not to be comfortable in Christ. Sometimes we just don't get it. The truth is, a life of suffering is a better benchmark of God's favor than a life of surfing. God's love is more likely to reveal itself in the presence of pain than in the absence of it.

In college I somehow became the favorite of the legendary head of our journalism department. W.L.T. Crocker was a demanding no-nonsense professor who never suffered fools lightly. He struck mortal fear into the hearts of engineering and other language-challenged students who displayed no imagination or appreciation for the written word.

Not an easy role, being his "elect." Crocker might over-look the intractable deficiencies of some for whom he had no hope. But mine he was all over like a spring flood over a dry creek bed. The man never gave me an inch. Oh, sure, he did encourage me whenever I gave him an excuse. But he never did gratuitously flatter me, and he did on more than one occasion totally flatten me—because he cared and wanted to shape me in his own image. That pain was a badge of honor; to be ignored was a sign of resignation.

It's something like that with God. His agenda is not to make our lives a trouble-free zone. His mission is to make us trophies of his grace. That goal requires some grinding on the stubborn outcroppings of our flesh. Never consider it a sign of God's favor when you regularly find yourself feasting on perennial abundance, soaking up constant fun and sun, and cruising along those carefree boulevards where pain and suffering are perfect strangers. This may come as a shock to "californicated" churchgoers, but the Christian life is not a beach; it is a battle from beginning to end. Godliness does not blossom on playgrounds; it flourishes in war zones. If we don't get worked over and melted down by adversity now and then, it doesn't mean God is blessing us; it more likely means he is disowning us (Hebrews 12:5–10). Remember *that* when you're feeling angry with God for allowing you to be pum-meled unmercifully. Christian soldiers are expected to face and endure hardness in the service of Christ (2 Timothy 2:3).

The second error is that there is a seam of willfulness in our character. We want life on *our* terms, not God's terms. We have our little image of the way life ought to be and we don't want God to mess with that. This is especially true when it involves our children, as in our case.

Maybe we reconcile ourselves to our own broken dreams, but it is so hard to see our kids' dreams dashed, their talents trashed, wasting away in bed for years at a time and living in chronic pain, with little to look forward to but just a miniscule taste of relief.

Anger takes over when our will is so stubborn that we emotionally deny God his sovereign right to do what he deems best. Oh, perhaps we acknowledge his right to do it, but still will not concede the wisdom of it. The anger stems from resentment that we can't have our way or that God is piling on when enough is enough.

We all have these moral aneurysms in the veins of our make-up. Those are the thinnest walls in our character . . . the areas where, under pressure, we are prone to break out in sin. Stubborn, strong-willed people are more prone to get hung up here than others. A persistent and unaccountable denial of our dream first frustrates, then angers us, especially when others seem to get a free pass where we cannot buy a break.

The answer here is the example of the submission of our Lord Jesus Christ, who in the Garden of Gethsemane prayed, "Father, not my will, but yours be done." We are not just God's family, we are his servants; it is our glory as well as our moral duty to give up our will to accommodate his. Besides, as that erstwhile theologian of the Chicago Bulls, Jalen Rose, once expressed on Jim Rome's *Last Word* TV show, "My arms are too short to box with God." Right! Nobody ever wins fighting with God. Far better to agree with God than argue with him.

What has always helped me drain my emotional tubes is to remember that anger is a spiritual corrosive and lethal toxin. Steaming inside and popping our corks doesn't change anything for the better. It is a destructive, cancerous emotion. Like jealousy, passion eats the guts out, if I may be blunt. It drives a wedge between us and God because ultimately it resists his will, objects to his disposition of our circumstances, and doubts his goodness and wisdom. We need to see it for what it is.

I don't have all the answers here. But I know that today several people are still standing, still walking with Christ, still serving, and still looking for the blessed hope because he gave us these answers:

"Polish those monuments, then put one foot in front of the other and do the next right thing. And don't let the sun go down on your wrath."

There may be more we can do, but with that advice you can never ever go wrong and you will always keep moving in the right direction.

Should you ever in a fit of melancholy grow weary of polishing your monuments and succumb to the notion that life has dealt you a bad hand, just remember you have all eternity to make up for it.

The sufferings of this present time are not worthy to be compared to the glory that is to be revealed to us (Romans 8:18).

Things which the eye has not seen and the ear has not heard, and which have not entered into the heart of man, all that God has prepared for those who love him (1 Corinthians 2:9).

In Ephesians 1:15–23 the apostle Paul earnestly prays for the church. The heart of his petition is that the Spirit of God would open their eyes to know God better. For if they do, they will understand what is most essential to carry them through the trials and tribulations of this present world. His desire is that they would understand 1) the riches of his calling, 2) the riches of the glory of his inheritance in the saints, and 3) the surpassing greatness of his power toward us who believe.

Translation: I pray that you will know God better and better, so that you will clearly see in the fury and fog of battle that 1) we are going to win, 2) we are going to win big, and 3) along the way we are going to have all the help we need!

To know God, we have to walk with God. There is no way to walk with God without going into a war zone and getting shot-up from time to time. Battle fatigue just goes with the territory. So fight the good fight and let faith take shelter in God's monuments. And always remember, doing the next right thing is submitting to God's plan.

Let me share with you a prayer I wrote many years back. I had it framed and hung on my office wall to remind me that life is not about *ME*.

The Unconditional Prayer of the Utterly Serious

Lord God, my singular ambition in life is to magnify you. I care not what the cost; spend me as you please. On your arrangements I place no conditions. You set the terms of my service. My prayer is simply that you ordain for my life whatever will glorify Christ most through me.

If my Savior would be honored more through my death than my life, more in sickness than in health, more in poverty than in wealth, more through loneliness than companionship, more by the appearance of failure than by the trappings of success, more by anonymity than by notoriety, then your design is my desire.

Only let me make a difference!

Y E A R S

16–17

March 1, 2004

Dear Friends,

Envision yourself receiving the horrific news that you've just been diagnosed with a newly discovered degenerative disease. Suddenly you realize that there is no qualified specialist virtually anywhere in the country to manage your specialized needs. You are desperately ill and the pressure is on you alone to figure out what's wrong, where to go, and what to do. There you have a small inkling of the predicament Juli and Paul have been facing for the past seventeen years. They've experienced through much trial and error how intractable the condition can be.

Yet as I've said repeatedly, I have never seen two people display more determination or discipline to take whatever steps necessary to get well. Often however, their only pay-back is utter exhaustion once their precious time and energy is expended.

What really drives their engines is their devotion to our Lord Jesus Christ and his master plan for their lives. Oh yes, they're human; they battle the depths of despair almost every day. But when the rubber meets the road, they understand that this whole mess is God's business and there's a mysterious reason for the mammoth testings they've endured.

Theirs is to do the next right thing. As one of their favorite Keith Green songs so aptly expresses this principle of obedience, "You just keep doin' your best, pray that it's blessed, Jesus takes care of the rest. Yes the Lord said that he'll take care of the rest." They are mindful that if it isn't God's time to heal, then they must trust his infinite wisdom.

At the present, so far as they can tell, God has led them to the next right thing. My last letter (dated December 31, 2002) ended with the news that Paul thought he'd found a new lead on the internet. After the UCLA endocrinologist reported back the negative results of Juli's second growth hormone stimulation test Paul wondered, "Since Juli's first GH stimulation test came back positive and her symptoms match the profile so clearly, are there any doctors who hold a differing opinion?"

Finally, he clicked onto an article by Dr. Paul Cheney, M.D., Ph.D., who believed that GH deficiency was an integral part of CFS. He thought the most accurate way to diagnose it in CFS patients was an exercise/stress stimulation test. In healthy individuals, GH jumps approximately fifteen points after such exertion, but in CFS patients, it stays the same or even drops. Thus when these patients exercise to a significant extent, they are unable to repair the typical muscle breakdown that occurs.

This is why, he explains in his many articles, CFS patients are so debilitated to the point of often being bedridden, and are weakened by activity instead of strengthened by it, as healthy people are. Here is another example of just one of the many aspects of this disease that the medical community, by and large, fails to grasp. It also explains why for years, Juli and Paul have been unable to trust local medical advice—to simply check in around the corner and say, "Please take care of me."

Dr. Cheney is one of the country's leading CFS researchers and physicians. He began his interest in the disease in 1985 when he saw an epidemic of a persistent flu-like illness in the Incline Village area of California/Nevada. He went on to devote his entire practice and research energies to deciphering the cause and eventually the treatment of the debilitating illness. Of course, Juli and Paul have known of his work from the beginning. But by the time Dr. Cheney began to implement his initial treatments (with limited success), Juli was too sick to travel.

But in mid-2000, he began treating patients with growth hormone. It was touch and go at first. Then as he became more familiar with the drug's effects on patients, he concluded that 1) their bodies needed to be prepped for a year with nutritional detoxifiers, 2) they must begin with the smallest possible dosage and slowly build their tolerance for increased amounts, and 3) after this occurred, they needed bovine growth factors to complete the healing process. Needless to say, if Juli had received the higher dosage that the UCLA endocrinologist would have prescribed, according to Dr. Cheney's experience, she might have become extremely ill.

So after Paul completed his internet research, he called Dr. Cheney's office for an appointment in mid-December 2002. He wasn't taking any new patients. How devastating! (He

255

later sent out a sad notice to *all* CFS patients that due to the immunosuppressant drugs he was on to reduce the rejection risk of his new heart transplant, he was forced to temporarily suspend his practice. However, he vowed to continue to benefit the CFS community through his research in the interim.)

Paul then contacted the leader of the Dallas/Fort Worth support group for CFS since her website had been the source of many of the Cheney articles he'd read. He emailed her, "Is there a physician who has studied with Dr. Cheney and is presently receiving new patients?" But she never replied. (Paul was unaware that he had the wrong email address.)

In the meantime, Juli's local OHSU endocrinologist called to let her know that he had received the test results from the UCLA specialist and he was going to use his influence to get her in an NIH Leptin study in Baltimore. When Juli visited him in early January, the doctor again found it difficult to explain the additional weight she'd lost (from the hips up) but confirmed that she was still suffering from lipodystrophy because of the lack of fat and muscle in her legs. He felt confident he could get her into the study.

But now they had a complicated quandary. Paul had finally reached the CFS support group leader in Texas. She was a very kind lady, who informed him, "Yes, there is a doctor here in DFW who has studied with Dr. Cheney and administers his program. His wife and son contracted CFS in 1987." As you remember, that's the same year Juli and Paul came down with it. In fact, it's the year when the highest percentage of CFS patients became ill.

So which way should they go? The decision-making process became even dicier when the OHSU doctor called again with the great news: He had contacted the director of the NIH study and was almost certain Juli would be accepted. If you can believe it, the tension twisted even a notch higher when

Dr. Larry Sharp's office called from Fort Worth to confirm that he was indeed receiving new CFS patients.

At this point, the stakes felt so high that Juli and Olsie had a rare blowout over which "fork in the road" to take. Juli explained the catch-22, "I'm very interested in participating in this NIH study. But if they are unfamiliar with the intricacies of CFS, I could have a major "healing crisis" with the leptin injection and it could backfire. If you'll remember, Mom, the UCLA doctor diagnosed me with a severely low adrenal hormone as well, but the drug he prescribed backfired badly, and if I hadn't discontinued it in time, I would have lost even more ground. Just because I test low for the brain hormone leptin doesn't mean I can tolerate the usual protocol full force."

Olsie said, "Well, why don't you ask the doctor at OHSU what he thinks?"

"I wish I could, Mom, he's a fine endocrinologist, but he doesn't know beans about CFS. Because he doesn't know the territory, he's unable to answer that question. Besides, just last week we read a recently published article about how many CFS patients are low in leptin and another one that explained how GH controls leptin levels. So if the root of my problem is really CFS and GH deficiency, then perhaps treating the CFS would take care of the leptin problem too."

Well, the Lord ended that family feud when the OHSU doctor called the very next evening and told Paul that unfortunately, Juli had been rejected from the NIH study because her blood sugars were normal even without medication. The vast majority of leptin deficiency patients have severe diabetes. Juli used to have it as well, but now that the diabetes component of her health was negligible, she no longer qualified for the study!

The next day, Dr. Sharp called from Fort Worth. Paul said it felt like they were two soldiers sharing war stories, hence two CFS husbands commiserating. The doctor was refreshingly humble after hearing Juli's extremely complex case and said, "I'm not a researcher like Dr. Cheney but I feel qualified to take her as a patient and implement his treatment program."

It took a two-week blitz to make all the necessary arrangements. The usual entourage of both moms plus Juli and Paul went in February 2003. Trips such as these are quite an undertaking for Juli. While she can take her "exercise" walks around the outside of the house for short distances, she requires a wheelchair for long journeys through airports. She also has to conserve every drop of energy by resting across three airplane seats. Still, in her early days of CFS, even this would have been too taxing, so we're thankful she can travel despite the strain.

When they arrived in Dallas, they were pleased to find Elaine's choice of accommodations perfect—close enough to the doctor's office, while in a newly developed area of Fort Worth with easy access to freeways and Olsie's favorite cafeteria, Luby's.

Dr. Sharp spent three hours with Juli and three hours with Paul. Paul wanted to be checked over thoroughly and have CFS-related tests done as well, because the stress of the previous two years had weighed heavily on his system. While Dr. Hulda Clark had helped Paul (and Juli) significantly, this hypothalmus/pituitary part of the equation was not her specialty. Anyway, back to Dr. Sharp. According to Juli, he has the personality of a Teddy Bear and he was very thorough with her CFS for a change!

He ordered batteries of tests (being ever mindful of their finances) to be run when they returned home. And what did these tests reveal?

1) Juli has thirty percent less blood volume and red blood cells than a healthy person—that's like an engine running on insufficient oil levels!

2) She has extremely low natural killer cells (a critical immune system component that kills viruses and bacteria), a hallmark of CFS.

3) She has immune system activation of coagulation. This means that the pathogens in her bloodstream are over-stimulating her clotting mechanism, another commonly found component of CFS that has just recently been discovered.

4) One additional clotting disorder Juli has can be genetically acquired, but this was ruled out when Olsie and I were later tested on her behalf. However, the levels were so pronounced, the clotting lab director told the doctor, "Her numbers are so high, I wouldn't be surprised if she hasn't had a major clotting episode already." Was it possible that in 1996 when her speech became slurred and she had a respiratory arrest, that she in fact had a stroke and pulmonary embolism (blood clot in the lung)? We'll never know for sure, but when Paul checked on the internet he found that it was possible for one to immediately follow the other.

5) Basically, she's tested positive for every pathogen on the planet—just kidding. But she does have the typical CFS pathogen profile. Even still, her genetic tests show, no surprise here folks, her genes are excellent for the most part—Olsie and I are healthy as horses. Speaking of horses, Dr. Sharp explained that in all probability, Juli's childhood physicians were correct in their prognostication regarding potentially serious complications from this accident, which has manifested itself in many directions. This includes not only the severity of her

GH deficiency, which led to the disproportionate body mass distribution, but also the fact that as a CFS patient, her brain tends toward seizures due to excessive viral activity that overstimulates the brain's electrical system. However, the few genetic problems she has inherited are consistent with other CFS patients.

This leads us to Paul. His genetic problems are slightly more extensive than Juli's—but it helps that he's never been bashed in the brain. However, they are almost identical to hers, and Dr. Sharp said laughingly, "You two are true soul mates, aren't you?" Though Paul functions pretty well, the doctor has still found some CFS abnormalities he hopes to correct.

Dr. Sharp said that during the first year, he would need to see Juli and Paul again in three to six months and after that, just once a year. They flew back last May while the weather was still amenable, and this time the entourage included Lynne Mackey. Juli and Paul commented again how refreshing it was to deal with a doctor whose family has endured similar circumstances. Sometimes in these appointments they laugh over the travails of the traveling patient and family members since he, his wife, and son had to travel to see Dr. Cheney. Juli says this reminds her of how we as believers in various trials have our great high priest who has suffered in every way we have, yet without sin (Hebrews 4:15).

They arrived home safe and sound and followed Dr. Sharp's instructions to a "T." He told Juli that if she was careful and patient, he thought she would become strong enough to withstand the GH aerobic exercise test at the next visit. He believed that both Juli and Paul, assuming they test positive as he expects, would be ready for small doses of growth hormone in about nine months. After a few months of GH, he planned to add bovine growth factors to the regimen.

So in late January 2004, the whole crew headed back to see Dr. Sharp. While Juli is still unable to walk long distances through the airport, amazingly, she was able to withstand the aerobic bicycle test. A year ago this would have been out of the question. It took quite a bit out of her but she did indeed recover. Paul took the test also and while he was in Texas, he took the opportunity to see a renowned dental surgeon who is, according to their Oregon dentist, "the world's best in his specialty." Dr. Sharp had referred Paul to him to correct a jaw infection that showed up on Paul's x-rays and was weighing down his immune system.

On their way home, while leaving the airplane, Juli had a touching answer to prayer. She was wearing a black and red cardigan sweater Paul bought her for Christmas. (By the way, all clothing tags now have an "S" on them.) After Juli walked down the airplane aisle and took hold of her wheelchair, the stewardess exclaimed, "Oh, is this chair yours? It's so small, I was expecting to see a child, but you're just a tiny lady."

Juli smiled and replied, "Well, thank you ma'am. You've just made my day; see, I haven't been for some time and I've been waiting to hear those words again!"

Two weeks later, Dr. Sharp called with the great news that both their tests were positive for GH deficiency. However, before beginning the injections, he wanted them to complete a month of the heavy metal detoxification protocol first. Then he believed both would be ready—even Juli. She still has miles to go, but the "prep" work over the past year has rendered a few positive developments besides her much welcomed weight loss.

As of last September Juli was able to sit up for longer periods of time. While she still has bad days, this has generally trended upwards. She's recently been walking on the treadmill again, albeit at the slowest speed for just ten minutes a day.

261

But what's meant the most to Olsie and me personally is that God has finally enabled Juli to use one of her talents for his Glory, even if it's in a limited way. You see, as I've said before, I'm a medical ignoramus. What's more, the complexities of this situation would make even Einstein want to blow his brains out. Both Juli and Paul are excellent writers, and for years now I've prayed they would someday be able to sift through and edit my letters to our church, and add supporting medical details to the originals. Well, as she's been able to sit up more, she and Paul have made this priority number one.

By way of explanation, one part of the brain that tends to be broken down in CFS patients is the word search area. Tasks such as writing generally make them extremely ill. So, this endeavor was only made possible because Dr. Sharp's treatments focus on healing the brain. Nevertheless, it has been a noble sacrifice for the cause of Christ for two reasons. First, Juli and Paul have experienced two perilous disasters this past year that I've been unable to cover within the space of these pages. The Lord delivered them from both crises, but it did significantly add to their years of wear and tear. Second, the effort still exhausts Juli, and some of the memories are so painful she would prefer to leave them buried beneath the Mariana Trench. However, Juli and Paul want nothing more than that their lives demonstrate to others in the throes of suffering, the transforming and renewing power of God's Word to attain and maintain perspective for minds tempted toward spiritual disillusionment (Romans 12:1, 2).

And what is our perspective on Juli and Paul's trial right now? Sometimes God's miracle in the midst of trials is not an immediate resolution but a demonstration of his provision, protection, and presence. We see this displayed in a time of drought when God sent Elijah to Cherith Brook to quench his thirst, and ordered ravens to bring him bread and meat. In our case, God has protected Juli's life many times over and has finally provided the oversight of a caring CFS doctor, which has led to Juli's relative stability.

We do not know when God will eventually say, "Now I will emancipate Juli and Paul from their tribulation." But sometimes when those, like Elijah, who wait for his deliverance begin to tremble from years of trauma, he reassures them through a "still small voice" (1 Kings 19:9–18).

Thank you for caring,

Pastor Jim

God's "Now"

The phone rang just after I arrived home. The caller informed me they had just heard on the local news that Damon Coates had been shot.

Damon, a member of our church, was a high profile Clackamas County deputy sheriff. A fit, imposing 6' 5" enviably handsome figure, Damon for several years had been the public information officer (PIO) for the sheriff's department. A very familiar face on local TV news, Damon was highly regarded not only by fellow officers and local media people, but surprisingly, by more than a few of the felons he had arrested over the years. As a testament to the consistency of his Christian character on the job as well as off, one inmate, whom another officer described to me as a "real bad dude," later wrote to me, "if all police officers were like Damon Coates, this world would be a better place."

The caller had no other details. With that call I learned that Damon had been air lifted to Emanuel Hospital, the very best trauma center in the city for gunshot victims. After notifying our associate senior pastor, I raced to Emanuel to find a frenetic scene a little reminiscent of the swarm at Dallas's Parkland Hospital when JFK was gunned down. One designated parking lot was already crawling with TV trucks and crews waiting for breaking news, police officers were converging on the scene from all jurisdictions, while friends and pastors rushed to the side of the families in total shock.

Earlier that night, Damon and his partner had responded to a call about an out-of-control fifteen-year-old teenager with a recent history of mental problems. With his usual cool and professional manner, Damon becalmed the youngster, who no longer, it seemed, posed a threat. According to police protocol, he started to handcuff the kid as a precautionary measure prior to patting him down. Suddenly without warning, the boy whipped around like a whirling dervish, brandishing a handgun, and popped Damon almost point blank in the face with a .45.

The devastating bullet penetrated maybe an inch or so below Damon's right eye and about the same distance from his nostril, fragmenting and tearing up jack all the way back. The damage was horrendous. For starters, it seriously messed up his inner ear, shredded his carotid artery, cost him a little brain matter, and left him with some (hopefully temporary) paralysis.

One officer at the scene told me afterward that of the shootings he had seen, this was the most gruesome sight yet. Damon would have bled to death on the spot but for the timely intervention of another officer on the scene. Even so, nobody really expected Damon to make it. In fact his chances were put at one percent.

For several weeks as he lay unconscious this story was the biggest drama in local news. As the family pastor, I was interviewed several times, and for several weeks TV crews were part of the Sunday furniture, so engaged was the press with the religious angle of the story. Because of Damon's cordial and accommodating professional relationship with the local media, they took more than the usual interest in this story. As more than one reporter confessed to me, Damon was a special guy and journalistic detachment was difficult. They took this tragedy as personally as if it had been one of their own struck down in the line of duty.

The story for a long while riveted and galvanized not only the whole Christian community in Portland, but also the entire city and well beyond, as many rallied to the support of the family, including the sheriff's department. Short of a major disaster, one seldom sees so many people touched so deeply for so long.

After taking refuge for several days in the bowels of the hospital from the bright lights of the media, finally the family's first news conference was arranged. When his wife Tammy, looking so pretty, so composed, in the most compelling and genuine way expressed compassion for the boy who had nearly killed her husband, and publicly extended her forgiveness, the whole city was dumbstruck at such amazing grace. The boy's mother Dawn was deeply touched, and a couple of weeks later she came to our church where the two women embraced and sat together in the service. When that word got out, everyone knew Tammy was not just blowing pious smoke.

What fascinated me in the middle of all this drama was the interest the media suddenly took in the subject of prayer. That curiosity was heightened, I think, by the resounding chorus of prayers being offered up in churches all over the state and the obvious fact that somehow "something" seemed to be sustaining the unsustainable. Later, one TV reporter came to interview me about the power of prayer as part of a feature the whole Coates story had inspired.

Clearly God was using Damon's tragedy as a divine sconce for the torch of truth in this city. God was using this as a kind of mirror to reflect the glory of Christ and the gospel. It was as if for a moment in time a great window of light opened in Portland. The truth broke through in space normally dark and unwelcoming.

It was weeks before Damon was even fully conscious. Given the vast extent of his wounds, the need to manage his pain and keep him quiet after so many extensive and delicate surgical procedures, Damon was maintained in a medically induced coma. Eventually as they brought him out of it, it was wonderful to find his mind and sense of humor fully intact.

On Valentine's Day, for example, Tammy came to see Damon and had just informed him of a Sweet Adeline group that came some distance to honor them on this special occasion. No sooner had she explained than he, suddenly sick, threw up violently through his feeding tube and spewed a stream of vomit like a liquid projectile that splattered everywhere. Once order was restored from the chaos and things settled back down, Damon, though still unable to talk, managed to write Tammy a note, "Real romantic, huh?"

After a while, with Damon's survival no longer in doubt, the media focus gradually shifted to other matters. Occasionally somebody will call me for an update, but by and large that big window of light has largely closed.

But the struggle for Damon and Tammy goes on. At this point the realistic prospect for a return to a normal, mainstream life for Damon seems remote, at least to me. The long, painful march to rehabilitation is underway, as I write. But so far, it is dreadfully and doubtfully slow, though we still pray for a better outcome.

As of this writing, Damon continues to endure all sorts of terrible complications from his various injuries. He suffers occasional grand mal-like seizures and, as mentioned previously, some paralysis on his left side, affecting also his vocal chords and swallowing. So far he is unable to sit up on his own, much less walk by himself. Speaking has tenuously returned, but it is very raspy and a great labor. Because he can't swallow yet, he still requires a troublesome feeding tube. That's not all. When phlegm or something else hangs in his throat, the poor man, with no way to relieve or expel it, will sometimes cough and hack all day and all night, unable to sleep or allow Tammy to do so. The damage to his inner ear makes him ultra sensitive to motion sickness. Thus, without warning he will throw up all over the place.

In an act a bit reminiscent of Jochebed, the mother of Moses, who discerned something special in her newborn son, Damon's mother, Judy, at birth laid him across her chest and dedicated him to God. All went well. Damon grew up, served God, married a pretty, Christian wife, fathered four nice kids, was devoted to his family, excelled at his work, was esteemed by all, lived modestly, and walked humbly. In short, Damon was a star performer in life and a light for Christ in every venue. Now this. In one terrible moment, the Lord signed that blank check Judy had written him at Damon's birth and spent it all over the Willamette Valley for his glory.

It has been easy for us on the outside to see the return on the Christian credibility the two of them had stored up so quietly over the years. This evil brought good to light that would otherwise have gone unnoticed. We should all be so blessed if in our own suffering Christ and the gospel would be so magnified before so many for so long. But seeing the aftermath and surveying the future, I wonder what Damon must really feel at this point. In his same circumstances, one would be sorely tempted to feel that his (or her) life is now reduced to an exercise in futility. How many of us in his place might not cry out, "Lord, why did you even spare me? My life has nowhere to go from here."

That response is only natural. But the *supernatural* response is to buck up and, as I call it, *wait on God's Now*. What that means will be explained later. For the moment just let me say that this posture is a great ally of monumental faith, for the reinforcing power of the practice of monument polishing always benefits from other good faith habits. One might call this "double-teaming" doubt. These are the functional equivalent of backup systems.

In the previous chapter we stressed the importance of linking monumental faith to an attitude of perseverance that just puts one foot in front of the other and does the next right thing. This newest tactic I am suggesting is another complement that helps us believers deflect onslaughts of doubt in times of trouble. It will prevent that "shortness of spirit" that so disabled the hope of the sons of Israel when Moses tried to encourage them with the promise of God's deliverance from their Egyptian slavery. "But they did not listen to Moses on account of [their] despondency (literally shortness of spirit) and cruel bondage" (Exodus 6:9).

If "waiting on God's *Now*" sounds like an anemic prescription, hopelessly abstract and impractical, trust me, it isn't. It's a spiritual posture that helps us, when we can't see the light at the end of the tunnel, at least to hear the whistle in the distance. This perspective in affliction has lifted the spirits of some of my embattled church people and has become a watchword itself that I sometimes hear echoing back to me, "Jim, I am just waiting on God's *Now*."

In situations where a sense of futility inundates us and such fundamental questions as "Why am I here?" or "Why did you send me?" haunt us, we are exactly where Moses found himself early on in Egypt. Entwined in his experience with the Lord are several important lessons for us, but none more than God's *Now*.

Let me unwrap them biblically. Way back in the desert where this palace-educated Hebrew had settled into the pastoral life of a lonely shepherd, one day God revealed himself (Exodus 3). On that momentous occasion the Lord called Moses to return to Egypt and to spearhead, on his behalf, the deliverance of the sons of Israel.

There was a history here. Forty years earlier Moses had been politically and emotionally burned when he tried to help his people (Exodus 2). In a providential twist Moses had been reared in the very court of Pharaoh as a privileged Egyptian, though (unknown to his adopted mother) his true mom was his Hebrew nanny. Through her guiding influence undoubtedly, Moses' heart and sympathies lay with his own people. In time he tried to intervene on their behalf but his initial effort to deliver them was rebuffed. The next time he tried, he went too far. Rejected by his people and now viewed as unfriendly by the Egyptians, Moses found himself in a political no man's land. Forced to flee Egypt, he wound up taking refuge with a Midianite family in the eastern Sinai Peninsula. At that point, Moses was not in God's *Now*.

After a whole generation living like a Bedouin among the Midianities, Moses still had a bad taste in his mouth from his earlier rejection by the sons of Israel. Then too the desert sands over those long years had blasted away much of his original court polish and with it all his former bristling self-confidence. This "desert" Moses was quite different from the earlier model.

One day out tending his sheep on the backside of the lonely wilderness, Moses experienced a life-changing encounter with the living God. Speaking from the midst of a burning bush, strangely unconsumed, the Lord introduced himself to a Moses almost frozen in fear and wonder. On this occasion the Lord gave Moses his marching orders. Initially, like many others since that time, Moses was quite reluctant to embrace his divine calling. Prideful rebellion was not what detained him. Rather, it was just a sense that the job was much too big and the man was much too small. This was a huge change in Moses, but one God could work with. That may be why all Moses' excuses met with more divine patience than we might have expected.

A CEO in our church once told me that part of his management style was to take away all excuses. For instance, when a subordinate blamed lack of performance on X, Y, or Z, his first tack was to do everything possible to remove the obstacle(s) presumably standing in the way of that employee's success. Then he would see if that employee would perform or if the real problem lay elsewhere.

Well, that's similar to what the Lord did with Moses. One by one he stripped away Moses' excuses. In fact, the Lord even equipped Moses with three supernatural signs for convincing the elders of Israel that the God of their fathers truly had met with him. God had really promised through Moses to deliver the sons of Israel from bondage.

At last Moses gave way to his calling. Arriving in Egypt, he executed his orders to the letter. The elders of Israel were duly impressed. They acknowledged his calling of God. Then, backed with their support, Moses got the people on board. They too were persuaded that the God of their fathers had visited them and had at last sent someone to deliver them from their cruel thralldom. So far so good. The next step: confront Pharaoh with a divine directive.

This conference with Pharaoh (Exodus 5) was a bust, or so it seemed. If Moses and Aaron imagined for a minute that the king was about to accede to their demand and release his entire labor force they were in for a surprise. If they thought Pharaoh would temporarily shutter the Egyptian economy so his good-for-nothing workers could traipse out into the desert to pay homage to some no-name God, they must be *on* something. Who the heck was "Yahweh" anyway?

But Pharaoh was worse than arrogant and defiant. He got cruel. That very day he decided upon a preemptive strike that would put a stop to any more nonsense. He had no intention of letting political activism clutter his administrative calendar. Clearly these people had too much time on their hands. They had become lazy. Anybody knows that one can expect only poison from standing water. So that very day Pharaoh issued a royal directive changing the work rules.

Previously the straw used to reinforce the mud bricks that the slaves were required to produce had been provided. That concession was to be terminated forthwith. Hereafter the Hebrew slaves would be expected not only to maintain their regular production schedule of bricks, but in addition, they would be required to scavenge for their own straw.

Same hours, double the work! A collective groan. Mission impossible. Try as they may, there was no way they could keep the pace. When they failed, slave labor became slaughtered labor. Through some protocol or other, the Hebrews managed to get a hearing with the king. Not understanding apparently that this new work regimen came directly from the top, they complained to Pharaoh that their failure to meet their quotas lay at the feet of his own taskmasters. More was required of them than they could humanly produce.

"No way," insisted Pharaoh. "You people are incurably lazy. Otherwise you wouldn't be sending embassies like Moses and Aaron to me with these ridiculous demands about taking time off for some religious festival in honor of some God. Now get back to work. And, no, the work orders will not be rescinded. Produce or pay the piper. That's final."

At that point the sons of Israel knew the jig was up. An already miserable life was about to become more impossible. They were past disconsolate. Naturally, when things go bad, it is always human nature to look for someone to blame. In this case Moses and Aaron, who had been awaiting the outcome of this parlay somewhere outside the court, got the black hats and the cold shoulders.

The unfriendly countenance of conferees said it all. Blamed for all the new troubles of the sons of Israel, suddenly Moses and Aaron went from the penthouse to the outhouse in the esteem of their fellow Israelites. Nobody believed in them anymore. All that talk about God's deliverance now sounded like Herbert Hoover's promises of two cars in every garage and two chickens in every pot just before the onset of the Great Depression.

This latest rejection by his people was for Moses, as Yogi Berra once said, *deja vu*. This ugly turn of events rocked Moses to his socks. When he returned to the Lord, Moses was lower than a beetle's bottom. He couldn't figure out what the Lord was up to.

O Lord, why hast Thou brought harm to this people? Why didst Thou ever send me? Ever since I came to Pharaoh to speak in Thy name, he has done harm to this people; and Thou hast not delivered Thy people at all" (Exodus 5:22–23).

As far as Moses was concerned, the Lord hadn't helped matters in the slightest. Actually things were worse than before.
And all this talk about deliverance seemed an empty promise;
it was nowhere in sight. To cap it off, Moses thought he was
useless. He had lost all credibility with this people. A thirsty
horse wouldn't follow him to water. "O Lord, why did you
ever send me?"

I suspect many readers can resonate with that question
or one similar to it. There is help ahead. But first, I want
you to notice what a smart thing Moses did with his doubts.
"And Moses returned to the Lord" (5:22) with his despairing questions. One mark of a truly walking faith as opposed
to a merely talking faith is where it goes with its doubts. In
the walls of faith there are always hairline cracks that great
stress exposes.

For example, we read in Psalm 10 where David cried out,
"Why dost Thou stand afar off, O Lord? Why dost Thou hide
Thyself in times of trouble?" (v. 1). Actually the Lord wasn't
hiding; David is describing his emotional perceptions not theological reality. To embattled believers it sometimes seems like
God is hiding. In reality the Lord has promised that he will
never leave us nor forsake us (Hebrews 13:5).

So what sets a living faith apart from a dead faith is not the
presence or absence of doubt, but the triumph of faith. Where
it is genuine, faith is deeper than doubt and in the rough and
tumble of life's battles, living faith always wins out. In the
case of the dead species, doubt is deeper than "faith" and
eventually prevails.

En route to our chief lesson, there are a couple of ancillary
points well worth noting. Observe, for instance, that the benefit
of knowing truth in advance does not necessarily shockproof
our faith in the trenches. The Lord had already forewarned
Moses that Pharaoh was not going to roll over and give in

except by divine coercion. Moses should have been prepared in advance for a marathon, not a dash. But, as with many life shocks, reality often jolts us harder than we expected. In those circumstances we may start coming a little unglued simply because we have forgotten that we were fairly warned.

Just as the Lord forewarned Moses, so the Scriptures forewarn us that the Christian life is not going to be a walk in the park, that we should not be surprised when fiery trials come upon us (1 Pet. 4:12), that through many tribulations we must enter into the kingdom of God (Acts 14:22), that we should not expect the world to love us (John 15:20), that many are the afflictions of the righteous (Psalm 34:19; John 16:33), and that various trials are both necessary and beneficial for us (1 Peter 1:6 and James 1:2). Still, despite all we should know and be well prepared for, we sometimes react as though, in the words of 1 Peter 4:12, some strange and unaccountable things were happening to us.

My friends, if anyone is intent upon taking up his or her cross and following after Christ, put this down: the *abnormal* state of Christian existence on this planet is an untroubled life. And, the truth be told, a healthy, vital spiritual life can ill-afford untrammeled peace and prosperity for long. For it is a law of life that all strength is born of resistance, not repose.

Secondly, in the gap between God's promise and God's performance, always expect unforeseen difficulties and disappointments that will challenge your faith to the bone. As I indicated, Moses should have known that his contest with Pharaoh was not going to be a first round knockout. What the Lord had *not* prepped Moses for was Pharaoh's cruel reaction and how ratcheting up his oppression would incite the sons of Israel, like angry pit bulls, to snarl at Moses and Aaron and refuse to listen to them any longer. That painful interlude between promise and performance, though hidden from Moses early on, was no surprise to God. All the unadvertised things were a crucial part of his providential design in the making of Moses. So bear in mind that between promise and performance there will be surprise items on the menu of providence. These may not be to our taste, but they are for our spiritual health. Just learn to expect the unexpected; some will be blessings, but others will be burdens. Both are friends.

For example, the Lord promises that if we seek first his kingdom and his righteousness that "all these things [the necessities of life] will be added to you" (Matthew 6:33). What he doesn't say (but we should expect) is that between promise and performance there may be some hair-raising crises. That is what Moses found. But wisely, in his extreme confusion and despair, "he returned to the Lord."

As long as faith has that well-trained reflex that takes all its troubles and doubts back to the throne of grace, we will be safe. That is precisely what Job did in his confusion and despair, "Have I sinned? What have I done to Thee, O watcher of men? Why hast Thou set me as Thy target, so that I am a burden to myself?" (7:20).

When Peter once debarked from his boat on the Sea of Galilee and briefly walked on water before his faith gave out and he began to sink, he turned for help not to his fellow disciples in the boat, but to the very Lord who had invited him onto the water in the first place, "Lord, save me, for I am perishing" (Matthew 14:30).

Well, that's exactly what Moses did. He took his doubts to the throne of grace, not to just anybody who would listen. After Moses had returned to the Lord with his complaints, notice the Lord's response, "Then the Lord said to Moses, 'Now you shall see what I will do to Pharaoh; for under compulsion he shall drive them out of his land'" (Exodus 6:1).

Get that "Now." All Moses had seen up to the present were the preliminaries. "Now you shall see what I will do," answered the Lord.

Ah, there's a huge, huge word! When life is in the tank, the habit of monument polishing is to faith what the late Woody Hayes's three-yards-and-a-cloud-of-dust were once to Ohio State football—the big, bruising strategy that wore the opposition down with steady pounding. But within his bulldozer playbook, Hayes had his share of pass plays, too, to offset the strategies of opponents who might want to load up on the line of scrimmage and frustrate his usual strong running game. And so do we.

I've called it "waiting on God's *Now*." Let me elucidate the concept and then I will share a recent story from our family saga that perfectly illustrates its application. God's *Now* is anytime the Lord breaks a stalemate, even temporarily, in a time of crisis. He picks his spot, breaks into our experience in a way that almost seems to echo his words to Moses, "*Now* do you see what I can do?" It could be the big breakthrough. On the other hand, it may not be the final resolution of troubles. Whatever it is, it is a timely intervention at some level that modifies our circumstances in such a way that makes us say, "Wow! This moment was God's *Now!*"

Waiting on God's *Now* takes patience. His *Now* never arrives before he has everything, including us, calibrated and disposed for optimal effect. The Lord sells no wine before its time. God's *Nows* more often than not arrive somewhere near our breaking point. Or, as I have put it elsewhere in this book, the Lord seldom saves the bacon until it's crisp. Patience must be our watchword. The Lord picks his spots.

Two recent events in the on-going drama surrounding Juli and her medical treatments were for all of us poignant examples of God's *Now* intersecting in timely fashion with

278

our critical need. The first event was a precursor. It merged beautifully into the second as a platform of hope when things at a certain point were desperate.

In May 2003, Juli and Paul returned to the Dallas-Fort Worth area to see the CFS specialist with whom they had been consulting since earlier that year. As usual, the entourage included Olsie, and Paul's mother, Elaine, who always goes ahead of them to make 1,001 logistical arrangements. Also along on this particular trip was Juli's dearest friend, Lynne, who has experienced some of Juli's afflictions and was along to receive treatment.

Owing to all the hurry, the hassles, the stresses, and disruptions of established routines on these trips, Juli's virtually zeroed-out energy base predictably plummets and her pain quotient accelerates. One has to be desperately in search of relief to consider putting oneself through this punishing drill. As the old saying goes, the "cure" seems almost as bad as the disease.

Anyway, of all her medical excursions outside Oregon that year, the one in May took the prize for drama as well as trauma. On this particular day of their five-day trip the weight had finally come down on Juli like a ton of bricks. Alone in her hotel room for a brief time, she bottomed out emotionally. Despair was all over her like hair on an ape. She looked sicker than a limp houseplant too long deprived of sun and water.

Moreover, she was due later that afternoon for an ultrasound to recheck her ovarian cyst that was discovered to have grown back (benign) in 2002. Juli, being already so out of sorts, suddenly had flashbacks of her traumatic 1995 "parking lot" ultrasound. Memories came rushing back faster than Noah's flood. Terror seized her, but much like Moses in Egypt, Juli returned to the Lord, crying out for help.

And then the voice of God . . . a God's *Now* moment. No, not an audible voice out of heaven, but one of those moments where God still speaks without saying anything. All who have walked with God for any length of time know exactly what I am talking about.

Out of nowhere, while construction work went on just below her open second floor window, someone, perhaps a landscaper or other hotel employee, started whistling. Initially Juli ignored it, assuming it was a worker whistling a pop song. Then to her amazement, it sounded exactly like her grandfather's whistling, with its distinctive, strong vibrato. Of all things the guy below her window was whistling "Be Still, My Soul."

From her Wheaton College chapel days Juli knew many hymns by heart, but not this particular one. Yet it immediately spoke to her like the voice of God himself. The ultrasound came out just fine that afternoon, even two centimeters smaller than the year before. Later that evening, Juli related to Lynne what had happened and that she felt the Lord wanted her to learn the verses when she returned home. It so happened that "Be Still, My Soul" was one of Lynne's favorite hymns and, knowing all three verses, she quoted them to Juli. What a message for her! Thus the Lord in a moment of profound discouragement sent an angel in disguise with just the encouraging words Juli needed to lift her sagging spirits. Those words the Lord sent her are these:

> Be still, my soul: the Lord is on thy side; Bear patiently
>   the cross of grief or pain;
> Leave to thy God to order and provide; in ev'ry change
>   he faithful will remain.
> Be still, my soul: thy best, thy heav'nly friend
> Through thorny ways leads to a joyful end.

Be still, my soul: thy God doth undertake to guide the
    future as he has the past.
Thy hope, thy confidence let nothing shake; all now
    mysterious shall be bright at last.
Be still, my soul: the waves and winds still know
His voice who ruled them while he dwelt below.
Be still, my soul: the hour is has-t'ning on when we
    shall be forever with the Lord,
When disappointment, grief, and fear are gone, sorrow
    forgot, love's purest joys restored.
Be still, my soul: when change and tears are past,
All safe and blessed we shall meet at last.[11]

That message was like a cup of cold water to a straggler
dying of thirst in the burning desert. Whoever that man was, he
will never know that he was an angel unawares. As they faced
the next crisis, that message of hope kept coming back.

But that was only the preamble to God's *Now*. As they
prepared to return to Portland, not only Juli, but everyone in
the entourage was exhausted. As my wife says, those trips are
only for calm souls (not my kind!) and even *those* get tried to
the margins of patience and endurance.

On previous occasions they had always tried to schedule late
flights less likely to be crowded. Times before they had even
taken the precaution of purchasing one extra seat so Juli would
be certain to have room to lie down. Since on those occasions
that costly measure had proved unnecessary, this time they took
the chance that things would work out as before. During the
entire trip, Juli was a basket case. But on the day they were to
return to Portland, she was so depleted that she could barely
hold up her head. Just to sit up in a wheelchair any length of
time was taxing. And she was just flat out ill after being hurried and hauled around over several days from this venue to
that like a sick dog dragged from a car bumper.

Given this circumstance, Olsie knew that it was imperative, just absolutely imperative, that there be an extra seat on the plane to allow Juli resting space during that long four-hour flight home. So they started praying early on. When they got to the airport and checked in, it was all Juli could do to stay upright in her wheelchair. At the desk they checked on the status of the flight and found to their alarm that the airline anticipated a full flight. Packed to the gills.

"Oh, no!" they all thought. No way Juli could sit up four hours. So they all prayed and prayed some more for a last minute miracle. Time comes to board. Oh, my, they are asking for volunteers! Not good at all. By now Juli was so out of it she was barely tuned in to what was happening around her, but she was aware they were all praying for at least one empty seat. When she heard the ticket agent's request for volunteers and knew they were close to boarding, Juli whispered to her mom, "God didn't perform a miracle for us this time, did he?" No. What were they going to do the next four hours? They needed a God's *Now* moment in the worst way.

Finally they are in flight. It has been a monumental effort for Juli to sit up even for this length of time. So before they even turn off the seat belt signs, Olsie sneaks into one of the restrooms to give her space. Her desperate plan, if you can imagine, is to hang out in the toilets (or wherever) for the next nearly four hours to give Juli lie-down space.

With a full flight, the flight attendants shortly caught on that this lady with the white hair was not in her seat. The male steward was a little agitated about this and had his female counterpart knock on the restroom door and ask Olsie if she was sick. Olsie comes out and explains briefly her dilemma. She had been in there now thirty-five minutes.

"Ma'am, we're very sorry but you can't stay in there," the attendant replies. "If you must stand, I ask that you shift around, maybe stand back here a little while, then move to the front near the First Class cabin and so forth. But if we hit turbulence, you must return to your seat."

Can you imagine three and a half hours of this kind of mental torture and physical strain on a woman who is close to breaking down in small pieces anyway?

Shortly Lynne, feeling sorry for Olsie and knowing Paul was frantically massaging Juli's sick muscles and giving her shots, gets up from her seat and asks Olsie to take her space for awhile while she stands. Lynne herself is somewhat ill with CFS and this was not an easy sacrifice.

But the move turned out to be providential. The position where she had taken Olsie's place at this time was back near the flight attendants' workspace. Naturally conversation turned to the problem about which they were quite curious. So Lynne seized the moment to unwind the whole Juli saga for them, including the stage in 1995 when Juli was diagnosed with ovarian cancer. It just so happened that the male flight attendant who had been the more unaccommodating one initially had just recently lost his mother to ovarian cancer. As Lynne unfolded the whole long and tangled narrative of Juli's trials and travails, both attendants teared up. They were deeply moved.

And then the most amazing thing! "And *now* you will see what I will do!" This was God's *NOW*. While this conversation was taking place, Olsie grew more and more uncomfortable about taking Lynne's seat and forcing her to stand when Olsie knew how bad Lynne herself was feeling. So she got up and walked back to where Lynne was talking with the flight attendants.

"Lynne," she said, "you go back now and take your seat. I don't want you having to stand."

Right there the male flight attendant, now swelling up with great compassion, broke in. "You know, I don't care if it costs me my job, but you (referring to Lynne) can sit right there in that jump seat."

By airline regulations it is a flat out no-no for a passenger to sit in a flight attendant's jump seat. The other flight attendants, however, agreed to share in the risk and allowed this breach in the rules. That freed up Lynne's seat for Olsie. Wow!

But this timely reprieve lasted only a moment, as right on the heels of this marvelous provision, the plane unexpectedly encountered severe turbulence. In fact, had Lynne not been safely seated mere seconds earlier, especially in her weakened condition, she surely would have gone flying through the cabin.

Immediately, the captain ordered the flight attendants back to their seats. "Where are these people going to sit?" Lynne wondered in horror, knowing she was occupying one of their places. But right here is where God manifested the full magnitude of his *Now* in their situation.

Remember, they had been praying for an extra seat practically non-stop for several hours prior to boarding. Since the flight was full, they assumed the Lord had said "No," when in fact, he had literally answered their desperate plea. You see, this particular plane was equipped with four jump seats and there were only three flight attendants onboard! The extra seat they needed was the very jump seat Lynne was already sitting in!

But God was not finished. After they were through the turbulence and the seat belt signs were off once again, Olsie came back to see how Lynne weathered the "storm." While she was there, the male attendant turned to Olsie and said, "Ma'am, I understand you can't eat?" referring to Olsie being so torn up over Juli that she wasn't eating much.

"Not much," she replied.

"Do you like ice cream?" he asked.

"I didn't know they had ice cream on airplanes."

"Would a hot chocolate fudge sundae sound good to you?"

"Oh, that's my very favorite!"

So, off he goes to the first class section and a few minutes later walks back past longing coach passengers with not one, but two high-stacked hot fudge sundaes in fancy tall glasses topped with nuts, and presents one to Olsie and the other to Lynne.

The rest of the trip they were all compassion. Lynne was even allowed to stay in her jump seat until the last possible moment, relinquishing her place only when the captain ordered the cabin crew to their seats for landing, allowing Juli the maximum time to rest. *"Now you will see what I will do!"*

For five days of the Texas trip it had been sheer torture. And then when it looked as though what was already miserable was about to become impossible, it was God's *Now.* My friends, there is always God's *Now* for every sufferer. I don't mean that in this life there is always some moment in time when, if we just stick it out in faith, the Lord will reverse all our misfortunes and make everything upright again. No, I'm not saying that. The truth is, some pain and suffering is going to be with us for the duration. In some cases there will be no reversals of temporal fortunes. God has his reasons. Some disasters we will have to live with.

But along the way, there is some special need, some great urgency, some crushing circumstances when something has to give, maybe not to fix, but perhaps maybe something God needs to finesse and ease. That kind of situation is the perfect set up for God's *Now* moments when he breaks in with provision and says, "Now, see what I can do?"

The ultimate God's *Now* is not in this life, but in the future when Christ returns and all the consequences of the Fall and all forms of evil are overturned. There is a day coming when God will say to all his servants in heaven and on earth, "*Now*, stand back and see what I will do to the kingdom of evil!" So we all wait on God's *Now* in its consummate form. For some, the extraordinary heaviness of this life will not be lifted until that in-breaking from above. But in the meantime, as we endure the pains and sufferings of this present world, there will be many of God's *Nows* on a lesser scale through which the Lord will display his glory to us.

So as we patiently endure and things become inordinately heavy, remember, there will be a day when we hear the Lord say, "*Now* you will see what I will do" and he will act in some way that refreshes our spirit. At the end of the day, we may not still be able to say, "Thank God, it's over!" but we will say, "Wow! Now I know you're still in this with me. Thank you!" And his timely reassurance will serve as a permanent monument to allay our fears.

I commend to you the words of the Psalmist who exemplifies both the need for and the spirit of monumental faith:

> I cried out to God for help;
>   I cried out to God to hear me.
> When I was in distress, I sought the Lord;
>   at night I stretched out untiring hand
>   and my soul refused to be comforted.
> I remembered you, O God, and I groaned;
>   I mused, and my spirit grew faint.
> You kept my eyes from closing;
>   I was too troubled to speak.
> I thought about the former days
>   the years of long ago;
> I remembered my songs in the night.
>   My heart mused and my spirit inquired;

"Will the Lord reject forever?
    Will he never show his favor again?
Has his unfailing love vanished forever?
    Has his promise failed for all time?
Has God forgotten to be merciful?
    Has he in anger withheld his compassion
Then I thought, "To this I will appeal:
    the years of the right hand of the Most High."
I will remember the deeds of the LORD;
    yes, I will remember your miracles of long ago.
I will meditate on all your works
    and consider all your mighty deeds.

(Psalm 77:1–12, NIV)

Epilogue

Update from the Furnace of Affliction

What are the secrets of life that enable us to survive trials? Why do some people "cave in" and others triumph? Our society looks for these answers, and as Christians we look for the answers that God has for us. How can we learn lessons from life and keep the eternal perspective that is our great hope?

In his popular business book, *Good to Great,* best-selling author Jim Collins talks about the "Stockdale Paradox," a law of survival that takes its name from Admiral James Stockdale, the highest-ranking American POW during the Vietnam War.[12] Inhospitably interned, along with other unfortunate military captives, in the infamously cruel "Hanoi Hilton," he was tortured more than twenty times over a period of eight miserable, sanity-challenging years. He never knew for certain if he would be set free or see his family again. Collins describes in detail the admiral's resourceful and successful survival strategies aimed at defeating the efforts of his captors to break him down and render him compliant for their propaganda purposes.

Reading *In Love and War,* a book relating the separate experiences of the admiral and his wife during those terrible years, Jim Collins was impressed with the mettle of the man, but puzzled about the secret of his endurance through so many horrors:

> As I moved through the book, I found myself getting depressed. It just seemed so bleak—the uncertainty of his fate, the brutality of his captors, and so forth. And then it dawned on me: here I am sitting in my warm and comfortable office, looking out over the beautiful Stanford campus on a beautiful Saturday afternoon. I'm getting depressed reading this, and I know the end of the story! I know that he gets out, reunites with his family, becomes a national hero, and gets to spend the later years of his life studying philosophy on this same beautiful campus. If it feels so depressing for me, how on earth did he deal with it when he was actually there and *did not know the end of the story?*"[13]

How does anyone deal with such a box canyon of onerous uncertainty in the midst of relentless agony? Collins eventually interviewed Stockdale personally and asked him directly how he held up in the face of all that isolation, deprivation, mental torture and physical abuse. The admiral explained:

> "*I never lost faith in the end of the story,*" he said. "I never doubted not only that I would get out, but also *that I would prevail in the end* and turn the experience into the defining event of my life" (italics mine for emphasis).

But what about others who finally gave out and gave up, Collins wondered. Could the admiral put his finger on what separated them? There Stockdale didn't hesitate:

"Oh, that's easy," the admiral answered. The ones who didn't make it out, he remembered, were "the optimists." They were the guys, he meant, who were always certain that soon it would all be over, that by Christmas they would all be headed home. When time after time their optimistic expectations were dashed, they finally "died of a broken heart." They had lost faith in the end of the story.

That was when the admiral articulated what Collins terms "the Stockdale paradox," a hopeful, but tough-minded mentality Stockdale always tried to instill in his fellow prisoners to shield them from getting dispirited by disappointed optimism. As he explained to Collins:

This is a very important lesson. You must never confuse faith that you will prevail in the end—which you can never afford to lose—with the discipline to confront the most brutal facts of your current reality, whatever they might be.

In his Hanoi Hilton days, his way of attempting to counter that optimism, ungrounded in reality, was to warn his fellow sufferers, "We're not getting out by Christmas; deal with it!"

With great insight of his own, Collins puts that bare-knuckled realism in the broader context of life in general:

Life is unfair—sometimes to our advantage, sometimes to our disadvantage. We will all experience disappointments and crushing events somewhere along the way, setbacks for which there is no "reason," no one to blame. It might be disease; it might be injury; it might be an accident; it might be losing a loved one; it might be getting swept away in a political shake-up; it might be getting shot down over Vietnam [or other war zone] and thrown into a POW camp for eight years. What separates people, Stockdale taught me, is not the presence or absence of difficulty, but how they deal with the inevitable difficulties of life.

Actually, this Stockdale paradox, if applied in terms of Christian faith, is, at bottom, living with faith in God. It is a crucial perspective for all those intensely and/or chronically suffering people who are rigidly trapped in seemingly endless misery, living out their own version of a tortured existence with no certain prospect that life will ever return to normal.

You don't know how my wife and I have prayed that by this time Juli and Paul, to use a metaphor, would be "out by Christmas." I had dearly hoped that by the time my publisher needed this epilogue I would be able to describe a happy story-book ending. I hoped I could inform my readers that at long last, after almost two decades of virtual house arrest and being subjected to a whole menagerie of tortures gleefully inflicted by a cruel enemy testing almost every conceivable way to break these two down, God had finally said, "Enough." So far that has not happened. The truth is they remain "afflicted in every way, but not crushed; perplexed, but not despairing."

They continue to hold up under it all because they instinctively live by that biblically grounded Stockdale paradox. In the admiral's words (though for perhaps different reasons) they have "never lost faith in the end of the story." Or, in the words of James, they remain certain of "the [wonderful] outcome of the Lord's dealings" (5:11).

Through it all, God's Word, which cannot be broken, assures them of his abiding love and compassion, of his timely provision and support, of his inscrutable wisdom and indomitable power, and of a perfect ending to the story. God is faithful and in the end he delivers on all his promises.

Yes, maybe someday down the road by means or by miracle the Lord will fix Juli. But neither they nor we have any way of knowing that. Then again, should this miserable marathon turn out to be a lifetime event, they can by faith deal with that brutal reality. Whatever the outcome, they aren't feeding hope on the husks of a hollow optimism that offers comfort where there is none. No, they carry on, staring straight in the eye the un-cheering possibility that this suffering life might last as long as they will. Yet they rest their hope on the almighty power of God, on his incomprehensible wisdom, and on his perfect moral character. So if they aren't home by Christmas, so to speak, they can deal with that. For in the interim, they polish their monuments regularly, they ponder God's promises, pray constantly for sustaining grace, put one faithful foot in front of the other and just do the next right thing, saying in everything, "not my will, but yours be done."

They are by no means alone in that spirit. Myriads of God's servants the world over endure unimaginable affliction in many different forms. For reasons totally hidden from us, the Lord has seen fit for the present time, some perhaps for the duration, to burden them, like Job, with a harsh existence. Even so, they trudge faithfully on, knowing full well that "the sufferings of this present time are unworthy to be compared to the glory that is to be revealed to us" (Romans 8:18). In the end they know they will prevail.

So, they never lose hope under the worst circumstances, because they never lose faith "in the end of the story." With the eye of biblical hope, they envision a future beyond anything the eye of man has ever seen, beyond anything his ear has ever heard, or beyond anything that has ever entered into his imagination. That vision enables them to reconcile themselves to the bitter and unyielding realities of the painful present.

If during the course of my ministry, and especially over these harrowing last twenty years, my wife and I have learned anything, it is that the people of God are by no means exempt from the whole distressing catalogue of human troubles. It is our hope and prayer that the biblical perspectives and habits I have shared with you in this book, combined with the flesh-and-blood example of the on-going pain and testing in our family, will strengthen and inspire you.

Notes

1. W. Glyn Evans, *Daily with the King: A Devotional for Self-Discipleship* (Chicago: Moody Publishers, 1991).

2. D.A. Carson, *The Difficult Doctrine of the Love of God* (Wheaton, Ill.: Crossway Books, 2000).

3. Harold S. Kushner, *When Bad Things Happen to Good People* (New York: Avon Books, 1981).

4. Ph.D. in Biophysics and Cell Physiology from University of Minnesota, cancer researcher, and N.D.

5. Louis Berkhof, *Systematic Theology* (Grand Rapids: Eerdmans Publishing, 1996), p.166.

6. Alexander Maclaren, *Expositions of the Holy Scriptures, Deuteronomy through 1 Samuel* (Whitefish, MT.: Kessinger, 2004), p. 801.

7. Leland Ryken, *How to Read the Bible as Literature* (Grand Rapids, MI.: Zondervan Publishing Co., 1985).

8. Millard J. Erickson, *Christian Theology*, Vol. 1. (Grand Rapids, MI.: Baker Book House, 1986), p. 357.

9. W. Glyn Evans, *Daily with the King: A Devotional for Self-Discipleship* (Chicago: Moody Bible Institute, 1979).

10. Bruce Ware, *God's Lesser Glory: The Diminished God of Open Theism* (Wheaton, Ill.: Crossway Books, 2000).

11. Katharina A. von Schlege, in *Neue Sammlung Geistlicher Lieder*, 1752.

12. Jim Collins, *Good to Great* (New York: Harper Collins, 2001).

13. James Stockdale and Sybil Stockdale, *In Love and War: The Story of a Family's Ordeal and Sacrifice During the Vietnam Years* (New York: Harper and Row, 1984, 2nd ed. Naval Institute Press, 1990).

Jim Andrews has led Lake Bible Church (Lake Oswego, Oregon) for seventeen years and hosts a daily radio program, *The Final Word*. Previously he taught for a total of twenty-one years at Western Bible College (Denver) and later at Western Seminary (Portland). He graduated from West Virginia Tech (B.A. in Journalism), the University of Colorado (M.A. Classics) and Dallas Theological Seminary (TH.M New Testament) Jim and his wife, Olsie, have been married forty-nine years and have two married daughters.